Guiding Recovery from Child Sexual Abuse

Good Practice in Counselling People Who Have Been Abused
Edited by Zetta Bear
ISBN 1 85302 424 4
Good Practice in Social Work 5

Counselling Adult Survivors of Child Sexual Abuse, Second Edition
Christiane Sanderson
ISBN 1 85302 252 7

Sexual Abuse
The Child's Voice
Poppies on the Rubbish Heap
Madge Bray
ISBN 1 85302 487 2

Boys: Sexual Abuse and Treatment
Anders Nyman and Börje Svensson
ISBN 1 85302 491 0

Child Abuse and Child Abusers
Protection and Prevention
Edited by Lorraine Waterhouse
ISBN 1 85302 408 2

Guiding Recovery
from Child Sexual Abuse

Horizons of Hope

Dave Simon

Jessica Kingsley Publishers
London and Philadelphia

The right of Dave Simon to be identified as author of this work has been asserted by him in accordance with the Copyright, Designs and Patents Act 1988.

First published in the United Kingdom in 1998 by
Jessica Kingsley Publishers Ltd
116 Pentonville Road
London N1 9JB, England
and
325 Chestnut Street,
Philadelphia, PA 19106, USA

Library of Congress Cataloging in Publication Data
A CIP catalogue record for this book is available from the Library of Congress

British Library Cataloguing in Publication Data
Simon, Dave
Guiding recovery from child sex abuse : horizons of hope
1.Adult child sexual abuse victims - Counseling of
2. Sexually abused children - Counseling of
I.Title
362.7'6'4

ISBN 1-85302-5712

Printed and Bound in Great Britain by
Athenaeum Press, Gateshead, Tyne and Wear

Contents

List of Figures

Acknowledgements

There are many people who I want to thank for their support in helping me write this book:

The survivors who helped me to understand their difficulties while I tried to help them with their difficulties;

the survivors who have given permission for me to include their experiences, poems and case history interviews in this book;

the staff and trustees of *ASCSA* (Adult Survivors of Child Sexual Abuse) the charitable Counselling organisation I set up on the Isle of Wight to take this work further;

the various staff of *ASCSA* and social services who worked with me in the various groups where these ideas grew: Mrs Ronny Temple, Mrs Janet Weinkove, Mrs Jeannette Wade, Mrs Vicky Townsend;

Jane for typing and Jen and Caz for proofreading;

my friends and family who have given me time and patience;

...and many others.

Notes

The 'clients' of this counselling programme are referred to as victims where the emotional tone of that word is appropriate to the way that person is likely to feel at the time being described. Otherwise, I have used the word 'survivor'. Discussing victims or survivors in general, I will usually put 'abuse victims' or 'trauma victims'. Thrivers are different again (see page 43).

I have given abusers the male pronoun 'he'. Victims have the female pronoun 'she' as this is the most usual situation. Recent research shows that there are significant numbers of female perpetrators and male victims, perhaps many more than has been thought previously.

I have used double quotes to show words and phrases actually used in the programme – we have refined them to be as clear and user-friendly as possible. They are always sympathetic to the victim and the speaker's tone of voice should show that.

I have used as many 'real life' examples as possible to show what I mean.

I have used confidentiality rules in this writing. Where I have directly transcribed a large chunk of a survivor's words, actions or experience, I have gained their permission to write the words I have written. Where I have used their poems or case histories, I have given them the choice of how to name it: 'Anonymous', with a code name, with their initials, their first name or their full name. Those who have used their full name do so in pride – some have already published these poems.

Where I have included poems and interviews, I have remained faithful to the writing and recording I received, only having suggested changes if I felt readers would be confused by some aspect of the poem. I have had permission for these changes from the writers. Any apparent misspellings are included intentionally. Please note: some poems do not rhyme as they come from letters rather than traditional poetry.

Where I have made a comment about the poem or interview, or have added, left out, or altered something written, I have shown it with square brackets [like these!].

Warning!

I have written this book for counsellors and therapists who are interested in working with adolescent and adult child sexual abuse survivors. This uses a talking approach, which I've called counselling. Therefore, it will not suit younger children but may help their parents and carers understand more about it all. Some survivors might be interested in reading it too, so I have tried to write with survivors, relatives and counsellors in mind.

I feel that a few words of introduction would be useful to explain why I have written the book in this way. I have based this book on my experiences in counselling with adolescent and adult survivors of both sexes, and of a wide age range, who have suffered a variety of sexual abuse experiences. It is not a research-based book nor is it a survivor's story.

I have written in a personal style that might take some getting used to. This is a textbook written for professionals, to show them how the counselling programme works. It is also a story presented in a factual style – as though spoken – to make it come alive. I also want to help survivors and relatives who are searching for answers to get as much out of the book as possible. I have designed it as a 'choose-your-own-order' book, to allow readers to follow their curiosity. I think this is the most useful way to learn about it – there is too much to learn it all!

Please use the Contents list (page 5), the List of Figures (page 6), the general Index (page 250), the Survivors Cross-Index (page 243), the Alphabetical Index of Metaphors (page 246) and the Cross-Index of Metaphors (page 247), to help you navigate around the book in the order that is most useful to you. Because it is so many things, people are likely to read it in many different ways and in different orders. It is likely to give readers different reactions at different times or in different moods. This is intentional.

So, all in all, I have written in a style that may:

- seem 'unscientific' to those who are used to reading academic textbooks

- seem a bit too personal at first to those who are themselves adult survivors

- seem to be a disorganised hotchpotch to those who prefer an orderly approach

- seem too slow and detailed to those who would like a glimpse – as if by video or one-way mirror – of what really goes on in counselling sessions and groups.

A Few Words of Preparation

I want to make a few points to the various readers who might pick up this book:

To Academics

This book is not a summary of a long research project. I have avoided statistics and kept references to other written work to an absolute minimum. The book is intended for survivors, relatives and practitioners and is, therefore, written to be relevant to them. I think there comes a point in describing things where you cannot watch from afar, you have to get close. This is the view from close up. There are many subtle weavings of facts, feelings and reactions. I cannot cover all of them, but I can hope to describe most of the important ones.

To Counsellors

The idea of this book is to help you take up the therapeutic programme described. It is not aimed at helping you understand all the details of abuse if you have not learned about it elsewhere. Neither the book nor the programme try to be a research-based training package. The subjects discussed here have been chosen to help people change. Also, it is important to remember that this is a very specific programme. Therefore, it will not help much in understanding the general approach of counselling either, but by all means read it and consider the implications.

To Non-Professionals

This book may give you an idea of what happens in a counselling programme specifically set up for survivors of child sexual abuse. This might be interesting reading because of studies, general interest or concern for victims. Comparisons with other forms of abuse, and/or with other forms of counselling, may be possible, but please remember that this was not why I wrote the book. But I would be happy for you to read it because the more people who understand what happens and what abuse does to people, the better – and it might help stop abuse happening in the first place.

To Survivors

This book will help you to understand the counselling programme, if you are going to enter it. If you try a do-it-yourself approach, it may not help as much. This is for three reasons:

1. In the counselling programme, group or individual, we choose how to explain the ideas to keep it as relevant to you as possible. We talk over all the implications and important connections that might help you – often in detail. And of course, as they say, two heads are better than one!

2. In the programme we repeat a lot of the information. It can take quite a few times before it starts to sink in. Most survivors have spent a lot of their lives believing the opposite of what we say here, or believing that there is no answer, so, to begin with, they often doubt the ideas we offer.

3. In the group counselling sessions there is the opportunity to see if other people react to the discussions in the same way that you do. This is why we use the group approach. It is so reassuring to see that you are not alone – especially to see for yourself – that it is much better than individual counselling.

In reading this book you will not have any of these advantages. But, if you are not ready yet to talk to professionals, or if you have not found a professional or service that makes sense to you, I hope this book can help you make progress.

To Survivors' Relatives

This book might be a useful way to understand what your survivor relative has gone through in their past, and is going through now. Counselling can be a very nervous time for the person in counselling and his or her relatives. Everyone wonders if, when and how things are going to change. Survivors often find it very difficult to explain the abuse and the counselling, even when they are in the counselling, so an outside source of information might help. Remember: you might be able to read the whole book quicker than they can get through the counselling programme, so try to avoid being too far ahead of them – if you do, you run the risk of putting them off. Counselling is very personal. No one likes a 'take-over bid'. Also, remember that other counsellors might work in a different way, so be careful what you say.

To All

Remember: these categories are artificial. Some people may belong to several categories. There is no rule to say that academics cannot be survivors or relatives. Some survivors have a good reason to become professionals: they want to help other people who have suffered too.

But, to all, I would like to say: read it anyway – why not? One reason why not is that something you read could remind you of frights, traumas or abuse experiences in your own past. Alerting you now is what I have called 'The Government Health Warning' (nothing to do with smoking!). Have a look at that soon, the ideas in this book may affect you in ways you didn't expect. But don't let this put you off, have a go. If you recognise any scary bits, give yourself time to think about them before going too much further on. Take your time. I think books are more useful if they are taken slowly and thoughtfully. This is their advantage, you can read any part several times to get it clear before moving on.

This book works a little like the counselling. It is a guide around the difficult area of helping people recover from child sexual abuse. Guides have to know about the geography of the journey – this is what I describe in the book. More than that, it is a guide for guides who have worked in other areas and want to know more about this particular area. I feel strongly that this area is very different to many others and care is necessary before changing areas.

Introduction

I would like to set out some background information to explain a few things before I start on the main issues for this book. I hope they are useful enough to read before going on to the more relevant parts, though I know some people might want to go straight on – I'm probably one myself!

A Single-Issue Approach

The majority of courses in counselling and related work provide a training in a method that is expected to apply to people with all types of problems. This is because most counsellors work in some sort of 'general practice'. In other words, they expect to meet people with a wide variety of problems.

I feel that this does not prepare counsellors for work with survivors of child sexual abuse. The effects of the abuse are far-reaching and complex. In some important ways, the problems they lead to are different to those caused by other things. To be able to help properly, counsellors need to know these differences and what to do about them. It makes sense to use a single-issue approach, one that concentrates on the problems that abuse brings.

A single-issue approach is likely to have a number of basic parts that apply to most people who go through the counselling, so it is sensible to think of it as a programme. It all fits together and it is difficult to use small parts of it on their own. This book describes the counselling programme I have developed for work with adult survivors of child sexual abuse. It is useful for individual work, group work, couple and family work. It draws upon ideas from all these areas and is, therefore, useful in all these areas.

In a small charity called *ASCSA* (Adult Survivors of Child Sexual Abuse) we have worked with the programme to provide a path of recovery that is as safe and easy as possible. It is still difficult and, often, slow. Survivors have been forced to be as cautious as possible, and even then many find their life moves from one crisis to another. The programme is built on a number of specific tools: a collection of relevant metaphors covering definite issues. I feel it is vital to make the counselling friendly and familiar in order to help as many survivors as much as possible.

These tools can also help counsellors. They have various concerns about helping abuse victims, especially if the area is new to them. They can get nervous about making things worse and/or about being upset about the injustices they will discuss. These metaphors will help counsellors familiarise themselves with the issues involved in counselling adult survivors of child sexual abuse.

As a way to start the book, I want to make some introductions and to work in reasonably logical steps from the topic of sexual abuse through to the layout of this book.

A Bit of History

I first knew that I had met a victim in 1972. She was a teenager who had a persistent headache, all day, every day. She was a patient living in an adolescent unit in a psychiatric hospital. Nothing helped: medication, counselling, living away from home. Although we knew she had been 'interfered with' (as it was called in those days), we did not talk about it. We assumed that she would not want to talk about it and counselling focused on the headache. Although I now have some idea of what she was surviving, I didn't then – nor did anyone else who worked with her in that establishment, nor many others in the 'helping professions'.

Later, during my years with the social services department, I had to get used to the idea that child sexual abuse happens, that it happens too often and that it leaves tremendous suffering behind. My managers asked me to concentrate on victims of child abuse, especially sexual abuse. The work increased as colleagues heard about what I was doing. I heard more and more about people's responses to having been abused. I heard similar responses being described more and more.

I worked alongside (but separate from) the child protection team who investigated allegations of abuse. I had previously been a social work manager heavily involved in investigation work. I began to feel quite confident that I was hearing the real human experiences and reactions involved. These were not made-up, dreamed or vengeance lies, these were the reactions of ordinary children who had been pushed off their proper development path by an extremely serious trauma. (A 'trauma' is a fright, shock, horror. It is the emotional equal of a serious physical wound. It has the same scale of harm.)

A1: Case example – Yes, it had happened

I talked with a social work colleague who told me about a woman in her 70s she had recently met. They had been making friends and found much in common. When the older woman asked about my colleague's job, she said that she worked with children who had been abused. She went on to describe the different types of abuse. When she came to sexual abuse, the 70-year-old said 'That happened to me'.

They talked more and it seemed that the older woman's sister had had similar problems in life: marital, financial, emotional, with her children... My colleague said; 'What if the abuser did it to her too?' This idea shocked the older woman, but later she said 'It makes sense, maybe it happened to her as well. I thought I was the only one'. She phoned her sister that evening and – yes, it had happened.

There are several things I learned from this one story:

Keeping it secret

Both sisters had kept it secret for 60 years or so, *deliberately*. This was not accidental. This was not amnesia. There must have been a good reason for keeping it secret. There was something about the nature of the experience that made it important to hide it away. This seemed an important starting point.

Avoiding support

Both sisters had kept it secret from the for 60 years or so *from each other*. If they had talked to each other at any time during or after the abuse, they could have supported each other. I felt this was an immense tragedy.

Changing reality

Sexual abuse can happen to more than one child in a family, *without the parents realising it.*

There must be something very unusual happening to have so many serious secrets in one family, something especially powerful must go on to alter family behaviour so much, something had changed the 'reality' of that family, something that made them actively work hard to stick to the changed reality for many years. This seemed so important that I felt I needed to understand it better.

I listened, read and learned more. I heard from men and women, girls and boys. I talked to children under ten and elderly people over 60. I met people from different classes of society, in different jobs, in various sorts of relationships, in all sorts of family situations. I read and watched videotapes of documentary interviews and child protection investigation interviews. I read poems and autobiographies and looked at drawings and paintings from survivors. I heard about a variety of abusers: men and women, parents and professionals, young and elderly, convicted and unconvicted – some victims themselves, others not.

I wanted to know how ordinary people react to extremely frightening situations – what are the normal results? I talked with a local psychiatrist who had a wide experience in this area. I began to feel I was making sense of a situation that other professionals were unsure how to handle. I began to realise that I was changing my usual approach to counselling when I worked with victims of sexual abuse. I used to start where the person (the client) is emotionally and with what he or she wants – traditional counselling practice. Nowadays, I start with reassurances to counteract the nervousness I expect survivors to be feeling when they start counselling. If they aren't feeling nervous, I move on a stage so the counselling is no longer 'client-centred', as my original training required, but 'programme centred'. But it is still paced for the client, and tailored to the client.

The programme developed as I started to get survivors together into a counselling group. I remember working with a particular survivor who had conquered many doubts and questions but who was still stuck with problems she felt no one else could understand. I realised that the sensible thing to do was to get a group of similar people together and let them explore the problems they all had. The idea was that they would find that they had more in common than they expected. I hoped that this would help them draw strength from this discovery and the discussions that would follow.

When we tried it, I found that the amount of support that they were quickly able to give each other was enormous. The support was knowledgeable, consistent and respectful. This was different to other forms of group therapy I have done, where individual group members can be much more selfish and demanding. In those groups everyone can say 'But my problems are different!'. Here they all knew that they had to face the same problems. Ironically, victims of abuse are often much less demanding and selfish than they worry that they might be!

In Chapter 5 there are five survivors' histories. Readers wanting to check on the realities of abuse and its effects can find more personal information there.

Child Sexual Abuse

I think it is important to say that, in some significant ways, people who have been sexually abused have some serious problems that are different to other people's problems. I think it is important for professionals to say this. If victims try to say it, they may be ignored. These problems develop from the way sexual abuse (usually) happens and how ordinary children – later adults – cope with it.

Going back to the example of the 70-year-old woman described above, I want to describe some of the details of the consequences.

Keeping it secret

Both sisters had kept it secret for 60 years or so, *deliberately*.

As I met more survivors, I discovered that there *was* a good reason for keeping it secret. Fear – usually with guilt, shame and grief mixed in – was quite enough to ensure their silence. I began to hear the ways in which abusers make children keep the abuse secret. I began to understand this as a *natural consequence* of the abuse: abusers want to avoid being caught.

I began to understand the trap that is almost always involved. I understood that I would react in the same way in the same circumstances – I would try to keep it secret if it had happened to me. Many of the symptoms (fear, alcohol abuse, marital and parenting problems) are *logical results*.

Avoiding support

Both sisters had kept it secret for 60 years or so *from each other*.

If they had talked to each other, they could have supported each other. They would have had to take risks in telling each other. Breaking the secret could have lead to all sorts of things going wrong. It could have lead to one suicide, or two, or more if their mother had found out.

They could have approached professional help. But we must remember that 60 years ago they would have run many risks – they might have been locked up in either the prison system or the psychiatric system. This point made me wonder whether it also explained some of those psychiatric problems that are still so hard to help with nowadays. If the patient does not want help, professionals get very puzzled and are tempted to feel impatient. This is understandable. If someone obviously needs help because they are so unhappy, why do they avoid using the help offered? Sometimes it's because it is not the right sort of help. But with sexual abuse (perhaps all child abuse), victims might fear that the 'help' will make things worse than they already are.

Changing reality

Sexual abuse can happen to more than one child in a family, *without either of them realising it.*

If abusers are related to the victims through blood or marriage, they are likely to have the opportunities to do this. They can abuse the children one at a time or together. Either way, 'divide and conquer' is the most obvious approach for the abuser to take. By telling different stories about each child, they can create jealousy, distrust and misplaced loyalties that alter everyone else's understanding of 'reality'. Therefore, the victims know two 'realities'. One reality is public, one is secret; one reality is morally correct, the other is wrong; one reality is ill-informed, the other is accurate to events. Put like that, this begins to sound like the things schizophrenic people say – maybe that's why both are such difficult problems for helping professionals to work with.

The Counselling

The problems described so far develop directly from child sexual abuse. They do not arise from the problems people have later in life after a happy and normal childhood. These problems also shape what counselling has to try to do, what its job is.

Changing reality

In a way, the job is to help survivors sort out the two realities I described above. This is not by ignoring either of the two realities or simply reversing them. It is more like making a new reality out of the other two by adding the understanding of why there are two. Counselling can help victims under-stand it better by describing how abuse happens and what it does to people –

by this I mean describing the processes involved rather than enquiring about the personal details. If survivors want to contribute their personal details, OK, many do, which is how I know enough to write this book.

Accepting support

To do this, people have to stay in counselling. If they do not, it cannot help them. People have a right to stop counselling whenever they want so we must design the counselling to be as easy to stay in as possible. This means that it has to be extremely reassuring to people right from the start.

Talking about the secret

The counselling has to be so reassuring that a victim who has not yet told anyone would consider starting now. It has to feel safe. The risk has to be low enough to try these counsellors – this may be after a lifetime's silence, as in the case of the 70-year-old woman described earlier. Sixty years of silence show a lot of determination to keep a secret. It is a long time for a habit of silence to have built up. (I have heard survivors say that even when completely drunk, they can still avoid that subject.)

The overall aim of counselling is to help survivors stand on their own two feet, stand up for themselves. We want them to design their own future as they want it rather than suffer what they feel trapped into.

The Programme Idea

Most training on counselling aims to help the counsellor to respond to distressed people with a wide variety of circumstances, problems and supports. Therefore, the methods of counselling focus on 'how to help' rather than 'what has gone wrong'. They help counsellors to be flexible and adaptable, so the method shapes the approach to the problem.

Usually, this provides the best sort of training. However, when a counsellor works in an organisation that specialises in helping people with only one sort of problem, this may not be the best way forward. In these circumstances, it seems to me that the problem should shape the counselling.

Counselling adult survivors of child sexual abuse is more about the abuse – how it happens and what it does to people – than about the problems that result. People may be depressed, anxious or having a nervous breakdown. They may be in collapsing marriages, having great difficulties with their children or unable to form or keep relationships. In all these cases, they have more in common through their abuse than anything else.

We have designed the programme so that it is fairly flexible. It can be tailored to each survivor's individual situation. It makes use of a number of specific tools: the Metaphors – descriptions of various aspects of the emotional experience of abuse. They are meant to reassure survivors about their reactions to the abuse. This is the start of the process of change. The Metaphors can be used in any order or combination according to the counsellor's judgement or the survivor's needs and progress.

There are occasions when a survivor says: 'No, I don't want to listen to your programme. I want to tell you about it all in *my* way!' This does happen once in a while and survivors have a right to say this. The programme was originally designed for people who were still Victims (i.e. paralysed in The Invisible Trap and unable or unwilling to start talking themselves). So, if the survivor knows where to start, we should not stop them. In these situations we either agree and hope it works or sort out a compromise (which is more likely if finances affect the issue).

Checking reality

The programme allows counsellors to grow confident that they can help survivors to check the emotional reality of their situation. The Metaphors will help the counsellor understand this reality in plain language rather than in research statistics or technical jargon.

Sharing support

Gathering survivors into counselling groups is a basic part of the programme. Working together, the survivors can reassure each other about their experiences. This is usually more effective than working with professionals who have not had the experience. The professionals become facilitators who help the group to work rather than relying on their own understanding of what abuse does to people.

Accepting the secret

In the end, there is a decision that survivors have to make. Will they keep the secret or will they make it public? Telling their original family, their partner, the police, etc., will mean that they lose control of the consequences. Things may get very difficult as anger, guilt, regret, shame and a host of other feelings emerge. Sometimes, survivors choose to keep it private. If it is their choice, they are in control: it is a secret kept private for good reasons.

The Metaphor Tools

Many of these Metaphors are descriptions of basic issues in the causes and consequences of child sexual abuse. This programme starts on what is, basically, an educative approach. This does not stop the therapeutic counselling work for each individual. It provides a starting place for adults who may be very depressed and despairing, although angry and frustrated. Often, they feel surrounded by a whirlpool of feelings that leaves them unable to make productive plans. By that I mean that they often go round in circles and find it impossible to plan and achieve things for themselves. What they do try, tends to go wrong. This leads to hopelessness, frustration and depression.

Some of the Metaphors will be useful for people who were not sexually abused, or abused in any way.

The programme started to take shape in 1991. At that time I was employed by a social services department as a family therapist. While I met many people on their own or in couples, I was always thinking about the relationships around them in the past and the present. So, many of the Metaphors are about the relationships that survivors have with other people and with themselves.

The Programme Itself

The programme has a three-stage format. In practice, these stages are not as clear-cut as they sound, it is not a teaching curriculum. Each survivor is likely to pass through the stages, each at their own pace. Each survivor learns, grows and changes through each stage.

Describing the secret

The Educative stage uses Metaphors to form a first bridge. We talk about the abuse, how it happens and what it does to people. We – the counsellors – describe as much as seems relevant. We give the survivor a chance to listen without committing themselves. This gives them a chance to check many of their own thoughts and feelings and to check whether we know what we are talking about.

Changing reality

The Future-focus stage begins to address current problems. We start to discuss what has gone wrong and what they want to do about it. We talk about answers, experiments, taking risks and so on. We warn them that this will not be a quick process.

Sharing support

The Support stage aims to give survivors the time and the patience to work on their lives. They have been in limbo ever since the abuse, coping as best they can, often in the same ways they used to as children. Other adults have developed and matured and found more confident ways to cope. Survivors have stayed stuck. They may have decades of delay to catch up with. This takes time – a year or perhaps two.

The programme can use individual counselling, couple counselling, group work and family therapy. If the same basic tools – the Metaphors – are used in each setting, Survivors can pass between these settings at different stages according to the match between the services on offer and their particular situation.

The Design of this Book

This book is, in some ways, like the programme:

- describing the secret – it tries to be open and easy to understand, written in plain language
- understanding the realities – it tries to reach as far into the human experiences of the situation as possible
- sharing the support – it takes a personal ownership of what is said and describes feelings in a feeling way.

But a counselling programme is not like a book. A programme needs reliable and consistent staff to be there for long periods of time. This book is unlikely to be as much help to survivors (whether they are professionals or not) as a counselling programme would. The following poem (extracts from a letter) describes the let-down feelings of a survivor when she learned that her counsellor was being made redundant. In its way, it shows just how important the staff in the programme are.

A2: Poem example – The Crime

To me the crime is being born.

Born into a family of those who sexually abused me and physically and mentally abused me. To me why was I put in this family – not because they wanted or loved me so what and why? I still don't know to this day.

No one wanted to know – who did I have? No one to talk to, no one to trust?

The hurt I went through. To me I was put in a cage never to come out, locked away forever and for what; just being born. No one ever wanted to know. (I was a kid.) and to me I thought everyone was like me, how wrong I was.

So it was me against the world. If I wanted to live I had to fight the whole world, and to me that is what I did. I had to fight to survive and that is what I did. To me by then I did not care who got hurt; to me I hurt every day so why shouldn't I hurt them back, to me if I let all these hurts hurt me any more then I could not live, so to me I lose any love I had for anyone. I lost all feeling, that everyone else has. To me I would fight all I can and do the things I wanted to do or I would die. And to me that is what I did for 31 years. Then something happened in my own family, that took my own world apart. How could I cope, so to me back in my cage to plan how to get everyone back again, until someone from the social services came along and she understood me and I thought at last someone I got to myself. Someone I can talk to, someone I can trust, someone to show me I am as important, to me she should have been around for me or someone like her for me when I was a kid, to me it took a long time to trust her, she gave me the hope I needed, but that was short-lived. She had to go away and leave me. Back on my own and deep in my bottle and gone was my feelings again.

Then I thought if I can be helped and there is someone out there to help me I got to try again. I got to have feelings, I got to be able to give love – what ever that is? I went to see a counsellor, it took me a very long time to trust him – I had to know he would always be there for me. I needed someone I could talk to and someone that understands me.

And I am slowly coming out of my cage. He has unlocked the cage for me. He has made me have feelings that I did not know I had. He gave me life to live, he has helped me to know what's right and what's wrong. And how to love. I don't know how to be loved yet but one day I will know, I hope. He has helped me more than my bottle. I know I can trust him – he has never let me down, he has always been there for me, I just had to ask for him, if only he was around for me or someone like him when I was a kid, but no luck, they didn't have them when I was a kid.

I had no one, I had a life of abuse, a life of crime, a life of prostitution (on the game), a life of ordeal, a life of problems, a life of being scared, a life of being sadness, a life of being on my own, a life of shock, and a life of being silent. No one to care, no one to listen, no one to care until I saw this counsellor; then my life has been changing.

I don't have to hide in my bottle, he is there for me any time I need him, but as luck with me no one is there for ever, I knew my life could not be so good for ever, my counsellor will not be here soon for me, it's quite frightening, what will I do, how will I cope without him. I need him, I don't want to be on my own again. Why is it when I get someone I need they go away – I don't understand, is that what the rest of my life is going to be like? I need him, I'm not ready yet but he has to go. He unlocked the cage for me, but, how long before I go back in the cage and stay there forever? Or do I die in my cage? I don't think anyone will have the answer to that – how can anyone hurt us, after all I did not ask to come into the world did.

This was written by me, Jenny, feeling very low on Thurs 3rd Nov. 1994.

I hope this makes sense to you who reads it, there is a good reason for me being like this, and why I don't trust anyone, because when I do trust them they go away and leave me all alone again, then what?

A Note

Where a complicated situation involving several people is being described, it may be difficult to sort out who the 'he' or 'she' is that is being talked about. If the sentence has a focus on feelings, these will be the survivor's feelings. Much of the writing in this book is mainly about understanding the complexity of the survivor's thoughts and feelings about the abuse.

CHAPTER I

A New Counselling Programme

The Structure of the Programme

This is a three-stage programme through which every survivor will pass in their own individual way.

The educative stage

If survivors arrive in counselling and are clear about what they want but are not sure how to get there, a Future-focus approach can be used immediately. But, too often, adult survivors of child sexual abuse do not know what they want. They are too frozen in their feelings of hopelessness, as many trauma victims are. So *we* should approach *them* rather than leave them stuck. We should build the first bridge using explanations about The Invisible Trap (see page 59) and its effects. We should offer more explanation rather than less. The aim is to reduce their anxiety and reduce their feelings of isolation and of being completely different to everyone else.

The future-focused therapy stage

Next, we should guide them to help them make their own choices about their future. This needs them to move towards identifying clear objectives for themselves. The aim is to encourage them to make plans and try to work with them to gain hope and confidence from achievements.

This may work in a series of very small steps. There may be a lot of uncertainty about the end result. Some people are able to decide very quickly what they want. Most feel that there are a number of vaguely understood options for their future but feel they have little power to choose – they need a lot of time. If this stage works very well, the next stage can include partners, family, friends, other professionals, clergy, and so on.

The support stage

Then they need help in continuing to achieve new objectives. They have so much catching up to do that they need to keep on sorting things out and try new ways of working at relationships and believing in themselves. This is likely to take much longer than it would for those with a good start in life and a trauma-free history. Patience and hope are essential.

Introductory Meetings

We start off by meeting everyone in individual meetings. We often go to their homes, perhaps meeting them with a partner or friend, or in some other safe and neutral place. These meetings aim to:

1. Introduce us to the survivor.

2. Allow us to introduce the ideas we work with (i.e. the Metaphors).

3. Allow the survivor to ask us questions.

4. Allow the survivor to work out whether she thinks we make sense or not.

5. Allow us to make a quick judgement about whether the survivor would fit into the group. (It would not be fair to her if things went badly wrong and it is the group leader's job to make sure this doesn't happen. It is extremely rare to find someone who would not fit in).

We usually meet three to six times – this is a decision based on a mixture of the survivor's needs, the finances available and the speed at which we cover the essential information.

We start the meeting with generalisations about sexual abuse and aim to become more personal and relevant to the survivor's experience. We go through the basic issues of how people normally respond to frightening situations. This leads on to the Post Traumatic Stress Response questionnaire (see Appendix). We discuss the various frightening and stressful situations during their childhood and then move on to the Unhealthy Childhood questionnaire (see Appendix). These questionnaires are useful to show the survivor how complicated the situation is and allow us to identify confusions and circles in their experiences and their thinking about it all. This helps us get closer to where the survivor is rather than continue in generalisations.

We describe how the group works, its confidentiality rules, and give a reminder about its being voluntary. We explain the 'start with listening' rule – this is permission to listen without talking for the first one or two groups. This is intended to help the nervousness people usually have in joining a group. It immediately shows a difference to Alcoholics Anonymous where new members have to stand up and introduce themselves and their problems. This is one of the most likely comparisons many will be making. We say that the other group members will know that a new member is not saying much and will be a little more careful than usual about personal things so it's OK to just listen.

Group Counselling

We usually use this programme in a group counselling approach, although we also use it in individual counselling. The group has significant advantages:

Seeing similarities for themselves

It allows people to see similarities with other survivors' reactions to the abuse. Survivors can gain a lot of strength from seeing for themselves that they are not the only ones to have reacted in the way they have. They can be reassured that they have reacted in a normal way, considering what has happened. They can begin to break out of the isolation imposed by the feeling of being totally different to everyone else. Breaking out of the isolation to start making meaningful friendships is the second step to change (the first is saying 'I was abused' or even 'I think I was abused').

Sharing support

Group members can receive support from other survivors. This will help them realise that other people do understand and do care and do want to help. Group members can also begin to give support and feel that they have a useful contribution to make, they can be of help to someone else. They are *useful*, not useless as they often think of themselves. This support can happen outside the meetings as well as during them – we encourage group members to contact each other by phone. This may be different to other professionally run groups where there may be concerns about short-term sorts of contact preventing more useful work for the longer term.

Cheaper and better

In the real world expense is an important consideration. Although some groups require as much work in preparation and the 'after-words' discussion of events because of their complexity, these groups are different. After the first adjustments to get used to the method, introduce the people and settle into a pace of discussion, these groups are relatively well behaved. There is rarely a great deal of argument between members, they usually agree a lot. There is seldom any jealously or resentment. They feel they are all on the same side trying to make the same progress. The issues discussed tend to be familiar and need repeating. This gives group members a chance to change their habit-formed attitudes. So, this sort of group is cheaper to run and provides a better level of support than a group for people who have very different problems. (For this sort of group, a reasonable membership means six or more.)

Individual Counselling

For people who prefer individual counselling, the advantages for them might include:

Keeping hold of privacy

They may have a fear of being 'the odd one out', which cannot be quickly eased. In our Introductory meetings we talk about this fear and tell people we are trying to reduce this fear because we know everyone thinks they are the odd one out. We say: 'If everyone thinks it, you can't all be right, so this is a normal fear to have!'

If this is not sufficiently reassuring, privacy becomes important. It is reasonable to say that a small number will be too slow to trust, too cautious to relax, too convinced of their differentness. These are often the results of the Post Traumatic Stress Responses – in other words, the Fright. At the time of discussing the idea of joining a group, they may not be able to accept this.

I remember one woman in her late thirties saying that she couldn't face joining a group. She hadn't talked to anyone about it before and she was convinced that all the group members would be in their teens and twenties. In other words, she thought that they would all have faced up to it and started to deal with it quicker than her. She thought that she was the only total failure and that they would all make her feel worse. This would be especially true if they tried to reassure her it was OK, which I would usually have encouraged them to do. Why? Because if they had the confidence to reassure her, that would prove she was the worst case of them all.

Control over the counselling situation

Some survivors are so worried about the implications of talking about the abuse that they feel they have to stay in charge at all costs. They might be afraid of being laughed at, or ignored, or not understood, or misunderstood, or even locked up or having their children taken away. They might be afraid that if they let the secret out, some consequences that the abuser threatened might come true. This could be especially important if there were several abusers who might have ways of knowing if the victim said anything about it.

One victim who impressed me with this concern had memories of what seemed to her to be some sort of ritualistic sexual abuse. She felt very worried that a circle of people would trigger off too many feelings. She was convinced that it would be easier to start off in individual counselling. She did say that maybe it would be important for her to face a group later on. She knew that at some point she had to force herself to believe that some circles could be good for her.

We make a special effort in the assessment sessions to tell survivors that they are in control. In other words, they can stop the conversation, delay the next session or even just not come back. Some do take this last option – we allow this even if we are tempted to try just a little bit more reassurance. If we are committed to the idea of people pacing the counselling for themselves, we need to accept some consequences. If some survivors are too anxious or frightened to try a group, that is an appropriate emotional attitude for them to hold. People have to decide for themselves if they are ready for counselling, we cannot force them to try it. In fact, forcing them would be too close to abuse, so we never do it. This might leave some people feeling uncared-for but we know that no professional programme is going to suit everyone who is eligible for it.

Deserving special treatment

One mother of four refused to join a group because she deserved time for herself. She said no one had ever treated her as an important person, they had always pushed her aside or trodden her down. She was very angry about this and felt that she wanted to be put first. 'Principle!', she would say – in other words: 'My opinion is more important, my wishes are more important'.

This survivor was saying that she deserved special treatment in her counselling. Abuse had always put her second or last (see Unhealthy Childhood questionnaire, page 223) so counselling had to be different. If it is financially justifiable, it seems a morally acceptable argument. If it is not financially possible, counselling may reach a very sad dead-end or, maybe (I hope) a compromise.

Using alternatives

Where someone has already started to talk in a counselling way, our Introductory meetings can give things a healthy push to speed them up. In this case, it might be better to encourage the talking that has already started rather than argue about joining a group.

One young woman turned down the group and said that the information we had given her in those first meetings had already helped her. She had talked to her mother and explained why she had done some things that had come between them. Her mother listened, encouraged and eventually admitted to being a survivor herself, much to the surprise of both of them! They formed their own little group and, because they didn't have to start as strangers, it was easier than joining a group. We did offer the possibility of both of them joining a group together but they preferred to continue as they had started.

After Counselling

When a survivor has done as much work as she felt she needed, it is time to leave the individual or group counselling. The aim of this programme is to help people live their lives as normally as possible. This means using the help that other people use: vaccinations, grants, complaints and so on. It means getting on without large amounts of help from health, welfare or other services.

The next stage

Getting to this stage may take a while, even when the survivor feels ready to leave the programme. We encourage survivors to stay in touch by phone, visit the group (if that's the form of help they used) occasionally and, perhaps, join a leaver's group that meets once every two or three months. Even chance meetings in the street play their part, they offer an opportunity to share progress, grumble about how hard life is and renew some energy.

Going on to helping others

There are also times when survivors can help other survivors outside or after the group. We support the occasional pairing up of same-sex survivors as friendships. Usually, one is further along their personal path than the other. We stay in touch with these supportive pairings to ensure that it is working fairly – it would be a pity if it went wrong and one began to feel over-burdened by it. Some pairings are just friendships, others are more like teacher and pupil – teaching drawing, for instance.

Being free to be independent

The overall aim of the programme is to leave survivors free to live their own lives as they want to, quite separate from the programme. The programme should be a temporary stage in their lives. The programme should not depend upon them for anything more than their attendance in the group or counselling meetings.

I feel quite strongly that we should not ask survivors to support the organisation or the group in any essential way. I feel that they have had enough to cope with already. It is an unfair responsibility to expect them to work for the organisation as well as work for themselves. The finances should not depend upon them – surely they have paid enough for society's blind-spot already. The organisation should be able to organise itself.

Some other organisations do ask for assistance from the people who use the services. When an organisation has financial difficulties, it is easy to understand the pressures on the organisers. An organisation that cannot stay alive cannot help those it intends to help. Even so, I feel there is a moral issue here.

However, if someone offers to help in a relatively small and achievable way, I would not turn them away automatically. We would talk it over and consider it for everyone's sake – the survivor's, the organisation's, the other survivors', etc. The idea of the supportive pairing above is just this sort of help. I realise that this opinion may be unpopular in some quarters used to self-help and community work. I shall only say that I hope any developments to include the survivors in the organisation's work – as staff or as volunteers – are done very carefully.

The most obvious way in which survivors can help is by giving good news of progress. This can then be passed on (with permission) to the group or put into a Newsletter or circulated as a poem (see The Result, page 243). One such case arose from a chance meeting in town:

1.1: Case example – Life gets easier

Once you've dealt with it [the abuse], life gets easier. Then you can decide what you want and work to get there. I'm doing a full-time job and training at college one day a week. I'm doing Welfare Studies and enjoying it – it's very rewarding. I learnt a lot meeting my Dad [after about 20 years, following his divorce and separation from the family; he was not the abuser]. It's made all the difference – finding out that I was wanted and loved after all – even though he died two years later.

To my eye, three years after our previous meeting, she had lost quite a lot of weight and looked better for it. She was not so brassy, she was more mellow and thoughtful.

Progress in the Programme

If we follow the progress we hope a survivor makes, we can find some stages.

Surviving the abuse

The way the abuse victim manages to survive emotionally during the abuse can play an important part in his or her future. Some people cope better than others. Some have to cope with worse abuse than others. Some have to cope alone, others with friends. Some cope by instinct, others by plan. All these factors will play a part.

Often, it is the way that the child deals with the pain that stays with them later. Hiding their anger, ability to love or feelings of guilt and shame influences their adult life (see the poem, *Hidden*, page 235).

Remember: some do not survive, they remain trapped, exploited and, in some cases, killed.

1.2: Case example – Counting the bricks

I remember a woman who said that there were times when she only survived emotionally by concentrating on counting the bricks in the wall. This went back to the days of the abuse, when she would distract herself by counting anything; bricks, patterns in the wallpaper, cracks on the ceiling. She was very ashamed of this as an adult. She could arrive at the individual sessions giggly and apparently relaxed. At home she could easily collapse onto her bed, shake and shiver with fear, and count things in the room. (Later, she told me that the giggling was another way of keeping the fear away).

Surviving after the abuse

When the sexual contact has ceased, the victim remains as an abused child. The teenage years and the twenties are often times when survivors try to 'forget it all and get on with life'. Sometimes this is successful, sometimes its failures bring suicidal thoughts and depressions. But, all the time it works, we should accept it. Many professionals recognise teenagers, young adults and young parents who are doing this and worry about it. They feel they should interrupt it and make things better. I feel we should accept it without challenge. The danger is that the survivor has a bad experience in counselling and then feels unable to try again when things get more desperate. It is vital to make sure that they know that counselling will be available if anything goes wrong with their plan.

One of the most important factors is the survivor's own opinion of their previous coping methods. If they believe themselves to be failures, they stay victims. If they believe themselves to be successful, they become survivors. Most seem to consider themselves failures and flawed. Victims they were made and victims they stay, in attitude.

Some of the coping methods victims try are more dangerous than others. In time, some may suffer from the risks: drugs and alcohol, prostitution and crime, self-harm and suicide attempts.

Asking for help

There seem to be two ways people get to the point of asking for help. One is to decide to ask and to prepare for this well beforehand. The other is that a crisis arrives suddenly and forces the issue. The difference is the months of

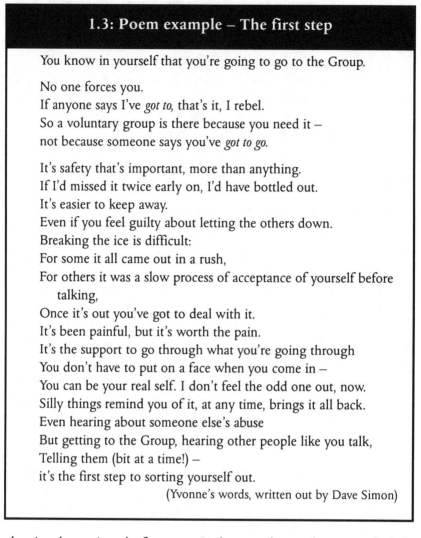

1.3: Poem example – The first step

You know in yourself that you're going to go to the Group.

No one forces you.
If anyone says I've *got to*, that's it, I rebel.
So a voluntary group is there because you need it –
not because someone says you've *got to go.*

It's safety that's important, more than anything.
If I'd missed it twice early on, I'd have bottled out.
It's easier to keep away.
Even if you feel guilty about letting the others down.
Breaking the ice is difficult:
For some it all came out in a rush,
For others it was a slow process of acceptance of yourself before
     talking,
Once it's out you've got to deal with it.
It's been painful, but it's worth the pain.
It's the support to go through what you're going through
You don't have to put on a face when you come in –
You can be your real self. I don't feel the odd one out, now.
Silly things remind you of it, at any time, brings it all back.
Even hearing about someone else's abuse
But getting to the Group, hearing other people like you talk,
Telling them (bit at a time!) –
it's the first step to sorting yourself out.

(Yvonne's words, written out by Dave Simon)

planning that go into the first route. In the second route the request for help is often made during the crisis or only days afterwards. Either way, it takes a great deal of courage and/or determination to break the habit of safety in silence. But this request can make all the difference in the world to their future.

Joining the programme

Saying 'I was sexually abused' is probably the most useful thing a survivor can say to an informed professional. It immediately provides the ground for active and reassuring work. Saying it to uninformed professionals could be a problem, and survivors know it all too well. The risk is that when they are desperate they are not in a good state to weigh up how the professional will react. If they have 'made mistakes' before, we take the heat out of it by reminding them of the desperate crisis they were in. We also remind them that it is the professionals who are trained to assess clients, not the other way round!

Saying the one sentence 'I was sexually abused' can totally alter the quality of help these people get. Before that is said they will get the best that professionals can do when they only know half the story. Some people ask for professional help but hide the reason for and the extent of the problems. I suspect that a large number of people in mental hospitals with unexplained depression were sexually abused, perhaps a majority. Perhaps it's the same for people with other types of emotional problems.

I have heard survivors admit that they previously hid the abuse from professionals (see the poem, *Hidden*, page 235). One woman said 'I got away with blaming my depression on my father, who physically abused me. I didn't tell them about the men who interfered with me. I couldn't, there was too much at stake'. This is not surprising. Most of their life has been a habit of hiding thoughts, feelings and memories, but they often regret deceiving professionals when they realise they haven't really helped themselves. They may feel tempted to blame themselves 'for being a coward'. We must remember that this is a most difficult thing to do. No one can do it for them and no one can guarantee everything will be OK. Fear of the consequences has kept them in silence for tens of years of pain and problems. Why should another crisis be any different?

Joining the *ASCSA* programme is a way of saying 'I was sexually abused'. For some people it is the first time they have ever said it. Being a specialist organisation helps this. We give a clear message about what we do. Having specialist experience allows us to start talking about sexual abuse very quickly, where other professionals might wish to go very slowly. Occasionally, survivors use the first meeting to reveal one painful memory or miserable question after another. It is as though the flood gates are opened. This can be very scary for the survivor, but we offer a lot of reassurance as quickly as possible. We encourage their courage. When this works well, it can make a very solid stepping stone for the later meetings.

For other survivors, the early meetings are a chance to check whether their memories are about sexual abuse or about something else. Some people really are not sure because they don't know the definition of sexual abuse. This definition can be difficult to find and many survivors would avoid those library shelves in case someone noticed their interest and jumped to (the right) conclusios..

Making progress through turning points

Progress takes time, energy and risks. There are turning points and hiccups. There are disappointments and triumphs. Apart from a counsellor – or better, a group – there are usually very few people who survivors can talk it all through with.

Progress can be fast or slow, orderly or chaotic, understandable or confusing, planned or spontaneous. Change can have many characteristics and it varies a lot from person to person. Sometimes these characteristics stay the same throughout the counselling, other times they vary in different stages. It is important to talk about the process of change itself, in case mistakes or misunderstandings make things worse. Therefore, we talk about the Government Health Warning, Vertigo and the Garden Gate (see Metaphors about Progress, page 111).

The process of change feels like a long and uncertain one. For most people it is a first, they are automatically in new territory, never having done this sort of thing before. It is normal to be anxious at the start of counselling and this can continue throughout the process. For survivors it can last a year or more, there is so much to sort out. This seems such a long time to be anxious that we feel we must help to reduce the uncertainty as much as possible.

The steps described by the section headings in this chapter are:

1. Surviving the abuse.

2. Surviving after the abuse.

3. Asking for help.

4. Joining the programme.

5. Making progress through turning points.

6. Deciding to leave the programme.

7. Successfully ordinary!

These are landmarks of a kind. They show the path of the survivor from childhood abuse through to recovery as a happy and healthy adult. To make the path as clear as possible, we look for landmarks to describe what goes on in abuse, survival, progress and recovery. This is the basis for the metaphor about the Fogbank (see page 91).

LOOKING FOR LANDMARKS

We try to offer landmarks so that people can have some idea of where they are and where they are going. The following counselling group discussion shows us talking about this – it is also an interesting example of how useful personal metaphors are.

A group discussion often leads to a series of metaphors being put together to explain the issues of finding, checking and understanding memories of abuse. I remember a discussion that jumped around a lot with several people contributing – typical of much group work. A group member called Julie described how confused she was about a lack of memories prior to the age of eight. Then she said that she had recently had one small and isolated flashback memory about that time. The conversation flowed around the topic, touching a number of her personal metaphors and some added in by others. Another member responded with the idea of a jigsaw, each piece being a small memory about a particular event. The first stage was gathering together clusters of jigsaw pieces. This then allowed her to see the whole picture. Julie likened this to her experience of building up chapters of the book of her life. Some chapters were completely blank and some had many pages, although some of these pages were half-empty. She reminded us that she'd written a poem that mentioned this:

1.4: Poem example – What happened?

What happened to the days
missing from my mind?
Like pages of a book,
glued together, impossible to find.

Julie Anne Holton

Once she had got the chapters clear in her mind, she had to sort them into the right historical order. Then it all became more like a video with lots of fast-forward – play – fast-forward – play – fast-backward – play, and so on, happening without her control. It was as though there was a search system trying to put it all in order for her. Nowadays, she still gets occasional memories or flashbacks or bits of a dream that she needs to slot into place, but it's much easier. The video only goes onto fast-forward until it reaches the right place and then slots the memory in. We said it seemed as though someone else had the video remote control to begin with but now she operates it. She is more in control of it all.

During this discussion we mentioned detective work as a way of describing how some people have to sort out *what* happened before they can sort out *why* it happened. Then we changed the metaphor to one of archaeology – digging into the past until you reach bedrock and then reconstructing events, what really happened in physical, legal and moral terms.

Writing about the discussion here makes the flow seem very disjointed. It doesn't appear as good literature, the metaphors seem to jump about a lot. But in live group discussions, this is OK. It feels relevant and real. It is made meaningful by the people there at the time.

Note: It is important to mention that we do not accept people who have no memories of sexual abuse onto the programme. This discussion occurred between survivors who were sure it had happened. One survivor could not remember when, or with whom, it had started. Another could remember a lot, but not always when or where. This area of 'forgotten memories' is a particularly complicated one, with important legal and theoretical problems.

It is interesting that survivors' own metaphors sometimes use landmarks of their own (see the poem, *The Lamppost on the hill*, page 242).

1.5: Case example – I wasn't embarrassed, just angry

At work, this woman talked about sexual abuse because she'd heard something on the radio about rising levels in the country. She said that she didn't know what all the fuss was about because she did it every day. And then I said to her 'What do you mean?' and she said 'I do it every day, I touch people'. She does, she's terrible, really, grabbing men's bums – even the boss's.

I swung round when she said it 'cos there was no one else she could be talking to – no one nearby – and gave her this piece of my mind – shouted at her – that that was sexual harassment not sexual abuse and swung back to my work. I wasn't embarrassed, just angry. Couldn't have done it a year ago – I used to keep quiet and make out I didn't know what they were on about and think 'You stupid bitch, you don't know what you're talking about'.

Mel

Quite often, turning points occur and need to be noticed as landmark experiences. A survivor's depression, pessimism and confusion can all mean that his or her positive achievements are overlooked. We point these out as they happen and try to build up confidence from them.

Deciding to leave the programme

Once progress is being made, there comes the question: 'How will I know I am ready to leave?' There do not seem to be any answers that suit everyone. Generally, the answer is: 'When you don't need it any more'. Better, the answer is: 'When you need other, happier things more'. We often find that attendance drops when a survivor takes up an educational course, changes their relationship, becomes a happier mother, finds a job, and so on. These are the best reasons for leaving the programme. It seems as though other things become more important in life (see Spring-cleaning, page 97).

One discussion I had with a survivor who had completely reworked her life told me a lot about how the final bits of change worked:

1.6: Case example – Yes, life is totally different

'You reach a point where other things become more important. It [the abuse memories and feelings] doesn't disappear, but it just isn't so important. It ends up more like other memories – you can remember them if you want to, but I don't! It's easy! My course is much more important to me. I want to keep working on it and get through it.

I don't worry about failing it – I would have done a couple of years ago, but not now. Now I just do the work, go to the classes, make friends. Relationships are totally different. Yes, the kids have troubles. But I can decide which to help them with and which to leave them with.

My relationship with my new partner is something else! I don't know what to call it but it's different to anything I've ever felt in myself and different from anything I've ever felt from a man too. I've been asking friends 'What is love?' to try and find out if that's what it is. I don't know yet, but I do know I want to keep it. Yes, life is different, totally different!'

Sandy

Because the programme is completely voluntary, people can leave at any time.

Successfully ordinary!

The next challenge is to stay away from any support system for abuse survivors and their problems. The eventual aim is to be self-sufficient in the emotional sense – able to look after themselves. This means they are able to use the ordinary support systems others use to help themselves – friends, family and appropriate health, welfare and educational services. Getting on with the rest of one's life, dealing with problems, coping with stress and improving the quality of life is what everyone wants.

One woman started a discussion in the group about being ordinary. She left shortly afterwards and has been happy knowing that the group is there but not needing it. She later agreed to support a group member in distress, after it became clear that they had a lot in common, despite 20 years' age difference. The discussion was arguing about the question: 'How can survivors be ordinary?'

One point was that survivors are just human beings, not Martians! True enough, but most of the group members said that they felt different to non-survivors. We reminded them about the Post Traumatic Stress Response of 'feeling separate and different' and that this could happen to any survivor of any trauma. 'But we were ordinary before the abuse happened! So why can't we be ordinary afterwards? I think you [the Group Leaders] should tell doctors and social workers, we're not freaks! We're ordinary people with big problems because of abuse.'

We then talked about 'The Wall' (see p.62) and how most survivors don't want other people – especially professionals who might be 'dangerous' to their freedom or their children's freedom – to know they are abuse victims. 'But some professionals are survivors too. How do they feel about it all?' And so the discussion continued. What was important was that they began to ask the question about how to regain ordinaryness – most of them had never considered it a possibility. The member who started the discussion was saying 'I think I feel ordinary' – quite a shock to her and the other group members!

1.7: Case example – Now it's because I want to

'Part of what has helped is my new job. It's great, it's boosted my confidence. I'm doing training for a specialism within three months of starting! I'm not a desperate workaholic anymore. I do work hard but now it's because I want to not because I have to'.

We have to remember to stay practical when we are sorting out where a survivor wants to get to, where she wants to end up. Sorting this out helps us to provide targets to aim for, which is much easier than only knowing what she wants to get away from. Sorting out targets needs everyone to stay practical, although that is not the only consideration!

It is useful to think of a stage after 'surviving' – 'thriving'. I have only recently heard this term and it fits the situation well. Thrivers often go on to educational courses, new jobs, better or improved relationships where they say 'I'm enjoying this!' It is wonderful to hear them say this and it shows the counselling job is done.

1.8: Case example – Room for mischief and fun

During a conversation with a survivor about her progress, I asked 'Whereabouts on a scale of zero to ten are you nowadays?' We had agreed that she had been at zero when we met. We said that ten was the most wonderfully peaceful and happy experience she could possibly have.

I asked 'Where are you now?' 'Six'. I asked 'Where do you want to get to eventually?' 'Eight or nine, not ten.' 'Why?' I asked. 'Because there's got to be room for mischief and fun' she explained!

The Reasoning of the Programme

The programme has some principles that guide how it works. These principles emerged and became clearer as we worked on it.

Using research

If we know that people who have been sexually abused are still in 'The Trap' (see page 59), we cannot realistically (or ethically) expect them to come to us, explain their problems or inform us of their intentions. They cannot behave and experience feelings within the normal range. The trauma has pushed them off course. They are unlikely to have enough confidence. They are quite different to someone who can explain their nervousness as being due to a mugging several weeks ago.

Therefore, we have to 'go to them'. This idea is totally in line with the original ideas of counselling: 'Start where the client is at'. But that used to mean 'Start your planning, your thinking, your intuition where the client is at'. We do all that and take it further: we start our *talking* 'where the survivor is at'. We 'go to them' by telling them what we know about 'how sexual abuse happens and what it does to people'. To do this, we rely on research – both national and local. We tell them what the general facts are. We admit they are generalisations and we accept that later in discussions we must deal with their particular problems.

In serious cases, survivors are 'Trapped' in 'The Fogbank' (see the Metaphors on pages 59 and 91). They will not disclose the sexual abuse unless given very urgent reasons to do so (desperation) or very strong feelings of safety (reassurance). To make them desperate, or wait until they are, would be re-traumatising unnecessarily. We can and should reassure them using our research knowledge. This is also likely to be quicker, which is better for survivors and better adjusted to financial realities.

Research should be described in the most easily understandable way possible. We need to use an anti-mystifying, anti-confusing clearness of communication to show a difference between counsellors and perpetrators. Scientific jargon may help academics. Professional jargon may help professionals. Plain language helps ordinary people.

Using definitions

One particular area we must discuss early on in the Introduction stage is the definition of 'child sexual abuse'. We are very aware of using a modern definition of abuse. This raises issues of 'was it abuse 50 years ago when it happened?' We have to tackle this question as well as we can. It is one thing to rely on a legal or professional definition of abuse, it is another to show that it is a useful and reliable definition. Definitions have changed as research findings have changed professional good practice. Other influences have been the legal precedents and political progress that have changed the laws of the land.

Our reason for using the definition we choose is that we can relate it to the modern actions taken to prevent child abuse. The investigations that happen nowadays are based on the most up-to-date definitions. This gives us a starting point.

- We may need to say that abuse was not called 'abuse' years ago. It was called different names: interfering with children, molesting children and incest, for example.

- We might possibly need to say that the abuse was not illegal at the time it happened, although it was immoral.

- We may need to say that some abuse is still not illegal but is immoral (child pornography is only illegal if distributed to other people, not if kept by the photographer).

Even so, if the abuse caused emotional, relationship and even physical problems, it was wrong and it should not have happened.

At the time of writing (1997), in the country of writing (the UK), the current definition of child sexual abuse says it happens when there is:

(a) an adult and a child, or several of either AND

(b) a duty on the adult to be responsible for the child AND

(c) any type of sexual intercourse – started by either –

    OR

        sexual touching – either on the other –

    OR

        sexual looking – either at each other –

    OR

        sexual displaying – either to the other –

    OR

        sexual talking – adults flirting with the child –

    OR

        involving pornography – showing or taking photos or videos

Most Survivors are willing to accept this definition. Sometimes it answers their questions about whether they were abused – they may have known what happened but been unsure whether it was abuse. Sometimes it surprises them because they thought what had happened was not sexual abuse. Sometimes it clarifies that the abuse was physical or emotional, even though it touched on the child's sexual parts. In these cases, children may have suffered violence to their genitals or have had their genitals or sexuality belittled through sarcasm or verbal aggression.

At this point it may be important to say that child sexual abuse often happens where neglect, emotional abuse and physical abuse have already happened. It may happen before, during or after the sexual abuse. It may come from the same person or a different person. It may lead to, or lead from, the sexual abuse or be completely separate from it. This all needs to be sorted out in the early Introductory meetings as it will affect the next steps.

It is also important to identify people who have not been sexually abused. These people may have great problems and may wonder whether they were sexually abused but have no memory of it. They might ask whether the counsellor thinks it is possible. We have to be very careful about this. While it might be true, if there are no memories to confirm it we have no evidence to help us decide one way or the other. Courts have been very careful about this area, particularly where there seemed to be physical evidence but no spoken evidence. Sometimes, defence lawyers can suggest that a professional has 'planted' the idea in the mind of the person enquiring about sexual abuse. This is an opportunity to 'question the evidence', as their job requires them to do.

It is also very important to the progress of the programme. Joining the counselling group depends on the person being clear in themselves and saying clearly to the group leaders that they have been sexually abused as a child.

If we meet someone and explain the definition of child sexual abuse and they then say they have no clear memories of any of those activities, we cannot invite them into the counselling group. Although they might hope that listening to others in the group would help them become clearer about it, or might bring back memories, we cannot easily take that chance. It would not be fair on other group members if there was someone in the group simply listening and not returning confidences. This would reduce their feeling of security in the common bond between them and could stop any meaningful discussion. Also, if a court suggested that the group had put the idea into that person's mind, this would threaten the other group members. This could damage the future of that group and, perhaps, the programme as a whole.

These issues are so important – although very rare – that they must be taken very seriously.

Using metaphors

The question 'why we should use Metaphors?' is one that we need to answer.

Some counsellors might feel more at ease using the 'facts of the matter'. Others might want to use more intensive methods of exploring personal and subjective experiences, such as psychodrama. By actively offering Metaphors in this way, we could be criticised by people who feel that we are closing the survivor's area of freedom to create his or her own Metaphors.

The aim of using Metaphors is to provide a gentle, meaningful and therapeutically useful bridge. This bridge reaches between survivors' unresolved, 'un-sorted-out' experiences and 'the rest of the world'. The idea is to enable them to achieve a better emotional health. In the language of The Fogbank, the Metaphors are the maps the counsellor can use to guide the people out of The Invisible Trap and the Impossible Jigsaw.

Metaphors have been used in many areas of counselling. Bettleheim (1976) wrote a large book about the uses of stories with children. A book about Milton Erickson, a master of the use of metaphors (Zeig 1980), gives a useful description of what metaphors are: 'For example, they can be fairy tales, fables, parables or allegories'. It is also very interesting that he includes the word 'parables' – this connects us with 'proverbs' and reminds us that the Bible shows us just how long a history this method has had.

There are great advantages in using Metaphors rather than talking literally about the 'facts'. I will go through some of them here.

METAPHORS ARE MEANINGFUL – THEY EXPLAIN THINGS

Some issues addressed by the Metaphors cannot be discussed in a factual way. Using the idea of 'The Trap', we intend to describe an emotional trap, not a physical trap like a prison. But they might *feel* similar. Emotions are invisible, they are names for feelings we experience or expressions and gestures we see others making. The Trap is an emotional fact, a spiritual truth that counselling must confirm as appropriate and true. As time goes on, The Trap ends up being inside the survivor's head – especially after the abuser has gone away or even died. So, Metaphors are more about subjective personal truth than about scientific factual truth. In counselling, this is useful, in its place. We use research too.

METAPHORS ARE CHALLENGING – WHAT IS REAL EXPERIENCE?

Openly using a Metaphor – or a Story – conveys an awareness of the fragility of the nature of 'Reality'. What feels real for one person may not feel real to another. This applies to feelings and 'philosophical' questions especially. Saying 'this is a Metaphor' suggests something like 'things are only as real as we think they are'.

This allows us to discuss what feels real (but shouldn't) and what shouldn't be real (even though it is). So, if survivors feel that abuse was their fault (but hear others say it wasn't), we can discuss issues like 'what is this feeling, who has the final say, how do we solve circular puzzles?'. Where they have flashbacks, hallucinations or bodily sensations that aren't 'real', we can confirm that subjectively they are very real and painful. Describing pain as a Painkiller (see page 106) is not logical but does make sense to survivors.

We can also discuss hidden feelings and artificial expressions. This can go on to areas of considering other people's 'Walls' and how much they camouflage their feelings.

METAPHORS ARE ADJUSTABLE EXPLANATIONS

We can modify a Metaphor to clarify or emphasise different parts of the message. With 'The Fogbank', for instance, we can focus on the various sections of the journey. There is a 'lost, lonely and miserable' message at the start of counselling. Then there is 'exploring the paths' and 'getting to know the map', and 'finding the beginnings of Hope' stage nearer the edge of The Fogbank. Finally, there is a 'breaking free' to make large-scale choices about life.

We can change the sensory medium we convey it in. That is, we can translate from one sense to another – so we can translate what we usually see into something we might hear or feel instead. For instance, The Fogbank can become The Pit or The Forest or The Maze. The Trap can become The Plastic Coffin, The Darkness, The Silence, and so on.

From time to time, survivors prefer to modify the Metaphor to make it a closer match to their experience. It is important to confirm their description as being more meaningful (to them) as long as the new one doesn't differ too much from the essential emotional and moral message of the old one. Many of the Metaphors listed in this book came from survivors – either directly or through an amalgamation of several similar stories. Some Metaphors appear as poems or in poems, which offer a slightly different and very useful medium.

METAPHORS ARE DISPOSABLE DESCRIPTIONS

The message contained in a Metaphor is not 'forever fixed' as though it were a fact (that is, right or wrong, true or false). So, if the message feels unhelpful to the survivor , we can leave it behind, temporarily or permanently. It does not make the counsellor or the survivor wrong or useless if we use a Metaphor that jars with the survivor's experience. We can simply say 'That wasn't useful, was it?' and move on. Some survivors have already thought out some parts of their experience before starting counselling, so we can find that a Metaphor is accepted without interest because it doesn't offer anything new to them.

All in all, I think Metaphors offer a very useful channel for the counselling communications that seem to help. Given that our main job is educating in the first stage of the programme, we have to use some basis to explain how abuse happens and what it does to people. The Metaphors are flexible, yet strong, tools with which to build that first bridge to survivors.

In the second stage, where people start to set their own aims, they begin to work in more concrete terms of what *they* want. The Metaphors become of much less relevance because 'Designing a New Future' (see page 99) becomes more important. Most of the Metaphors are about the past and survivors will only occasionally remember them in the third stage. This is a good sign!

I have grouped the Metaphors described in the next chapter into areas that change through time. They are about abuse, about counselling, about surviving and about progress. This roughly follows the order in which we might use them, or at least the order in which they are likely to come up.

The Time Perspective

Timing is an important issue in any discussion of the programme. Timing issues might relate to the delay between the abuse, or when the victim was made safe, and the start of the counselling. Or it might concern the length of time the counselling takes.

These issues might be discussed between a counsellor and the survivor, the relatives, the counsellor's manager, other critics, or other interested professionals.

Part of any discussion about the time taken to do the counselling has to be about the decision to pace the programme to the survivor's speed. Some educational programmes go at their own speed, following the curriculum or the course week by week, term by term. They do not slow or stop for anyone. Students have to speed up or drop out. This programme is trying to include everyone and to work at the most productive speed for each survivor. This inevitably takes time.

Several sources of delay

These issues are important when we are talking to both survivors and professionals. There is more relevant discussion in the Technical Note on page 153.

SURVIVORS SUFFERING DELAYED SHOCK

In considering the delays between the abuse and the victim asking for help, we must understand that the reaction to a fright will often include a stage of shock.

Shock may delay the realisation of what has happened after a fright, so that it is only some time later that the victim realises what has been done to her. This might mean that it is some while after the first incident (if there is a clear 'first' one, which there may not be) or some time after the end of the period of abuse. In either case, victims may blame themselves for not having realised earlier and 'done something about it' quicker.

Strong feelings often follow the shock stage but these may be delayed by that stage, which might create a feeling of unreality and of being 'disconnected from the world' for some time before the fright hits home. These strong feelings may turn the victim away from talking about it into sadness or anger, grief or depression.

Also, we must remember that shock may not follow the incident immediately. It is possible that a survivor doesn't realise she has been a Victim until years after the event because of delayed discovery. This might be because:

- The memories were completely buried in the Storage Cupboard. This is a very difficult area to understand and to react to. There are various theories about how memory works and the legal questions about 'False Memory Syndrome' (as it has been named) do not help us in counselling work. Rather than untangle things for a survivor, this syndrome complicates and confuses things more. We take a practical approach to the Storage Cupboard (see Spring-cleaning, page 97).

- The memories were confused because the victim was so young or confused by the abuser. I have heard people say that it was only five years later in Biology class, or Social and Moral Education at school that they realised what had been done to them. The confusion that an abuser creates is discussed later.

SURVIVORS AVOIDING HELP

Because victims have chosen to stay in The Trap out of fear of the consequences, there has been plenty of time for problems to get worse. New attempts at coping may have failed, new problems developed, hopelessness grown and grown. Many survivors have been stuck in The Trap for four or five decades or more. For instance, in the case example I described in the Introduction, the two sisters had both kept the secret from each other for sixty years or more. This is plainly tragic. If progress through counselling can stop this, one or two years of hard work is well worth it. We are talking about a fairly small fraction of the time that many survivors have been suffering in silence; this makes a year or two seem quick by comparison.

Even when victims do start to talk about their experience, things may go slowly. Because victims usually choose to hide their problems, and develop a habit of hiding them, professionals will not understand just how bad it is. Victims often seem to describe only half their problems – or less – so it is not surprising that professionals can say 'Look, no problems!' Unfortunately, we have to remember that abusers can and do say this too, so for professionals to say it (or even think it) is a continuation of The Trap, leaving the victims very little choice but to put up with it as best they can. Nowadays, professionals are getting a better idea of just how bad it is and encouraging victims to say how they feel and ask for relevant sorts of help. (But, remember, around 5% of victims say they have no problems.)

The seriousness of sexual abuse

This programme may take one or two years. While this might seem a long time, we need to set it in perspective. I originally aimed to work in a 'brief therapy' approach, trying to work as quickly as possible, for example over a period of two or three months. I was used to this with counselling people and families with a wide variety of problems. So, when I started this work I struggled with the fact that a year seemed such a long time in comparison. However, I realised that it was due to two things:

1. the seriousness of what child abuse often does to the child

2. the length of time most victims have been stuck in The Trap.

It is not because of incompetent counsellors, or because of survivors being 'useless' in the counselling (see The Fogbank, page 91).
Survivors need many opportunities to test their judgement of the counsellor(s). They need to check the arguments. They need 'thinking time'. They need to take several goes at sorting some things out because parts of it are so complicated (see The Confusions: Sexual Abuse is Always Complicated, page 115). They need opportunities to test their new ideas against other family members, other group members or other sources of information (TV, magazines, books).

It may take two years before a survivor *really feels* that they have survived. This is not surprising, many of them were caught in The Trap of abuse lasting as many or more years. Most adult survivors have stayed in the emotional trap for decades before asking for help. I will not attempt to offer an average period here, but let's point out and emphasise that two years of counselling is quick compared to 20 years in The Trap.

The Philosophy of the Programme

There are different moral approaches to working with people. Generally, they are to punish, reward or rescue them – in work with child abuse we might want to punish abusers, rescue victims and reward rescuers, for example. There are other possibilities though. Some people would rather rescue abusers (perhaps from themselves) to prevent them ever abusing another child. Sometimes, victims are punished (or nearly are) for speaking out – by ridicule or violence, at home or in Court, privately or in the media. We have to be aware of our moral starting point when we decide to work with survivors, especially because of the immorality of the abuse done to them.

In counselling and therapy generally, we are on the 'rescuing' side. There are some aspects of this that we must be clear about. We must be careful to avoid thinking we are the *only* means of help for them. There are many. We must also be careful not to think that everything we do must be helpful. It is not that simple. We must aim to help them to help themselves, otherwise they may need rescuing services longer than necessary. This is why we try to change, heal, cure people to reach an independent and self-sustaining lifestyle.

As a general statement, counsellors want to help because they think people should not have to put up with problems. They assume people would rather not have problems. It is difficult to believe that anyone would happily keep a problem.

But there may be exceptions. I think one is when survivors believe that things will get worse if the 'problem' gets better. In other words, what seems a problem to us may actually be an answer to them. So we must be careful to do the right thing – for them and for others. We have to check as we do it.

In working with adult survivors of child sexual abuse this is especially important. There are usually many problems and many answers already around. Society has had answers. Families have, partners have and survivors have too. These could have been any combination of punishing, rewarding or rescuing the various people involved. If someone is asking for counselling, this usually means that the answers they have already tried have not been helpful enough. So 'helping' has not been a simple matter so far.

A clear philosophy

I feel it is very important for survivors to know quickly where the counsellor is with all these issues. They half expect people – including professionals – to blame them and tell them off. Alternatively, some might half-expect to be told 'It wasn't your fault, so cheer up and forget about it'. For most survivors, neither of these responses is new and neither is useful. We must be clear about where we stand about the abuse so that the survivor quickly understands us.

So the options for counsellors are:

- to be moral-free – 'we don't discuss the good and the bad of what happened' – or
- to be moral-driven – 'we have opinions about the unfairness, and we say so'.

I prefer to be moral-driven. It is clear and recognisable. It gives survivors a choice about whether they accept or argue with the moral messages. It gives them the freedom to decide for themselves what they think about the morality of the abuse, their responses, other people's reactions to their responses and so on.

In practical terms, this means discussing the issue in the first or second interview. I think we should mention it briefly and quietly. It can sometimes be appropriate for the counsellor to show a small amount of emotion and to say that any form of child abuse is *wrong for the child*. This follows most naturally from the early description of the emotional results of the abuse: 'Child Abuse almost always harms the child's development, and that is why it should not happen, and that is why it is illegal'. We must remember to say that it is the adult who was doing wrong, not the child. As adults, we can now understand that the child didn't understand the moral issues at the time – even if they had been taught the physical aspects of sex during the abuse.

It is important to clear up any thought the survivor might have that they also did something wrong – after all, they were there too, they will say. Although it is simple to say this, some survivors will continue to feel guilty and ashamed for a long time and we must often repeat this message several times over a year.

This moral position will not suit all readers of this book. Some will feel we should discuss it more during the counselling, others will say less. Morality in psychotherapy and counselling is an important subject that is still open to discussion. Morality in counselling the adult survivors of child sexual abuse who are safe from abuse is an area people are likely to have strong feelings about.

The moral-free approach may be more useful for people who are not sure exactly what happened. It may also be more useful for those who had extremely complex sorts of abuse that are the exception to the rule, including brother and sister sex.

ASCSA's philosophy

At *ASCSA* we have developed a philosophy that we can believe in and can describe reasonably easily. It has three basic components.

MORAL: 'YOU DESERVE A HAPPY AND HEALTHY LIFE'

I prefer that we say 'You deserve happiness and health. You were not born this unhappy/unhealthy. This is the result of what was done to you. People who suffer other big frights, even natural ones, end up with many of the same feelings'. We need to repeat this. Many survivors feel they don't deserve happiness and health. The abuse taught them this. Even when they begin to accept the idea, they daren't get their hopes up (one of the Post Traumatic Stress symptoms is pessimism). But, as we keep saying to each survivor, this is true of the survivors of many different types of stress, fright and trauma.

This moral point of view will reappear in various parts of this book.

HELPFUL: 'WE WILL FIND YOU IN THE FOGBANK'

Counselling usually starts 'where the client is at'. I said this earlier about the research base we use. This one of the things that separates counselling from teaching. In teaching, we start from where the curriculum is at – the pupils have to fit in or fall off the course. In counselling, we start from where the client is and proceed from there.

In a programme that has both counselling and teaching, we need to be clear about what we are doing. The Fogbank (see page 92) is where most survivors are when they start counselling. It is usually where they have been for many years – perhaps ever since the abuse started. They seek help through counselling because they can't get out of the Fogbank, so we have to go to meet them in it. It is no good saying 'we will help you once you are out of the Fogbank and in safe territory'. Counsellors have to get to know the Fogbank and a lot of its issues. The counselling then has a real chance of getting going.

Most of the Metaphors are useful in this process of finding and guiding the survivor in the Fogbank. The next chapter goes into these in detail.

PRACTICAL: 'GO SLOWLY AND CAREFULLY'

This programme is not a quick one. We cannot do it in a three-month period of weekly meetings. The effects of the trauma are too great for 95 per cent of survivors. Intensive rapport-building and persuasion on any important issue are to likely to raise feelings of distrust. After all, this is what most of the perpetrators did. They said 'Trust me, it's OK' and then abused that trust. Counsellors cannot afford to say anything like the same thing because survivors will never trust them.

Because the perpetrator was acting in response to his own sexual need, it is important for counsellors to show that they are not acting from any similar needs. Therefore, working at the client's pace, rather than any other, is important. If there are external constraints on this, we should say what they are very early on. Some survivors may walk away on hearing this. They should be free to do so. If the proposed programme does not suit them at the time, it is best to accept this quickly. This may be hard on counsellors or their managers but to hope for anything else is to put the survivor's needs second, which is unfair and unethical.

Converting a philosophy into practice is probably a complicated process. I will give more examples later.

CHAPTER 2

Using Metaphors to Explain and Reassure

These metaphors are the 'tools' that I have found useful for counselling survivors of child sexual abuse. They help me explain various aspects of 'how it happens and what it does to people'. I think these explanations are crucial to a survivor's recovery. While they may have serious and scientific foundations, they have been set in 'plain language' as the most useful approach for survivors to learn in counselling.

Some of these metaphors can be useful in counselling people who are survivors of other frights or other types of abuse. Some may also help with people who have problems that seem to have grown slowly rather than arrived suddenly.

Listing these Tools

I have listed the metaphors by grouping them together by their general area of explanation – that is, the metaphors in the same group are likely to be used together and be linked to each other. Some describe how we think sexual abuse usually happens, others relate to what we think it does to people and there are a few about counselling itself.

We do not use them like this. We choose them according to what the survivor is talking about at the time. Some are most useful at the beginning of the counselling and others come into importance later. The groups follow the likely order of use in a very rough way. I think The Fogbank, The Invisible Trap, Serious Fright and Government Health Warning are essential – especially in the early stages of the counselling.

I think it is worth mentioning that many metaphors are connected to each other. For instance, The Wall is very closely linked to The Storage Cupboard, and both of them with The Bruise. We can link others for a particular reason where it is relevant to a survivor. For instance, The Circles of Hopelessness, The Boomerang and The Monty Python Foot are all about mood, desperation and depression. Sometimes we can use metaphors inside metaphors. For instance, inside The Fogbank metaphor is The Guide metaphor. It would be easy to put Vertigo and The Compass into The Fogbank too.

Describing these Tools

I have set out the description for each metaphor in sections (this is an artificial form of description organised only for this book):

1. Name and description: The first part is the story as I would tell it to a survivor in counselling. I have written in the way that I would speak. The idea here is that other counsellors could imagine themselves saying it. This will help them learn how to explain them. Survivors reading this book can read them as though I am actually saying them. This may help them understand their abuse and their reactions to it. Academics and scientists will get a chance to understand both the nature of abuse and the way we do this sort of counselling.

2. The reasoning behind the metaphor: The second part describes the reasoning for each metaphor. When survivors ask, we can explain any of this to them. Few ever ask – the metaphor either makes sense to them or means very little. My experience is that the metaphors make overwhelmingly good intuitive sense and survivors can be very relieved by the fact that someone else can talk about their experience and seems to understand it. The reasoning will be important to other counsellors and to academics. This programme does take a value position on the wrongness of child sexual abuse. Some parts of the reasonings are based on research, others are based on legal and moral issues.

3. Notes on how to use the metaphors: The counsellor should alter the actual style of presentation to suit survivor's with different educational, racial and religious backgrounds, gender and orientation and other factors. I have also included some suggestions about the timing and combinations.

4. Variations and alternatives: Occasionally, I have added a fourth part: Variations. Some metaphors seem to describe relevant experiences so often that survivors have already given them other names. I have included some here to help recognition.

5. Additional descriptions: I have occasionally included a case example or a poem to show how I use the metaphor. These can be useful in the discussion of the issues – they make it 'come alive' and it can be easier for survivors to think about someone else's situation than their own.

Any reader can skip the parts that are not of interest. They can also return later to read more detail. For instance, some may want to read all the metaphors first and then return to read the reasonings and usages.

My experience is that a few survivors need to hear all the metaphors, many survivors need to hear most of them and a few will only need some of them. Listing them in a book might give the impression that they are all used in every case. This is not true to the programme.

About Abuse

The largest collection of metaphors is used to explain how the abuse happened and what it has done to the victim. This is a major part of the counselling as it is the major source of confusion, depression, and isolation.

The Invisible Trap: The emotional place where the abusers put the victims

The Trap is the place where you end up after abuse. You are stuck, unable to sort out your life and unable to put up with it either.

It is where you stay all the time that the abuse remains a secret, even after the physical sex has finished. Therefore, it may last months, years and decades – perhaps half a century. Even when survivors tell someone they were abused (and stop the secret), they may still remain emotionally stuck in The Trap. In this situation, it is your reactions to being a Victim that keep you in The Trap even as an adult.

In The Trap, you continually go round in circles – blaming yourself, putting yourself down, half-heartedly trying to solve your problems, failing and going back round the circle (see Circles of Hopelessness, page 88). This isolates you, keeps your confidence down and stops you really hoping for anything better. This *is* a Trap.

Twenty years ago (or more) people did not know what we know now about sexual abuse, so a perpetrator who said 'No one will understand' was right and you probably knew he was.

The Trap is invisible because no one can see it. They may notice the victim's struggles but they won't understand what is causing those struggles unless they know about the sexual abuse (and understand it). Because The

2.1: Case example – Through the tunnel

Early in my period of specialising in counselling adults who had been sexually abused as children, I worked with a woman whom I had briefly met as a teenager. She had three children – girls – and had a new relationship with a man who had been lodging with her mother. When she had met him, they had very quickly found they had similar feelings about love, fairness, loyalty, justice, parenting and so on. They believed in each other; they trusted each other. This was something quite new to them both.

Problems with the children had started off worries about them surviving as a family unit. The children were noisy, demanding, chaotic. There had been a concern in the Social Services about the man – an incident reported about a possibly sexual approach to a teenage girl. No one took any action but the questions left things unsettled. She asked for counselling to help settle herself, her children and the relationship. Her depression became a large issue in the early stages of the counselling. She said 'I can't see the light at the end of the tunnel, someone keeps building another mile on the end'.

We discussed The Trap in some detail. I put suggestions about the likely implications for her levels of trust of him and his responses to her caution. I got it right so often that they started to laugh and say 'Hit the nail on the head'. This discussion left the Metaphor behind quite quickly and we explored their personal thoughts and feelings about each other in the light of the difficulties they had both had in childhood. Because of his emotional deprivation by an alcoholic mother, he was as cautious as she was. They were both wanting the other to be reassuring and offer guarantees about the future of the relationship before committing themselves. Then they saw the funny side of both waiting for the other to start.

Counselling got her through the tunnel and out of the other end. The Trap had effectively enveloped them both. They broke free. They had a child together – a boy – and are much more relaxed, in control and able to laugh real laughter.

Trap is invisible, victims can sometimes forget it's there. Over the years they will become convinced that their problems are caused by their own stupidity or craziness (see the Impossible Jigsaw, page 67; Circles, page 88).

How do you get into The Trap? Well, you are put there by the abuser. It is his way of making sure you keep it a secret. I will go on to the details of this later (see Stealing a Pencil, page 84).

REASONING

The Trap is a simple description of the emotional feeling of most victims – they feel trapped.

We are also interested in the Catch 22 situation of the Double Bind theory (Bateson *et al.* 1956). This describes the interactions of sexual abuse well. The theory says that:

1. The victim should not be able to escape from the situation, which they can't because of age, emotional immaturity, financial dependency, etc.

2. The perpetrator should be sending a message (or a set of messages) which is contradicted by another message (or set). In sexual abuse both sets of messages will be of an uncomfortable or distressing nature. These may be, for instance:

   it is OK for me to do this to you AND this is secret and you are not to tell anybody
   it is your fault that I am doing this to you AND if you tell anyone it will break up the family
   we are enjoying this aren't we AND I will hit you if you tell anyone about it

3. Because the victim is a child, she will not be capable of analysing the situation like this. She will not be able to protest or refuse to accept these arguments.

The fit between the dynamics of child sexual abuse and those of the Double Bind theory go a long way to explaining the difficulties researchers found in proving that theory. Because of the nature of the secrets, supporting evidence from undetected perpetrators or non-abusing carers is extremely unlikely to be available to the scientific inquirer. Victim Psychology speaks of Learned Helplessness (Seligman 1973) and, more recently, Learned Optimism.

The moral statement implied in this metaphor is that 'The Trap was, and still is, very real' – that is, it is recognisable by other people and they also feel it is wrong. It is not 'all just your imagination', which is what many survivors feel it is, or fear others would say. Civilised society says no one should have to endure that sort of cruelty and has had public laws to stop it (where possible) for a long time. This cruelty results in spiritual pain.

It is also noticeable that many writers speak of suffering in silence. Silence is both a sign of The Trap and, in its own way, a cause.

USAGE

We often discuss this issue of entrapment throughout the counselling programme. The metaphor of The Trap is very emotive, therefore we can usually agree on it quite quickly. It rarely needs very much explanation. It is an early signal from the counsellor that he or she has an understanding of the victim's experience. This is often important to help establish a rapport on which victims can build trust.

We can discuss the 'invisibleness' of The Trap early on in a straightforward and matter-of-fact way. While no one knows about the abuse, no one knows about The Trap. However, some of the implications of The Trap must be left until later, when other metaphors have been explained. We can also widen the discussion to include The Confusions (see page 115) if appropriate to the thoughts or feelings of a particular survivor.

VARIATIONS

We often shorten 'The Invisible Trap' to 'The Trap', as it has been above. We can bring the term 'Invisible' back if the discussion turns to other people's reaction to The Trap or the victim's reaction to it. The Plastic Coffin, The Darkness, The Silence, and so on, are other variations on the name.

The Wall: How useful psychological defences can also create problems

Everyone has a Wall. The Wall is what we use to keep people out of our minds and to hold our secrets in. Sexual abuse survivors have a higher and stronger Wall than most other people of similar age or situation. This is necessary to keep in all the secrets that have become so important to them. Of course, everybody has secrets of some size or shape.

Also, a survivor's Wall grows an 'automatic pilot' that decides when to bring the Wall up and keep people out and when to come down. One problem survivors often have is not trusting their Wall's autopilot – it sometimes does the wrong thing and the result is panic! In marriages and in relationships with children, survivors can have problems based on The Wall being too quick to go up, or too strong or too hesitant to come down. The issue is not the existence of the Wall, it is control of the Wall. We can describe the aims of counselling as working towards the survivor being in charge of the Wall, not the Wall being in charge of her.

2.2: Case example – The Wall

An extremely angry mother of four children asked for counselling. Problems with the children brought her to me through the Social Services Department. She window-shopped; she checked her opinion of me and disappeared for some months. She later came back with the support of her husband and social worker. She would never say the counselling was helpful or made any sense but she would listen and she always demanded an appointment for the next session.

She came with a reputation of verbal aggression towards authorities, towards her children, towards her husband. She had a long-term alcohol problem and a leaning towards occasional theft and deception over financial matters. She began to allow a conversation about the various ways in which she kept other people out of her mind and out of her life. Alcohol, aggression, always too busy to stop and talk – these were the ways she kept her privacy, as she thought of it. 'Principle!' she would say, meaning her principle was to keep as independent as possible. This was to stay in charge of her life and ensure that she never again fell into anyone else's power.

We began to describe it as a Wall. This allowed us to think of the alcohol, aggression and busy-busy lifestyle as methods of staying in control rather than ways of losing control. She was frightened of losing control within herself. She was also frightened of the authorities removing her or her children. However, she really did not want to admit this – it meant that I was starting to have some control over her by understanding her – so I told her to keep her Wall up as much as she wanted to.

This woman has now virtually stopped drinking after several decades of fairly continuous alcohol misuse (see Painkillers, page 106). She has relaxed in her relationships, has 'found herself' in family life, has stopped arguing and fighting and has become much more law-abiding.

2.3: Poem example – My Wall

I've been hurt a long time.

My feelings have been hiding inside me. I've never let any one get too close to me as I have been hurt too much. Now my feelings are coming out as I've put my trust in someone who had the time for me, who liked to help. It took 38 years for someone to know how hurt I've been and to know there is good in me, as I didn't ask for anything I got. I've just been used, then put to one side to be used again when men wanted it. I was so young, how was I to know?

All through my life I get feelings of guilt but I never asked for anything that I got. The wall that's in me and the box that's in my head that holds all my past – all my hurt – and all my feelings, is being emptied. There is someone I can trust. I gave him a key to the box in my head, to get all the bad feelings and all the hurt out of the box in my head. But as far as the wall inside me, that will take time. But in time I hope I won't have to hide behind the wall again. I don't want that wall to go just yet as it keeps me safe from the outside world, because it's the world and what's out there that put me behind the wall all those years ago, and I don't want to be hurt like that ever again.

I am not mad, just hurting at what I have missed in my life. But with the help and trust of someone I will have a life to live, and one day all the hurt and all the bad feeling will go and I will live like anyone else in the world. As for now, it's too soon to take my wall away – it's my wall and I've got to keep it to keep me safe. I've had my wall a long time.

I hope there is someone out there who can understand me. It's not me that's mad but others who wanted me to think I was. There is a lot of sadness in my box and behind my wall. If only I was shown love and happiness then I could have given to my kids and loved one man, instead of sadness. But for my sake I hope I can learn to love and to care and one day to sleep, and all the bad dreams go away that upset me because of what happened to me.

So for now I will keep my wall to hide behind.

Written by me, Jenny.
How my world is and what it's done to my life.

Because The Wall has an autopilot, it can start to get in the way of progress. It's as though you have to pull it down and jump over it at the same time to come out of yourself and have meaningful relationships with other people. While it is in the way, The Wall becomes The Trap.

However, The Wall also keeps in the feelings of anger and guilt. These can turn into depression, which means that The Wall becomes part of The Trap. While they are safe, they are surrounded by misery (see the poems *Is there no end, Living in my mind* and *If you bought damaged goods,* pages 233, 234, 239). Being alone on the inside feels very lonely. This is connected to the sense of isolation that is one of the Post Traumatic Stress responses that survivors of any serious fright might feel (see The Fright, page 106).

People can put a different face on the outside of The Wall: angry and aggressive, cheerful clown, devil-may-care delinquent, depressed and despairing, nervous, etc. These are all ways of keeping people out, keeping them away from the truth of what is going on inside the survivor.

Some faces are professional faces: the concerned professional working in law, health or social services, the professional entertainer working on stage or in the media, the professional academic or the professional financial expert, and so on. Links between The Wall and the Workaholic (see Painkillers, page 106) are important here.

2.4: Case example – My Wall is coming down

'My Wall is coming down – yes. It's more mobile, more responsive – that is what I mean. It's not up all the time just in case... It's as if life is becoming more happy and I'm becoming more me. It's taken so long...'

What we are aiming to do is to help people use their Wall better. We do not want to get rid of it, bend it or fasten it down. We want it to go up when it's needed and come down when the survivor wants it to. We want them to be more in charge of it. We have to be a bit careful about talking about this as 'down' is often thought of as 'good', so we check carefully.

REASONING

Psychoanalytical or psychodynamic theories use descriptions and explanations of personal problems based on ideas about the person's mind.

Many survivors fear they will be told that they are crazy or something similar. They are worried about not being understood. They are worried that the counsellor will not know how The Trap works and then blame them for having 'mental' problems in some way.

I feel we must remember that the entrapment process that the perpetrator constructs is very real. There is no other way of sexually abusing children and getting away with it. In this process he is deliberately surrounding the victim with suspicion and uncertainty. As well as using confusion, he sows the seeds of doubt. He says 'no one will believe you, even if they do believe you they will blame you and, anyway, your mother will die of a broken heart' (see Stealing a Pencil, page 84). In situations like the child ends up with lots of reasons for keeping the secret and preventing anything being discovered. This means hiding feelings and reactions to things like sexual abuse articles in papers or on the TV so that nobody becomes curious and asks questions that lead to 'dangerous areas'. The irony of The Wall is that the nearest and dearest become the most dangerous – they might discover the secrets.

The problems are directly caused by the perpetrator's actions. The problems are reactions, not wishes or fantasies. Their cause clearly comes from the perpetrator. This issue must be clear for counsellors for two reasons.

First, there are cases where the victim is accused of inventing the memories of abuse because of an evil or perverted mind. She is accused of wanting such things to happen. We must have a clear understanding about this. We think it is reasonable to say that for an ordinary human being brought up within her society's rules about sexual behaviour, such desires are very unlikely. If we are asked to believe that a person has these wishes, there must be a reason, even if it is hidden from us. Sexual abuse is a very likely reason. Let us remember that a child may be 'properly brought up' by her parents and yet still be sexually abused by someone else, and if the parents are not told then they, too, will not know the reason. In this situation, the accuser may be the abuser or may be some very disappointed and confused parents or other carers.

Second, having this issue clear allows us to start tackling the self-blaming circle. 'I must have made it happen/liked it/gained out of it or it wouldn't have happened, so I must be bad and, because I'm bad, I probably deserved it anyway'. Describing this self-fulfilling circle of argument as clearly as possible is an important task, although it can be difficult as it varies from person to person so much. Putting it into ordinary words is an important reassurance that their 'sillyness/crazyness/depression' can be understood (see Circles, page 88).

This metaphor is much less emotive and can take a fair amount of explanation. The fundamental point about the normality of having a Wall is important but the growth of The Wall to unusual size must be put down to a reaction to the trauma. This gives rise to the Post Traumatic Stress response of feeling detached and separate from the rest of the world (see Serious Fright, page 72).

The Impossible Jigsaw: The confusion experienced by the child during the abuse

Imagine that a four-year-old in playschool is given a box of jigsaw pieces and asked to put the picture together. Everyone else in the class is asked to do the same. But the box given to the this child contains pieces from two different jigsaws, but no one ever says this. Let's say half was a portrait, half was a landscape. Embarrassment stops the child from asking about this, especially since everybody else in the class seems to be getting on with their jigsaw quite happily. Most people in this situation come to believe it is their fault they cannot do the task, they think *they* are the 'failure'.

REASONING

The original cause of the child abuse trauma in sexual abuse results from the actions of the perpetrator. Much of the lasting confusion about this trauma results from the conflict between the perpetrator's actions and the wider social context of rules governing such behaviour. For the child, the two parts of The Jigsaw were the rules that the abuser applied about sex between people in the family of different ages, and the rules that she had picked up from television, newspapers, friends and stories. In other words, the child is very aware of the contradiction, even at an early age, *and yet this contradiction is set up by one of the people who should be obeyed at all times.* (No attempt will be made here to define an age threshold.)

These ideas are again connected with the Double Bind theory. Here the perpetrator's actions are put in the context of comparison to the surrounding social rules about sexual activities. We must remember the difference between the 'known reality' (i.e. the Secret) and the 'shown reality' (i.e. Normality) – some perpetrators show very anti-abuse feelings in public, with

2.5: Case example – I must be stupid!

A middle-aged mother started counselling because her young teenage daughter had begun to get beyond her control. She had become increasingly depressed and was using increasing amounts of alcohol to cope as much as she could. She used food as a comfort, a Painkiller. Later, when she attended a counselling group, she always brought a packet of biscuits or cakes 'for every body' (see Painkillers, page 106). She had a younger son whom she tried to protect from the growing chaos. He became seriously overweight during her period in the group (but it reduced later). Her second husband had left some years before and she had an on–off relationship with a man she described as an alcoholic.

The biggest problem for this woman was not being able to understand how or why the abuse had happened. When we talked about her childhood in general terms, she mentioned frequent violence from her alcoholic father, suffered by all her brothers and sisters too. And some of her sisters had been sexually abused as well.

Reassured that it was normal not to be able to understand it completely, she rapidly relaxed and accepted that she could take control of other parts of her life. She began to say 'NO!' to her children, her partner, her mother, and so on. She began to make new friends, found a sense of humour and started to actively help other people. She eventually said 'Yes!' to her partner, who had been away. He had stopped drinking and dried out because he believed her 'NO!' for the first time ever and, because he knew she was important to him, he did it.

We began to untangle her thoughts about it all – she had been convinced that she *should* be able to understand everything about the abuse. All the time that she couldn't, this was proof (in her own mind) that she was stupid (see The Confusions, page 115). This kept her going round in circles.

regards to other children. This makes for increased difficulties for victims to convince others.

The Impossible Jigsaw makes an explicit description of the two sets of morals colliding and the child alone being at the centre of this collision. Discussed in this light, it becomes possible to move on to the issues of the responsibility felt for the adult abuser's life. The Victim is the only person in the whole world who can say he has done this wrong and help herself while punishing him. (Because there are very rarely other witnesses to sexual abuse, the child (later adult) victim is usually the only witness.) This is an enormous burden to bear. It means an eye-for-an-eye morality that is often very unattractive to survivors, despite their anger at the abuser.

USAGE

This metaphor is useful for explaining why survivors regularly end up feeling confused and concluding that they are 'stupid' or 'thick'. This happens because both halves of The Jigsaw are, in their own way, right, legitimate and commanding. They also know that they conflict with each other. Since nobody else seems to talk about these rules very much, they are thrown back on their own thoughts and feelings about it all. Some think that no one else has been abused quite like this, despite hearing that others are victims too. Many think that the conflict is 'all in their imagination' – which proves that they are crazy and/or stupid (one woman said that she thought she was an alien, so she ended up taking an overdose). Others are tempted to think that other victims of child sexual abuse have coped well with it all, therefore 'there is something wrong with me if I feel hurt and confused and trapped'.

This is useful as a way of elaborating on The Trap and may be used before introducing that metaphor if the survivor appears reluctant to talk about it. Again, it is important to recognise this as likely to be for fear of being thought stupid – or even crazy – and to say so. This is extremely understandable given the confusing nature of the conflict and relates very clearly to the original formulation of the Double Bind theory as a positive causative factor in mental illness. If victims present with a mental illness diagnosis and have not disclosed the sexual abuse to any professional, they will remain in The Trap, and they may prefer The Trap because of the imagined and real consequences of such a disclosure.

The 'Flu: 'Flu symptoms as a comparison to reactions to sexual abuse

Let's use a comparison between 'flu and sexual abuse for a moment. The usual symptoms of 'flu are temperature, dizziness, perhaps nausea or diarrhoea, sore throat, runny nose, etc. The same 'flu bug takes different people in slightly different ways but if there is a 'flu bug going round, nobody worries too much about slight individual differences in symptoms.

Nobody talks about sexual abuse in the same sort of way. The information is not really available. What is written in magazines is mainly written for those who don't know it exists, not for those who do, so that doesn't help much. Therefore, people who are sexually abused do not know what to expect and how much symptoms vary. Also, while they know that 'flu may last three days, they do not know how long the symptoms of being sexually abused will continue.

Here we are saying that there are normal reactions to sexual abuse, just like there are normal reactions to 'flu. We can go on to talk about these reactions in detail (see Serious Fright, page 72). The aim of counselling is to separate 'You' from 'It'.

REASONING

The first gain from this comparison is to reassure people that we can think of reactions to child sexual abuse as symptoms caused by the abuse. We are also saying that they last for a temporary period, even if that is a long time. Second, we can reassure survivors that it is quite normal to feel confused and – at the same time – feel very ignorant of the symptoms of child sexual abuse because nobody talks about them openly.

This 'depersonalisation' of the symptoms (calling them 'it') may strike some academics or counsellors as an avoidance of what are called the psychodynamic issues. However, considering the research information on 'normal reactions to any trauma' (e.g. multiple motorway car crashes, house fires, being held hostage, etc), it appears that this *is* the relevant issue and 'normalisation' is the appropriate treatment response. It is also important to remember that some survivors feel a bit depersonalised themselves (see the poem *The auto-thoughts of a robot*, page 237).

This metaphor does not imply that a purely medical problem description is considered to be useful. However, it is useful to use the word 'symptoms' as a name for the reactions to the abuse because we can then bring a new understanding to them. We can establish and reinforce that the symptoms are temporary and that they are not of the essence of the real person, they are responses to external events. They can be responded to in ways that help. Sometimes, they are the person's way of dealing with the problem (for instance, a temperature is as much a part of the body's defence against disease as the disease's effect on the body). While confusion and ignorance are caused by sexual abuse, The Wall is created as a defence.

USAGE

This metaphor can be used quite early in the counselling, for instance in the first session or two, if survivors arrive for counselling fairly soon after a disclosure or with a very full conscious awareness of the events of the abuse and the opinion that it was unfair. It is used to directly address issues of trauma and is, therefore, an easy part of an approach towards going through the PTS checklist (see Serious Fright, page 73).

If survivors are in a different situation, this metaphor may be necessary as part of a slower approach – for instance starting with 'Is something wrong?' and going to 'What are the symptoms?' Some people start counselling without saying they have been sexually abuse and, if it emerges (hesitantly) later, The 'Flu metaphor may be useful. However, we must be very careful about diagnosing sexual abuse when the person has no memories.

When the idea of separating 'You' from 'It' is mentioned, it is useful to use an empty chair as 'It' and point at 'You' and 'It' to emphasise the difference.

Bumped Knees and Broken Legs: A comparison between serious and slight problems

Having a bumped knee is a bit like having 'flu – you expect a bruise to grow, for it to go brown, to ache a little, and then to return to normal. You can limp back home and put your leg up, put it under the tap and get over it. But a broken leg is different – it hurts too much to move, it won't let you stand on it and you have to wait for the ambulance. It will take months, not days, to return to normal and, even then, it may not feel 'quite right'.

Sexual abuse is not a bruised knee. It is more like a broken leg. It is not something that can easily be sorted out on your own. It needs help from other people. It can be sorted out but it will leave some mark from the experience, maybe for the better.

The trouble with the emotional abuse that goes with the sexual contact in sexual abuse is that the child can hide the hurt and confusion and can pretend that it hasn't happened. So they don't get help from other people, they are left to fend for themselves. The feeling of isolation can last through decades, several marriages, various sorts of counselling help, etc (see the poems *Is there no end?* and *Living in my mind*, pages 233 and 234).

Worse, they can pretend to themselves that it is only a Bumped Knee, a small confusion, a short business best forgotten. Many seem to try this. Maybe it works for a few people, but it doesn't work well for most. The temptation for them is to keep trying to sort it out and thinking themselves stupid because they keep being disappointed (see *The Impossible Jigsaw*, page 67, and *The Confusions*, page 115). Realising that it's not a Bumped Knee is a major step forward.

USAGE

This metaphor is linked to The 'Flu and A Serious Fright. They work well in the order 'Flu-Fright-Knees but there is a danger of offering too many metaphors in a row in the first two sessions (especially when the counsellor knows them all off pat!) so it may be best to leave a gap between the last two and then refer back to The 'Flu (i.e. the idea of symptoms).

This order is not crucial, it can be changed around in any way to follow the flow of conversation.

Many teenage survivors seem to have an understandable reaction of wishing to 'forget about it and get on with life' once they are reasonably safe. They may decline offers of counselling. This, coupled with a fairly natural teenage embarrassment talking about things sexual, makes it a particularly difficult area. It can become very tempting for the counsellor to try too hard to work with this area.

This may be especially true in circumstances of a fragile counselling relationship. This may be weakened by their caring parent (or other carers) persuading them against their will to go to counselling (for all the right reasons). It may also be worsened by difficulties within the counselling relationship if there are prominent triggers for flashbacks (see Painkillers, page 106) or if the development of trust follows too close a line to that of the abuse. Where there is a danger of the teenager deciding to stop attending the counselling, the 'more haste, less speed' problem must be remembered.

The counsellor's temptation to address this area arises from an understandable hope. If the first few tentative relationships can be weathered reasonably well, normal adolescent psychosocial development with regard to sexual relationships will have a chance of emerging properly. This argument makes sense, yet, because of the normal dynamics of adolescence and the recent nature of the trauma, this may remain one of the most difficult areas to work with. It has been useful to write small leaflets entitled *Ready for counselling* and *How counselling can help after child sexual abuse*. These can be given to people likely to refuse counselling offers and to parents and other carers to pass on.

It is important to say that counselling will be available whenever the survivor feels ready, with some reassurances and explanations. If nothing else is achieved in a contact between survivor and counsellor, I feel this is crucial. Survivors must hear that help can be found when they want it, when they feel ready.

A Serious Fright: the idea of trauma and its symptoms

We must talk about how ordinary people react to a serious fright. Child sexual abuse is frightening, for several reasons. Other examples of serious frights include things like a multiple motorway car crash, an aeroplane or train crash, a volcano blowing up near a town, forest fires, a passenger ferry sinking, a space rocket blowing up, a man with a machine gun killing people in the village, a rape or a mugging.

Any normal person is likely to go through some fairly set reactions in one order or another. The reactions are: shock, anger, sadness and getting used to it. It is important to know about the biological effects of frights, the actual physical reactions we have. These reactions were 'designed' by nature to keep us safe. The reason for this, as far as anyone knows, was to make sure that the species survived. When we see, hear or feel something frightening, messages get sent to our brain about the threatening thing.

Imagine that we are living in prehistoric caves and we see a sabre-toothed tiger. When we understand the danger it is as though an alarm bell goes off in our head. A message then goes down our backbone to some small glands just above our kidneys called the adrenal glands. They make adrenaline, which most people have heard something about. This is a small hormone that goes into our blood, gets pushed round our body very fast and, on the way, causes two main effects:

- it makes our small blood vessels shrink in size and
- it makes our bigger blood vessels open up wider.

These changes mean that our blood gets re-routed towards our muscles, especially the ones that move us about. This means that when we want to run away, we can run faster or further. If we want to climb a tree to get away, we are more agile and flexible. If we want to fight back, we can fight stronger or longer. The trouble is that nowadays most causes of frightening situations are not sabre-toothed tigers, they are people. Occasionally, a car might nearly knock us down when we are crossing the road but mainly it is other people being unfair in some way. In most situations we cannot run or fight back physically, so our body is ready for action but has nowhere to go. Instead, we get fidgety, we get the shakes and we get restless.

Our blood supply is changed to push oxygen and blood sugar into the muscles for action, so the oxygen and sugar do not reach other parts of the body in the usual amounts – the guts, the skin, the genitals and the brain all suffer. All of these show some effects at the time and, if the after-effects go on (perhaps a bit less alarming, but still anxiety making), these parts of our body can develop problems: ulcers, acne and eczema, sex problems and thinking problems. In frightening situations it gets difficult to think straight. In very severe cases we can end up in panic and we can do the wrong thing – even put ourselves in danger – because we cannot think straight. This means it is more likely that we put our experiences into The Storage Cupboard (see page 80) because we cannot sort them out at the time.

Sexual abuse is a bit different from the more obvious serious frights listed under the heading. It usually lasts for some weeks, months or even years, so it is not exactly the same as a single shocking event. It can go on for long enough for the child to begin to get used to it. Therefore, there are more similarities with being held hostage in a bank robbery or kidnapped as a political prisoner or months of fighting at war. Anyone facing these traumas will react in similar sorts of ways. Like 'Flu, of course, different people will react in slightly different ways. A trained soldier will be different to an eight-year-old girl, but soldiers do get 'shell shock' – even brave people who have been trained to cope in frightening situations can be affected.

The seriousness of a fright is a very personal thing. There is no one way to react, there is no 'right' way to be. Also, the nature of the event can alter how people react – for instance being trapped in a burning car for twenty minutes might be different to a three-second glimpse of a car before it drives off a cliff. Both might be just as shocking, especially afterwards when you have had a chance to consider how you think and feel about it.

It is useful to know the story of how we came to understand how people react to serious frights. Humans do get frightened, we're not robots, so it's natural if the fright is big enough. But how big? Some time ago, when people sued for compensation, the courts found themselves facing difficult issues over what was 'emotional injury'. If someone tripped over a pavement and hurt themselves, it was easy to find the X-ray results from the hospital to sort out how bad the injury was. But when people said they were too upset to go back to work, this was more difficult to sort out. The courts said to the doctors and psychologists: 'Find out for us how we can tell what is a serious reaction to a fright' and the Post Traumatic Stress Reactions list is the result.

This is a list of possible reactions that ordinary people might have if they get too frightened by something – it doesn't matter what it is. You don't have to have all the symptoms but some are normal if the situation did frighten you. The number and pattern of reactions will show just how serious the fright was *for you*, because it was *you* that was frightened. We can compare with the reactions of other people who have been sexually abused.

Going through this list:

2.6: Questionnaire – Post Traumatic Stress responses (see appendix for the complete format)

INTRUSIVE MEMORY PROBLEMS
1. Distressing memories getting in the way of ordinary life
2. Distressing dreams repeatedly waking you up – nightmares
3. Flashbacks; suddenly finding yourself back there
4. Intense distress when meeting or seeing something similar

WANTING TO AVOID IT ALL
5. Trying hard to avoid thoughts & feelings about it all
6. Trying hard to avoid situations that remind you of it
7. Getting upset because you can't remember some aspect of events
8. Serious/sudden losing interest in work, hobbies, skills, pets, etc.
9. Feeling separate from the rest of the world, being isolated and lonely
10. Unable to have some feelings; feel blunt or stuck in a vice
11. Unable to see far into the future, expecting things to go wrong more
17. Bodily feelings to similar events (shakes, butterflies, headaches, pains)

2.6: Questionnaire – Post Traumatic Stress responses (continued)

NERVES AND JUMPINESS
  12. Difficulty in falling asleep, or staying asleep
  13. More irritable, or having more outbursts of anger than other people
  14. More difficulty in concentrating than other people
  15. Edginess; always watching or listening out for someone or something
  16. Jumpiness; very easily startled, more jumpy than other people
  17. Bodily feelings to similar events (shakes, butterflies, headaches, pains).

One area that is very important to talk about is that of triggers (see page 106). In the list, the last question in the first and the third sets of questions are about small events prompting large reactions in the survivor. Sometimes, this means very small events and it can mean prompting very large reactions. These can be very scary as they bring the temptation for the survivor to feel that they are going mad and, if they tell anyone, there is a risk that other people will also think it is madness.

A parallel situation is the widow who is just settling down after months of upset after the funeral and then finds a cufflink under the chest of drawers. Let's imagine they had been married happily for 60 years and his death was not really a surprise, but, even so, she is grieving. She has already managed to clear his things out of the wardrobe with the help of one of her children, the support of her friends and a small whiskey to strengthen her nerve but finding the cufflink throws her completely. She dissolves into tears, retires to bed, gets depressed, stops eating and doesn't speak to anyone for a week. Everyone worries and says 'Why is she so upset? It's only a cufflink. She emptied the wardrobe last month'. But the wardrobe was planned and prepared for, the cufflink was a nasty surprise that had more emotional significance than all his clothes: 'The silly man, he was always dropping them, he would have lost it under there and he wouldn't have asked me to reach for it because he knows my knees are bad' (notice the change of tense from the past to the present. Memories do time travel like that, especially when they are highly emotional).

The other responses listed have important connections. It is important to go through them carefully and understand their meanings for people and their connections to each other. For instance:

- concentration problems (14) might be a result of sleeplessness(12), which might be caused by nightmares (2)

- edginess might be connected to pessimism (11) and sudden loss of interest in important activities (8)

- irritability (13) might be connected to flashbacks (3) or triggers (4) interrupting the train of thought

- feeling socially isolated might be mainly due to (9) as a response to the fright or it might be added to by anxiety about other people's reactions to panic caused by triggers, flashbacks or nightmares, or by fear of other peoples impatience at jumpiness, edginess and avoidance of possible triggers.

Considering all these normal reactions to serious frights, we have to think about how people react to them. There may be some things that survivors have done that they could be ashamed of. They might have felt these things were necessary at the time but later they regret them. This is not surprising, people do the best they can in extremely difficult circumstances. We encourage people to be gentle with themselves over the few failings they may have had. It is more important to remember how well they have coped with enormous difficulties than a few failings. Because they are used to being victims, they are too quick to blame themselves for what has gone wrong and too slow to give themselves credit for their successes.

The poem in Figure 2.7 was written by a woman who frequently saw the abuser – her dead father – laughing at her in a chair in the same room that she was sitting in. She would often leave the bedroom light on when she went to bed. She would stay up into the early hours washing, ironing and listening to loud music to avoid going to bed. This poem says very little of the feeling of being haunted she had, the questions about whether she was mad or the fear that she would be laughed at.

I told her about another woman – younger – who always turned the bedroom light off because whenever she got ready for bed the abuser would

2.7: Poem example – Couldn't sleep much...

Not sleeping at night –
too many bad memories
keep coming back to get me
Then very tired in the morning.

Will the feelings ever go away?
Will I ever be like everyone else?

Why do they keep coming back
– after all these years?
Why should I be hurt
– again and again?

Was it me –
should I have stopped it when it started?
how could I?
I was too young to understand
all the hurt that followed.
I didn't do wrong –
why should I feel like this?

Will it get better?
All I wanted to do was live like anyone else
– now I still suffer.

Couldn't sleep much –
in the dark feeling very on my own.
A lot of hurt keeps coming back.
Keep thinking of the past,
very scared, don't like the feeling.

Hope one day I will be able to sleep,
without all the hurt and bad times coming back.

Jenny

stand in the doorway and watch her undress. The abuser was her father, who was still alive but living 400 miles away.

Both of these women had anger problems, feeling it was all so unfair that they took it out on all those around them. These hallucinations were intrusive memories, like flashbacks. They seemed to have a life of their own because they did more than simply repeat old memories, they acted as though 'alive'.

REASONING

This area is based on the research into Post Traumatic Stress Disorder. This term is used in psychiatry to describe normal reactions to severe frights. The last word is an unhelpful labelling in this country; I replace it with 'Responses' or 'Symptoms'. In the USA, where the term originates, people may not perceive it so negatively.

The list of symptoms comes from the Diagnostic and Statistical Manual of the American Psychiatric Association (DSM-III-R 1987). The list and the method of use have a useful authority in defining this area. It allows us to talk about normal reactions. No one enjoys owning up to being frightened and this list of reactions – while not a metaphor – helps us start discussing this area.

It is important to notice that PTSR research should be split into two settings: military and civil. This affects the design of a counselling programme a great deal. In military settings the emphasis is on rehabilitating soldiers as quickly and effectively as possible to return them to their job (fighting wars, etc). The frightening situation is usually public knowledge and the soldiers have had training – and their 'fright' may be a relatively short-term one compared to years of sexual abuse.

Critical Incident Debriefing is a technique developed for this area of work and it is best used as quickly as possible after the trauma. This may not be possible in sexual abuse situations – some survivors wait twenty or thirty years before talking about it for the first time. It also uses a method of encouraging the survivor to remember as many memories, feelings and sensations as possible. I feel that this is a form of reliving the trauma and is unnecessarily painful. I also feel its use is very questionable in use with a sexual abuse counselling programme in civil life. Gentler methods are possible where speed is not essential and may help more when survivors are free to choose whether to attend counselling sessions or not. (This point also brings into question parallel techniques of 'flooding', 'catharsis' and 'guided fantasy work'.) See also the Technical Note on page 153.

USAGE

These ideas connect with 'Flu, The Bruise and Bumped Knees and also with The Trap and The Wall. Often, they all interweave with each other and form different patterns in each counselling session as they are repeated through a Survivor's programme.

Abuse can be compared to bereavement. It is 'the sort of fright that you can get used to but can never get over because the world will never be the same again'. In this way it is different to 'Flu and Bumped Knees. It is useful to have introductory leaflets about 'Normal Reactions to Fright' to present with this idea. Leaflets can make these ideas more permanent after the session. Most useful is a checklist of PTS responses that we can tick to show survivors a clear picture of their own responses (see Mirrors, page 99). It is very useful to keep a permanent record and give it to the Survivor to keep and look back over later.

It is important to emphasise the human aspect of being frightened, it can happen to us all. Sometimes it helps survivors to remind them that other forms of child abuse are also frightening. It can even happen to the bravest people if something frightening enough happens to them and, in child abuse, the child's age means that they are much more easily frightened than adults, so we may need to remind adults how young they were when it happened. They may need help to avoid the temptation of putting an old head on young shoulders when they think back to the abuse. We must challenge the idea of 'I shouldn't have been frightened'. We can also make links to Courage and Confidence (see pages 156 and 157) – 'you must have lots of Courage to get through so much fright for so long'.

The Storage Cupboard: How the memories stay so able to get in the way

When we are under great stress in traumatic situations our minds have to find unusual ways of coping with this. In this emergency it is as though our mind says 'I can't deal with all this important and extra-worrying stuff that is happening'. It goes on to decide that 'I can't completely ignore it because it is too alarming, so I will put most of it into a Storage Cupboard and sort it all out later'. But the trouble is, being human, we get nervous about what we put into the Storage Cupboard. It becomes very tempting to leave it where it is and hope to forget about it, so we can end up leaning on the door of the Storage Cupboard trying to make sure nothing gets out. However, because the experiences that are in there are so stressful, they keep trying to get out. But, every once in a while, they push open the door and say 'Hi! we're here!'.

REASONING

Bearing in mind that a traumatic situation is, by definition, an experience that is too much for us to cope with, it makes sense that these experiences would overpower us. We must also remember the Post Traumatic Stress formulation: the survivor's reaction depends upon both the events and the personal history and emotional balance. Therefore, what one person decides to put in the Storage Cupboard another might cope with at the time. Soldiers, nuns and three-year-old children will all react differently.

The immediate coping method is what creates the conditions for the flashbacks, dreams, nightmares and hallucinations. But, later, survivors may become frightened by the dreams and flashbacks and then start to think that the other memories in the Storage Cupboard must be even worse and 'try to sit on the door even harder!' This builds up a fear that may be more in the survivor's imagination than in the truth of what's in there. All of this will contribute to the survivor staying in The Trap for fear of what's inside the survivor as well as the possibility of embarrassment from outside.

This metaphor really speaks for itself. Rather than trying to explain things on an 'as if' basis, it is describing what some of the current research thinking actually suggests. The metaphorical bit is the idea of part of the mind being a Storage Cupboard – which describes long-term memory or the unconscious, depending on one's point of view.

USAGE

We can slot in this picture wherever it seems appropriate. We will often need to repeat it as a reminder that trauma has biological, psychological and social effects. This metaphor is best told as a bit of story, with some humour, in pointing out the absurdity of the situation. The image of someone sitting on a Storage Cupboard in the back of their own mind invites the possibility of survivors laughing at themselves a bit. This is an opportunity to show the humanness of the 'caught in a trap' situation.

VARIATIONS

Some survivors feel themselves more haunted by the memories and feelings. They think of the stuff in the Storage Cupboard as being more like The Monster. This Monster charges about unexpectedly and unstoppably, leaving them feeling worried about their temper, their sensitivity, their sanity or all of these. The Monster variation may apply more to those people who have feelings triggered more than visual memories. They may tick more Post

Traumatic Stress Responses in the third category than the first. In these situations we must be careful about our own preconceptions of what the intrusive phenomena may be.

This variation is more useful than the Storage Cupboard in discussions of separating 'You' from 'It'.

The Bruise: Why survivors can be extra-sensitive to small things

Imagine you are walloped on the arm and you get a large bruise. You are not surprised to get a bruise but you would rather be without it. You know it's there and you try to protect it. You walk around twisted up so that you don't knock your arm on a doorway or a cupboard. You hold your hand over the bruise to stop anything touching it. You end up all twisted out of shape trying to cope with the bruise. It's not that you're a twisted person, the bruise has made you look after yourself that way. And then, if someone prodded you in the arm, on the bruise, you would leap through the ceiling with the pain. It would hurt you much more than being prodded on the other arm where there is no bruise. You are extra sensitive because of the bruise.

2.8: Case example – The Bruise

A fully competent hotel manager said: 'Why can I deal with lost and lonely children, and angry or complaining or sick or drunk people, when I can't even watch the news on the TV. If something comes on about rape or abuse or injustice to children, I run out of the room. I make an excuse, like making a cup of tea. Sometimes – especially if I'm on my own – I burst into tears. Why is this?'

After explaining the Bruise and discussing many other Metaphors, she began to believe that it was possible to separate the effects of the abuse from the real person she originally was. Over the three Introductory meetings we had, she changed quite a lot. She started to look me in the eye, confident I wouldn't laugh at her or tell her off. She started to slow down when she spoke about these things and was less anxious. She started to leave pauses in the conversation, being able to think deeply about what we'd said. All this led her towards Hope.

REASONING

This metaphor is closely linked to The Serious Fright. It is explaining the increased sensitivity victims have to similar or symbolic events or perceptions. This is necessary because they often become acutely aware of their increased sensitivity and are embarrassed by it. They can end up feeling that their responses are disproportionate and, therefore, 'irrational' or 'crazy'. They may be told this by partners, family or professionals for either well-meaning or unfair reasons.

In many ways, The Bruise summarises the Post Traumatic Stress Responses (see Serious Frights, page 73). It covers the three areas of response:

- intrusive responses – e.g. memories, flashbacks, nightmares and sudden distress

- avoidance responses – e.g. avoiding situations, places, people, feelings and thoughts

- nervousness responses – e.g. lack of sleep or concentration, irrittation, extreme jumpiness reactions.

USAGE

We can use The Bruise to follow Serious Frights and the PTSR information or we can reserve it for use with examples of increased sensitivity when they arrive. We can then usefully tie in The Government Health Warning (see page 110).

For instance, as progress is being made, survivors' Walls start to come down and their hopes start to go up. At this stage they are specially vulnerable to disappointments. Previously, they had immunised themselves against disappointment by refusing to hope but once they do hit a difficulty, whether related to their problems or a completely new one, they are tempted to give up. 'What's the point? I knew counselling wouldn't work'. The Bruise can explain why they become *more* hurt by difficulties instead of *less* hurt.

The Bruise also reinforces The Broken Leg – this is why victims react differently to other people to cuddles, startles and TV programmes about rape, sexual abuse or other injustices.

Gesture and demonstration work well with this metaphor, emphasising its parallel with the experience of physical pain. Hitting your own arm, prodding it or twisting your torso out of position can all give a more lively portrayal of what we mean.

Stealing A Pencil: The abuser's responsibility for putting the child into The Trap

Imagine the abuser has stolen a pencil from a fellow student in college. He leaves it on his side of the table to use it soon. When the owner misses his pencil, he sees the one lying on the table and says 'Isn't that mine?' At that point the thief has a choice. He could own up and say 'Yes I borrowed it, thank you very much' or he could lie and say 'No, it's the one my sister bought me for my birthday three weeks ago'. If he wants to get away with it, he has to tell the lie to explain where it came from.

People who abuse children sexually have the same decision to make after the first time they abuse a child. It makes sense that many abusers would realise this before they abuse a child. If they want to get away with it, they have to cover it up. Abusers will want to get away with it. Unless they have very serious mental illness or very serious brain damage or are very young, they will know it is wrong. (If the abuser is in one of these categories, a lot of untangling still needs to be done to understand what has happened.)

Pencils don't talk, but children do. They could tell someone what has happened. So the abuser has to make them keep the secret. There are several ways that this is done:

Violence: actually hurting you to frighten you more. This might be outright violence – punching, slapping, burning, and so on – or it might be little pinches, scratching or pushing you off-balance and getting on your nerves. It might be in front of other people or in private. It might be once in a while or it might be regular. It might be when the abuser is drunk or when he is stone-cold sober.

Threats of violence: this is similar to actual violence. It works especially if someone else in the family is already violent to you.

Bribery: this might start with small things for small children – kindness, a few pennies or a sweet. Later it might become lifts, presents, extra help with hobbies, permission to stay out late, and so on. This can be very confusing later on with the idea that the victim might have become a sort of prostitute by accepting these bribes.

Confusion: anything that confuses the child enough to prevent them from telling other people will help the abuser. This can happen through confusing (usually untrue) stories or by lying to them or other people or by giving alcohol or drugs to confuse the child's senses and memory. Any form of magic could be used to confuse.

Emotional blackmail: this is when an abuser says anything like 'someone close will suffer if the secret gets out'. An example is the abuser saying 'If you tell anyone, your Granny will be so upset that she will die and your Mum will be so angry with you that she'll send you into care'. It is impossible for children – even young teenagers – to judge whether this would all come true or not.

Or a combination: sometimes emotional blackmail and violence are combined: 'If you don't let me [abuse you] I will hit [or kill] your hamster [or rabbit or goldfish or whatever]'.

In our experience, emotional blackmail seems to be the way that abusers most often choose. It seems to do the most harm to the child because it is so 'invisible' (see The Trap, page 59).

None of this is accidental. Somewhere in their minds, abusers know they are doing this. Of course, they might not think about it as we have described it here. In fact, research shows that they don't. They think of it as 'loyalty', 'kindness' and 'co-operation' from the child. If they ever say so, or show this attitude, this will add to the child's confusion more.

REASONING

We must tackle the guilt that most survivors feel. It is unethical and unfair to ask survivors to identify their 'own' reasons for feeling guilty when it is quite clear that child sexual abuse is an interactional problem. Abuse is not a one-person situation. The perpetrator caused the child's emotional responses, they are not a product of the survivor's imagination or unconscious. By giving a clear message that the perpetrator has decided somewhere in his mind 'to get away with it', we place the responsibility with the adult. It is also important to remind them that they were a child when this adult was doing these things. He *was* being unfair. This is a clear moral statement, consistent with the law and with society's moral standpoint on the subject.

USAGE

This metaphor is useful in the early middle stages. We must already have done enough work to build a rapport and reassure the survivor that her responses are 'normal, considering what they have been through'. This is necessary for two linked reasons: the reassurances are an important part of the rapport-building stage and this Metaphor is particularly challenging. There

2.9: Case example – The Trap

A young mother came for a few counselling sessions. She wanted to sort out her feeling of guilt. She understood a good deal of what had happened and how it had affected her. She felt she had a feeling of guilt that she shouldn't have, didn't deserve. But since she did feel guilty, perhaps she did deserve it, she wondered. She felt so bad, she had isolated herself from her whole family, even though she wanted to be friends with her younger sister.

I started off with reassurances about my understanding of sexual abuse and its effects: The Trap, The Confusions, The Circles, and so on. As we talked it became clearer that she was particularly upset about her sister, even though her sister seemed to be getting on better than she was. I wondered whether it was more to do with jealousy from childhood, perhaps from a 'divide and conquer approach' her stepfather might have used. Eventually she told me that she had good reason for these feelings.

What had happened was that after some years of abuse, her stepfather had told her that she could stop worrying about the abuse because soon her younger sister would be 'ready for him'. To try and stop this, she submitted to more and more abuse for some time until she couldn't stand it any more. She told a teacher and the stepfather was prosecuted and jailed. But, at the trial, her sister said that she *had* been sexually abused by the stepfather. All that sacrifice for nothing. She felt she should have told someone when he mentioned her sister.

We had to sort out that it was already too late by then, she was already in the Trap. She couldn't easily talk to anyone about it anyway. Saying 'I should have…' was dragging her down, and this understandably awful teenage burden made a lot of sense of her current feelings. She stopped feeling so guilty toward her sister, felt more able to talk to her, and started to settle down and feel more comfortable with herself.

are few punches pulled. It goes very much to the heart of the conflict that most survivors have: 'Was I wrong or was he wrong?' (this is often over-laden with 'Or were we both wrong? Or did I start him off anyway?').

Even if the survivor accepts that the abuser must carry the responsibility, they then come to a depressing realisation of loss: the parent who broke the rules. This has often been delayed for years by the guilt of the possibility of having been the one in the wrong. The survivor could hang on to the idea of a nice parent by saying 'he had a few problems' or 'he didn't really mean to' or 'he didn't know how much it upset me'. Putting the responsibility on the adult can then lead to questions about non-abusing carer(s): 'Why didn't she/he/they somehow know/guess/stop it?' In some ways, it can be easier to blame yourself, especially if the abuser is still alive, still caring for some part of the family, or even undetected. Even if the abuser is dead, it can be difficult to put the responsibility on him – you can't tell them so.

Why Me? – The Answer: the reasons why victims are picked by abusers

Survivors often feel very confused about why the abuse happened to them – they ask 'Why did this happen to me?' They often feel they have no right to ask this, but they wonder about it all the same. They are tempted to feel that the answer must be obvious to everyone else – especially other survivors – and get embarrassed that they don't know the answer. They think it might be because they are bad people who somehow deserved to be punished or that they are perverted themselves or that they were stupid. This turns into hopeless circles of confusion. I think there is an answer, and a relatively simple one that is better discussed than avoided.

When someone wants to abuse a child, they start to look for a suitable one. What is a suitable child? Not the school bully! The quiet, lonely, sad child is the one who is going to be easiest to trap into silence. This child is often starved of love already. Often, they have less confidence than other children their age. They have fewer friends to ask if the abuse or the abuser is normal. They are likely to have little 'good love' and 'quality time' with their parents, so they can't talk to them about what is happening.

Often, the child has already been physically or emotionally abused. This makes them extra vulnerable, especially if the abuser already knows this because they are a relative or a family friend. This makes the abuse seem doubly unfair to the survivor – that the sexual abuser seemed to offer help to begin with but then cheated (see the poem *He picked me*, page 236). It is not surprising that, afterwards, these survivors are greatly wary of people offering to help, even if they are professionals.

All this helps the abuser put the child into The Trap so that the sexual abuse can start and then continue. This suits the abuser, so he is likely to make the child more confused to keep them in The Trap.

REASONING

Much of this explanation is straightforward common-sense. It is backed up by research from abusers who have described how they choose victims (see Figure 2.10).

USAGE

'Why me?' is one of the questions in the Unhealthy Childhood Quest-ionnaire, so we can raise this issue after we have been through those lists.

2.10: Case example – Neil's story: a child sexual abuse perpetrator

(Not his real name)
taken from Personal Column, Night & Day, *Mail on Sunday*, 5/3/95

Neil knew he was 'a freak' at the age of 16…he began to satisfy his desires at the age of 28…

Neil's desire was for both sexes, but he abused only boys. 'I thought of boys as being tougher, girls as too delicate. Of course, all children are delicate, but I thought boys could handle it more easily. I was wrong, naturally.'

Over a three year period, Neil abused seven boys, aged between 8 and 13. [When he was 30 or so] he married… 'It was all a front', he explains, 'I was impotent with women, with adults, but I thought I'd be less suspicious if I had a wife. The marriage was a total sham.'

Circles of Hopelessness: Helpless in confusion, getting nowhere fast

A lot of the confusion comes from the experience of going round in circles trying to sort it all out. This is the experience of The Fogbank. Too much of the experience is just not logical. A major circle relates to:

REASONING

Most survivors agree that one of the most difficult things to sort out is the confusion that seems to affect so many parts of their life. It affects everything that has to do with people. This means that it changes social reality. But if it is hidden – a natural temptation – then it is a private reality (see the poem

2.11: Case example – But I was there

I don't understand why it happened
even though I was there

There must be something wrong with me perhaps I'm just crazy
and all these thoughts and feelings and memories are made up

If I'm crazy, maybe that's why it happened
– it was all my fault

And I don't think I'll ever understand it
So I'll probably stay crazy and they'll lock me up in the end

And tell me it didn't happen –
I must have a dirty mind to keep thinking about it
if it happened or even if it didn't

So perhaps I deserve to be crazy and miserable
But I was there…

I know what happened.

Hidden, page 235). This can lead into problems if the survivor starts to make decisions and take actions on this private reality.

These circles are very reminiscent of Laing's 'Knots' (1970) (see *Untangling*, page 95).

USAGE

The word 'crazy' can be replaced by the word 'stupid' or by 'crazy and stupid'. These Circles are, in effect, a place in The Fogbank. They are also related to The Boomerang. Further responses to Circles can be 'The Confusions'.

The Monty Python Foot: Confidence crashes; putting yourself down

Part of childhood is about the growth of confidence. It is important that it grows in the right way. Part of a parent's job is to help this. It is part of the duty of anyone who has the trust of a child. This is a generalisation but it is difficult to argue against it.

Sexual abuse bashes a child's confidence down. This means they are slow to learn how to do things that other children their age can do. There comes a time when the abused child realises this, by comparing with class mates. They begin to use this as evidence that they are stupid. They then begin to tell themselves off, put themselves down and discourage themselves. This can then make their failures worse. Some children fail at particular things, others at many things. Some children find an escape in school work, or pets or hobbies, and get very involved and do well. Others seem to shrink into the smallest space they can, trying to be as unnoticeable as possible.

Once your confidence has been bashed down, it is easy for it to be bashed down again. Life brings all sorts of things that do this. We call this the Monty Python Foot after the big cartoon foot in the opening sequence of the 'Flying Circus' TV programme in the 1970s. Survivors quickly grow to expect it. It all gets to be a habit, trying things half-heartedly, plans only half-working, failures seen as proof of stupidity, squashing your own confidence even more. Another circle!

Later in life this can have big effects on relationships. You let yourself be chosen by someone with problems because you don't think anyone 'really sorted out and together' will want you or you choose someone with more problems than you, so you can become a workaholic (see Painkillers, page 106) by worrying about them. And you expect the relationship to go wrong – and it does (and maybe the next one does too).

Even if you choose someone without too many problems, someone who is content to help you from time to time, it feels like it's only a matter of time before it fails. It's difficult to live with someone who is always pessimistic. You can only cheer them up so many times. After a while you run out of energy, ideas, optimism. And the relationship gets into trouble. And you tell yourself 'I knew it would all go wrong/I didn't deserve anyone so nice/(s)he would get bored of me eventually'. Back round the circle! (see Circles, page 88).

REASONING

This metaphor again relates to Learned Helplessness (see The Trap, page 59).

USAGE

We hold a hand up in the air and push it down to represent the foot coming down and blow a large raspberry at the same time, as Monty Python did.

It is most useful to talk frequently about habits of thinking and circles of thought. This saves jargon and reminds us that anyone could go round the same sorts of circles. It may be that there have been times when we have gone round in circles about some relatively small (and humorous) situation that we can describe. I would discourage personal disclosures about more important and intimately personal problems as this confuses the counselling. Who is helping who? The balance must be firmly and clearly in the correct direction.

VARIATIONS

A quicker and more direct way to talk about this area is to describe a Missing Foundation Stone. The confidence that children should build up during childhood and teenage just isn't there, so it is difficult to build the rest of life properly. (This leads onto Designing a New Future.)

About Counselling

The process of counselling is relatively artificial. By this I mean that it is something that we only do when necessary, for a purpose – it is not part of everyday life. And yet it works through talking, which is very much an everyday thing. Explanations of what goes on in counselling are important to forewarn and reassure people about to start.

The Fogbank: Acknowledging survivors' lost and lonely feelings

When survivors start counselling they frequently feel lost. They don't know where they are but they know they want things to change. They feel miserable and lonely, unsure which way to go and yet desperate to move. This is like being stuck in a fogbank up a mountain. A step in any direction might lead to a fall over a cliff edge, but staying cold and miserable and lonely isn't a nice idea either.

Towards the edge of the fogbank, the fog gets thinner and the sun begins to shine through. This is hope. The possibility of getting somewhere makes you feel more confident (see The Compass, page 112). You start to be able to see some way down the path, although you might not be able to see all the way to the end.

Once you get to the edge, you can see the horizon – your hopes can be as high and as big as anyone else's. Your horizons of hope are much wider than they were before. You see the choices in the future, the different possibilities, and you can start to sort out a plan. It's as though you can see several ways down the mountain and where the roads in the valley lead to.

Let's say you see a village, a town and a city. Then you might say 'I don't want to go to the city. I like the idea of the village and I'm going to try it but I'll probably end up in the town'. This is what life is like for normal people, people who do not have a big bruise that traps them. They make decisions, they hope for the best, they try their hardest and, if it goes wrong, they sort things out, change their minds, keep going. They allow themselves some flexibility and expect small disappointments.

The counsellor is a Guide who knows the paths and can advise you about where they lead and what obstacles are down them. But the Guide doesn't know which ones you want to try or where you will end up. It is your life, you have to decide where to go exploring. The Guide will accompany you. Because Guides have been around the fogbank before, they have a mental map of it and they have some knowledge of other people's journeys around it.

REASONING

Aims that are most likely to be achievable are practical, definite and realistic-sized. But most survivors find it very difficult to identify 'well-formed goals' (de Shazer 1985) at the beginning of counselling. Emotionally, they still feel themselves to be more Victims than Survivors. We could say that they feel their life is controlled by something outside themselves. They do not feel in control of their lives. This should not surprise us, given the man-made (and, later, self-made) trap they are in. Therefore, they might *appear* to be 'window shoppers', 'unmotivated' or 'resistant' in counselling. However, if we start by saying that this is a natural place for a trauma survivor to be, the responsibility is then on us to respond to this.

The first step is to reassure these survivors that we know where they are, at least in general. The next thing is to accept their relatively passive position and build a rapport to allow the survivor to decide whether she trusts us enough to listen. All this is within the metaphor of The Fogbank and The Guide. The Map and The Journey are parts of this Metaphor that are almost so obvious as not to need to be mentioned.

This metaphor is a distinctly 'feeling' level one. It is about being blinded by the confusion that surrounds the survivor and about 'out in the cold' feelings of being very lonely. It also sets the victim in a context and acts in a 'start from where the survivor is at' way, as traditional counselling values recommend.

This is a flexible metaphor that we can use in various different ways at different times. Early on, it can help reassure survivors about their difficulties in knowing what to ask for help with. 'It *is* difficult to know what to do. The things you've already tried haven't worked well enough. But this is to do with the child sexual abuse, not you. There is no such thing as simple sexual abuse. It is difficult for *all* victims to understand, especially as sexual abuse bashes your confidence at an early age and you end up being very unsure of your judgement of people (yourself included)'. (See also The Confusions, page 115.)

We can use it later to describe the difficulty in choosing paths when you can't see where they lead to or end up and it can help to identify the turning point – that is the beginnings of hope appearing. 'You may be very nervous about what you want to do and cross/hurt/sad that you have to do these things (which your school mates haven't have to do). You might also be concerned about other peoples' reactions to your new answers to the situation. But it is only fair on yourself to go slowly and cautiously. Stay careful'.

We must also remember that some survivors *do* arrive with reasonably well-formed goals, or with the possibility of reaching these. Not everyone starts from the centre of The Fogbank, but survivors who have been stuck in The Trap for 10, 20 or 30 or more years might well be there.

The Guide is really a metaphor in its own right and can be useful in training counsellors as much as describing the role to survivors.

The Fogbank can become The Maze, The Forest or The Marsh (or Bog – see Stepping Stones, page 209). The nice thing about The Marsh is that the city/town/village are all on hills around the marsh, so progress is going uphill and getting a clearer and better view of the world. The Maze is good because it portrays the confusion well. If feels as though there is only one exit/entrance. Remember that people have to find their own exit – when you are outside you can see there are actually lots of exits.

Separating 'You' From 'It': Emphasizing that the symptoms of sexual abuse are temporary

In the early introduction meetings it is important to describe what the counselling process aims to do. Sometimes, survivors have very strong worries about how counselling works. They worry about whether counsellors can read their minds. They worry about whether the counsellor might think they are disgusting, or stupid or crazy. So, as part of the general policy of working to reassure people as quickly as possible, we describe what counselling aims to do.

The problems that have brought the client to counselling are often all lumped together with the results of being sexually abused. It all feels enormous, unsolvable, unstoppable. We call this big lump of problems 'It'. Counselling is about finding 'the Real You'. To do this we need to Separate 'You' from 'It'.

REASONING

Again, we are giving the picture that although the abuse has influenced the person's growth and development, and their health and their happiness, for

2.12: Case example – Sexual abuse is always complicated

A middle-aged woman started the Introductory meetings very tearfully. She turned away, glanced occasionally, said very little. It seemed that this was very different from her usual self. She said it was. She had a responsible job working with people all day, every day. It turned out that part of her anxiety was because she had only recently made a connection between marriage problems and violent relationships with sexual abuse in her past.

When we came to it, she was quite convinced that all other survivors would have sorted things out by their mid-twenties. This meant that – in her mind – she was a failure who deserved to suffer. I raised the issue that sexual abuse is always complicated, which made her sit up and listen. Going on to describe separating 'Her' from 'It' gave her more hope. In a matter of three weeks she was more self-contained, self-controlled and optimistic.

We discussed various other issues as well, as usual in these meetings.

the worse, this is not permanent. The symptoms are temporary (see The 'Flu, page 70).

A major part of this metaphor is the issue of control. At the point of beginning counselling, victims invariably feel controlled by their experiences. It all feels hopelessly inescapable. While they may think of it as 'It', they also think of it as 'me'. They are worried about saying things like 'I feel like I am two people'. This is the popular idea of schizophrenia, but they often do feel that way, or they feel the Monster rushing about inside them, creating feelings they don't want.

A great deal of this is often the 'intrusive memories' of Post Traumatic Stress Responses. Some people have some recognisable reactions more specifically concerned with the sexual side – rejection of boy/girl-friends, sexual problems, sexual health problems. The aim is to gain control over 'Its' effects, rather than continue with 'It' doing what it wants, when it wants. This is clearly related to The Wall.

USAGE

We can accompany this metaphor with a hand movement showing a separation between 'You' (pointing gently in their direction) and an empty chair that we can use to park 'It'.

Untangling the Bowl of Spaghetti: What we are trying to do in counselling

To describe the process of the counselling we use the idea of 'untangling' the tangles caused by sexual abuse. This follows on from the 'The Confusions' idea; abuse always leaves complicated reactions behind.

The Bowl of Spaghetti is a description of all the loose ends that somehow join in the middle in a great big knot. Trying to untangle it is not easy, the spaghetti is slippery with sauce. It takes time and hope and determination and courage and victims find it very difficult to have confidence that this will help in the end. After all, they have already tried to sort it out for many years!

Fortunately, this observation allows us to say 'If it was simple, you would have sorted it out by now'. We use this to remind victims that 'There is no such thing as simple sexual abuse to you'. Sometimes it is extra complicated because it seems so simple to begin with (for example, see the poem *Someone*, page 239).

Sometimes it is useful to point out some of the 'other side of the coin' issues. For instance, when we are talking about The Trap, we can point out the helpful aspects of the different ways in which the abuser made the victim stay silent:

Violence: The only good thing about violence having been used is that it is easier to say 'He hit me' when sorting it out with the police or with a counsellor. Threats of violence are basically the same. If they are going to work, the abuser has to know that the child understood about violence and pain and would want to avoid it.

Bribery: Remember, little children do not know enough about bribery to ask for a bribe or a payment. It is offered by the adult, then the child learns how it works. The victim cannot have been a prostitute by accepting these bribes, she did not know enough about sex to 'sell' it. Imagine a seven year-old who signs a cheque for a Rolls Royce. Yes, she can sign her name in joined-up writing but, no she cannot legally buy a car that way.

Confusion: Anything that confuses the child enough to prevent her from telling other people will help the abuser. This can happen through confusing (usually untrue) stories or by lying to her or other people or by giving alcohol or drugs to confuse the child's senses and memory. Any form of magic could be used to confuse.

Emotional blackmail: Although it is impossible for children and teenagers to judge whether blackmail threats would all come true or not, they do know that the situation is unfair. This feeling usually stays through into adulthood and we can discuss it to show that she wasn't as naughty as the abuser said she was. *He* wanted to convince *her.*

Or a combination: Sometimes, survivors are very clear about which threats were used when. Things might have started with bribery, then emotional blackmail, and then violence or threatened violence. When these stages are identified, the survivor begins to understand that these were the abuser's attempts to keep her silent. And when we begin to think about the abuser's fear of discovery, it becomes clear that he knew that what he was doing was wrong – which means that she was not to blame.

REASONING

Because we are always offering hope and optimism, we need to use ideas that tie in with this. Other approaches talk about the damage and disorder done by sexual abuse. These ideas immediately bring pessimism very powerfully. Yet they are only ideas! These words may be of use in a courtroom or a doctor's surgery, but they are counter-productive in counselling. They can

can actually get in the way and slow down progress. When survivors ask – and they do – 'How do I have any hope?', I answer with two points:

'I couldn't do a counselling job if I was pessimistic all the time' and

'I've seen survivors grow, change, settle down – sometimes rapidly'.

The idea of untangling brings with it some hope. It implies that although things are tangled, we can untangle them. This will need patience, determination, courage and, perhaps, some skills, but it is not an impossibly difficult job. This is an important aspect of the programme – survivors often reach a point where they feel hopeless, and The Boomerang (see page 105), The Circles (see page 88) and The Monty Python Foot (see page 89) may increase this. This is called as Learned Helplessness (see The Trap, page 59). We learn that we are helpless if it comes true often enough and then refuse to tackle something that we are not helpless in because we believe we are. It is this aspect of a survivor's responses to abuse that makes us talk explicitly about Hope and spell it with a capital letter. Hope is mentioned in The Fogbank and The Bruise. I discuss Hope in more detail later.

It's like a bowl of spaghetti – you can see the loose ends and somewhere in the middle is the big tangle that is holding it all together. By hanging on to one or two loose ends and tracing them through, things get straightened out.

USAGE

When survivors return to their hopelessness, we need to agree that it does seem hopeless. To them it is hopeless and has been for some time. If it weren't, they probably wouldn't be starting counselling!

We then need to explain the hopelessness as being due to the complications of 'how sexual abuse happens and what it does to people'. Sorting this all out needs the untangling approach. This metaphor links to Circles, The Boomerang, The Fogbank, and many others.

Spring-cleaning: sorting out all the memories

The process of sorting out all the thoughts, feelings and memories is a bit like spring-cleaning. No one likes doing it. The amount of mess that gets behind the fridge can be enormous over the year. Pulling the fridge out can produce a nasty surprise. Clearing out all the mess can be unpleasant, but it's got to be done. It is something most people prefer to put off for as long as possible but when we do finally start it, it turns out to be easier than we thought. To begin with, it can be tempting to give up and hide it all again. But we get used to it.

It's a bit like sorting out the washing basket. To start with you look at every bit you pull out. Then you start to understand what's in there and you change the way you sort it out. You start to deal with things according to their category, so all the whites go in one pile, the woollens in another and the new coloured articles that will stain or dye other articles in another. The white pile might include sheets, shirts, underwear, hankies and curtains – it doesn't matter because they are all white. In this way, experiences get easier to deal with once you have got used to the first few of each kind. For instance, the first experience of being disbelieved when you tried to tell someone about the abuse feels awful but later memories of the same sort of experience hurt less. This is to do with the order in which you try to deal with the memories, not the order in which they happened.

It is important to talk about this because survivors often fear that they are going to start off dealing with the easy bits and that it is going to get harder as they go on. The worry is that the worst experiences have been pushed to the very back of the Storage Cupboard. That means that they will explode once the easier stuff is out of the way. Practical experience of counselling tells us that this rarely happens. Occasionally, people talk about the easy bits first, knowing that there is worse to come because they are not sure how much they trust us at that point. They know that they will tackle worse issues later. In these cases what usually happens is that once these worse issues are out in the open, it gets easier, as we have said.

It seems as though other things become more important in life. The memories and feelings about the abuse do not disappear. They may even be sharper. But they get out of the way, they stay at the back of your mind, they get filed and, when you want to remember them, you can, but the rest of time they stay out of the way. Much more important is that this allows other things – nice things – to come in to your mind. Good experiences start to happen.

REASONING

These ideas come mainly from practical experience. Knowing what worries survivors encourages us to develop ways to talk about these worries. 'Will my fears, flashbacks and feelings get worse?' needs to be talked about.

USAGE

Survivors often want reassurance about how the process of dealing with the memories works. They fear the worst and they fear that it will get worse than it already is. The Government Health Warning can emphasise this fear, so we need to be aware that we must address this issue to counter-balance it.

One particular point to make is about the puzzle of 'forgotten, or unconscious, memories' and 'false memories'. Sometimes, people do forget about some aspect of a trauma (or any experience, come to that) and later remember some part of it anew, which other people can confirm. In this highly charged area, where each memory might be crucial, a central issue is whether we can remember accurately. To respond sensibly to this, we divide legal and therapeutic reasons for remembering. In the legal situation, for court hearings, proof of each memory is required – although not always available. In the therapeutic situation, for personal emotional health, it is more about what is reasonably convincing to the survivor and counsellor.

Mirrors: Methods of looking at your whole self

When we use questionnaires or checklists, we call them Mirrors. They reflect back our emotional and mental self, like a glass mirror reflects back our physical self. It gives us the chance to look at those aspects that are usually only thought about one at a time. Mirrors show several aspects together and remind us that the combination of problems explains why progress is so difficult. For instance, 'lack of concentration' might be an obvious cause for school work suffering, getting poorly paid jobs and never having enough money to go round. Memories and flashbacks will obviously interfere with concentration and will lead to efforts to ignore these memories or to avoid their triggers.

Putting these all together shows how complicated the whole situation really is. This allows the counsellor to reinforce perspective for a survivor's normal reaction of feeling a failure: 'Who wouldn't, considering just how much has gone wrong for you?'

REASONING

It is useful to have papers that the survivor can read between meetings. Survivors spend a lot of time thinking about it all and will use poems, leaflets and questionnaires to remind them of different aspects to think about.

USAGE

At the end of the meeting in which we have used a questionnaire, we offer it to the survivor to take home and re-read later. Most survivors accept this. A few have partners/children/parents who might discover it, so they ask if the papers could stay 'in the office'.

Designing a New Future: Planning where to go with life

What do you want to do with your life? If you had a fresh chance to sort things out – a clean drawing board – what would you put on it?

REASONING

In the future-finding stage of the work we need various ways of encouraging people to move the Compass from the past to the future. The phrase 'Designing a New Future' has all the components needed to get people thinking – though it is easier said than done! Quite often, it needs to be said to allow the survivor to get a clear idea about a new future. It is as though we give permission for them to consider the possibility of a new future. Certainly we encourage them to think about it.

USAGE

This question can be very useful in groupwork, almost as an ice-breaker game. It is not a game but could be used as one if the need arose. For instance, we could change the question to 'What is the silliest/funniest sort of future you could make up for yourself?' Even if used 'seriously', some humour can emerge from people who let their imaginations roam. This humour can be a relief of the tension created by the idea that perhaps the future *can* be different.

Breaking the Chain: Responsibility to children and future generations

The great worry of so many adult survivors is that they will make their current or future children the same as themselves. In other words, they worry that their children will turn out to have as many problems too, that the children will mess everything up, be miserable and make bad parents a generation later. Sometimes they are even more specific: they expect their children to become sexual abuse victims, or even perpetrators.

Many survivors become aware of the part played by their own parents – even non-abusing parents – in reducing their confidence and discouraging their growth. This often comes from discussion of the way their confidence was bashed down.

The reaction against this is well described by the picture of Breaking the Chain. In other words, they want to get away from the inevitable feeling of abuse spreading down the generations. This is described as the 'cycle of abuse' when professionals talk about it. Survivors want to take responsibility for starting a happy and healthy growth for future generations. Even so, breaking the chain can be hard work, as Cheryl's Interview shows (page 184).

One way to break the chain is to help other survivors in some way, even at a distance. Being a friend, or a teacher, to a survivor can help both of them. Writing poems and stories also helps (see the poem *The Result*, page 243).

REASONING
We can use this metaphor to confirm that these worries are understandable and that the aim of breaking the chain is appropriate and deserves respect.

USAGE
We can show the general picture of this idea of breaking the chain through a hand movement that shows a significant change in direction. I point my hand forwards, moving 12 inches forwards, and then moving diagonally off to the side to a (relaxed) full arm stretch.

About Surviving

Victims have to respond to the frights and injuries of abuse to survive. These responses may then cause further problems. As part of the untangling process, sorting out the difference between the first effects of the abuse and the later effects of these responses is an important area. It is useful to point out the steps the victim had to take, because this shows that the abuse was a frightening, dangerous experience. This brings the idea that they have *already* been working hard to cope and get better. Counselling is just the next step.

It's Very Easy to Sexually Abuse a Child:
Reassurance that it really is difficult to understand

Now we are adults, we can think back to when it happened and talk to ourselves as we do this. We can tell ourselves off for not having said 'NO!' louder, more often, more forcefully and so on. We can change the story plot in our minds and organise it so that we would have done it all differently or so that it never happened in the first place. Then we become more critical for having let ourselves down by not following the story plot (as a child)that we have just written (as an adult).

Now we are adults, we can stop and think about how adults can affect children. As adults, we know how to cheat, we know how to lie, how to pretend, how to get away with things (even if we are not very good at it). We know how to impress children, how to punish them, how to hurt, surprise and worry them. Even if we haven't done it, we've seen others do it. TV programmes do it and we can imagine how to do it. Adults also know about sex, about relationships and about how the world works. They know all sorts of things that children don't so it becomes quite easy for adults to do things to children that make the sexual abuse happen, The Trap happen, The Wall happen. Once these have started, it must be very easy for an adult to keep them happening. Once the helplessness has started, it is very simple to encourage.

Why didn't you avoid The Trap? Usually, the answer is that the abuser has taken a long, long time about gradually pushing you into it. Only occasionally might abuse start with a sudden rape or seduction, which is then used as evidence for blackmail. More often, the touches start very innocently and easily and slowly become more personal, more sexual. This might take months or even years. It can be very difficult to know when to say 'Stop, that's far enough!' Remember, adults find this difficult too and, from time to time, people make honest mistakes, because what started as relaxed friendly tickling might suddenly feel 'too far' and result in someone getting shouted at 'Stop' or slapped. If adults can make mistakes, how can children expect to get it right first time?

We need to remember this to stop us telling ourselves off: 'I should have stopped it, it would have been easy if only I'd been braver or cleverer...' NO, IT WOULD NOT HAVE BEEN EASY! The adult had the easy bit, you had the difficult bit.

REASONING

There are times when the survivor is going round and round in The Circles in The Fogbank and is Trapped and seems to be digging The Pit deeper. We may need to interrupt this. Putting the issue this way round (it's easy to be a child abuser) makes it clearer that it's very difficult being a victim.

USAGE

The contrast in this metaphor can be challenging. We often intend it to be when we want survivors to snap out of their all-too-familiar circle. This is very much a companion metaphor to 'The Confusions'.

The Crossroads: Choices about love and sex are difficult

When a child or teenager has been sexually abused they will probably have understandable difficulties when they reach their first few sexual encounters. They may know more about sex than their peers at school. They may know more about sex than the boy they have met. But sexual abuse mixes up love and sex, which is confusing. There is a crossroads where these teenagers end up. They have to make choices that their friends do not have to make. (This is not fair.) There are four roads out of the crossroads. They affect large sections of later life.

One road says: 'I want love. I want someone to care for me and help me get over everything that happened. I want to give love and make someone happy. I don't want sex because it reminds me of bad experiences too much.'

The opposite road says: 'Don't talk to me about love, that's where people start to lie and cheat and let me down. Sex I can understand, I can control and I can enjoy. A good honest cuddle is much better than a pile of words that disappear into thin air leaving me alone again.'

Another road says: 'I'm going to keep away from love *and* sex. They're both bad and I just can't cope/don't like/get upset by them. I'll keep myself busy – in a convent, in a workaholic job – or become a social hermit.' (See Painkillers, page 106.)

The fourth road says: 'I want love and sex. I deserve to enjoy them both. I want to enjoy them both. I know it may take some sorting out but I'm not going to stand still and put up with miserableness all my life.'

With the first and second roads, some people find a fork in the road that concerns the difference between giving and receiving. For the first road: 'Can I love someone? Can I cope with being loved by someone?' For the second road: 'Can I enjoy sex? Can I give enjoyment in sex?' These might be the next questions after discussing the crossroads or they might come later with questions about The Boomerang, The Monty Python Foot, Painkillers and so on.

In the first telling of the crossroads story I end up by saying 'My own preference for you is the fourth road. I hope for health and happiness, good love and good sex for you. But, it is your choice, it's your life. I can only help if that's where you want to go.' The Guide cannot decide these things.

REASONING

The traumatic sexualisation effects of sexual abuse leave a great mark on the victims, it cannot be ignored by either survivors or counsellors. It is both fair and productive to acknowledge that these teenagers will know more than their friends at school. Victims *know* that they are different from their friends – their friends do not have the same crossroads. (Some victims of physical or emotional abuse may reach a similar crossroads.) The knowledge of being different will amplify the detachment caused by the trauma (see Post Traumatic Stress symptoms, page 76) and will continue to undermine the confidence.

Similarly, it is right to acknowledge that later in life survivors feel the effects of having been pushed into a road that is a long diversion. 'It has not been a waste. You have learnt more about survival than any of your friends will ever know. You have had to live on your courage and determination on your own.'

USAGE

This crossroads is very recognisable to survivors. They know which road they are on. They also know if they have tried several roads.

With younger survivors, it may be important to describe this crossroads to them to point out the importance of coping with a first heartache (like all teenagers) and allow themselves time to find another boy- or girl-friend. The first partner, the first sexual contact with him or her, the first row, the first break-up are all felt to be crucial turning points. If they have too much invested in the *first* one, we must discuss the danger of the self-fulfilling prophecy starting. Their first relationship 'problem' does *not* prove that they are a complete failure, totally unattractive, a man-hater or whatever final/ultimate/totally bad thing they feel tempted to call themselves. By reminding them that the *second* experience of any of these is as important, or more important even, because it allows them to make comparisons, then they are not so likely to jump to the conclusion that the problems in the relationship were 'all their fault'.

Also, it is worth reminding them that there is a natural period of life where many people experience difficulty in relationships. It is called teenage or adolescence. Their friends have to go through all that too!

Older survivors can get a perspective on some of the previous choices of partner or lifestyle through discussion of this metaphor. Hand-in-hand with it goes our belief that all humans do the best they can in difficult circumstances. Be gentle with yourself over your regrets. Therefore, a clear link with The Pencil and The Impossible Jigsaw is useful.

The Boomerang: Memories, thoughts, feelings and problems keep coming back

When people have had a problem or set of problems for some time – especially some years – they end up with a relationship with the problem. They have thoughts and feelings about it. They get to know it, hate it and expect it to appear 'on schedule'.

This becomes particularly important when they have decided that they are the only ones who have the problem, no one else in their family or current relationship. They are the only one with a *big* problem, everyone else suffers from a smaller difficulty or from difficulties resulting from 'my' problem. They become aware of the problem as an 'It', which they wish they could 'throw off', so they try to throw it off, push it away, stride over it.

The trouble is that when they try to throw it off, they find that the problem comes whizzing back, just when they were beginning to hope that it had gone. Like a boomerang, it hits them on the back of the head just when they'd started looking forward to some progress.

The result of this is that they learn they can't get away from this problem, and this confirms what they'd found previously – 'don't get your hopes up'.

REASONING

This hopelessness stems from the trauma and is shown in the Post Traumatic Stress responses 'Mirror' (see pages 72 and 99). Having it confirmed is proof that there is only one way forward and that's round the circle.

The powerfully negative experience of this suits the notion of a boomerang hitting you on the back of the head unexpectedly. This allows you to say 'I knew it was a boomerang all along. Why did I ever try to throw it off? I should have known better!' This creates a mental circle as powerful as the boomerang's circle.

USAGE

This metaphor is likely to be used only occasionally. It is probably best used to emphasise a survivor's own discovery of the circle of 'try – fail – give up on yourself'.

In describing The Boomerang, I make an arm movement to suggest the way it works. I gesture throwing it away, tracking the boomerang in a circle and then hitting the back of my own head to show the return of the boomerang. Changing to a facial expression of surprise helps to show the general idea and can also lead to some humour.

Painkillers: No one likes pain, we all cope with it as best we can

One of the results of child sexual abuse is the memories, feelings and flashbacks that are triggered by seeing or hearing a reminder of the abuse. This reminder can be a very small thing. The smaller it is, the more scary it is. It feels as though you are losing control of your own mind.

This can go on for years or decades. It tempts survivors to think they are mad. They can't forget the things they most want to forget. They wonder if they are perverted for having these memories going round their heads so often.

To try to stop this they often use various painkillers. This is what we call them. They are ways to keep The Wall up, even inside the survivor's own head. Painkillers are often based on normal things that everyone uses once in a while but are used more frequently or more strongly than usual. People will use almost anything to take their minds off these horrible memories. The main point is that they are distractions and that they cheer survivors up a bit.

It often doesn't matter to them that their painkillers can create more problems – the new ones aren't as bad as the old ones. Even if the painkillers only work for a while, that's better than nothing. Many drug users say they don't know why they do it. I suspect that for some – maybe many – they do know but can't or daren't admit it.

Painkillers include:

Alcohol, and other drugs – street drugs or prescribed drugs: Some painkillers are strictly legal and orthodox – such as prescribed anti-depressants or tranquillisers or alcohol and tobacco. Others are illegal – cannabis, amphetamines and stronger drugs. It would not be a surprise if many heroin and crack users are sexual abuse survivors (or survivors of other forms of child abuse). The poem *Is There No End?* on page 232 shows the connection. I see compulsive eating as a form of drug-taking – eating calms the nerves in the same way as other drugs.

Workaholism: Some painkillers appear to be very positive and respectable at first glance. For instance, workaholism seems to be good because it is pushing a career ahead, earning lots of money, helping others in need, advancing education, etc. In fact, some workaholics are professionals – social workers, doctors, lawyers, police officers and so on. They may be trying to 'put things right' a bit, but it may also be hiding the pain and so tempting people to do too much and then get exhausted and fail.

Obsessive housework, mothering lots of children, compulsive dieting, compulsive sports and working long hours for voluntary or charity organisations are all variations of the same thing. These are, basically, distractions that keep thoughts, feelings and memories at bay.

Pain: another form of painkiller is pain. A different sort of pain can seem a relief from the emotional pain the abuse leaves. Overdoses, cutting and scratching, fighting, starving or vomiting – they're all distractions. They also have many other useful effects, as the poem *Why do I hurt myself?* (Figure 2.13) shows.

It may also be that a rare form of self-harm called Munchausen's Syndrome is a painkiller – the survivor invents an illness and pretends to have the symptoms through various forms of deception. A similar situation is to do this through children, to pretend the children need medical help (Munchausen's Syndrome by Proxy). In these types of painkiller the sympathy and kindness that can arrive from others (nurses, doctors, other helpers) because of the problems may help as a painkiller. If survivors feel they deserve the help but cannot ask outright because they cannot mention the sexual abuse, this accidental gain of sympathy might become very important to them.

Fighting: Violence and fighting is yet another form of painkiller, using the bottled up anger to fight other people. The fights might be with strangers, 'the authorities' or partners (see the poems *The Crime*, page 25, and *Doing without the Painkillers*, page 110). Some survivors channel it into sports or other competitive activities. Sometimes it can turn into crime.

Hiding: Sometimes people get to the end of their tethers and feel they have to get away from everything. They want to hide away from people, traps, triggers, responsibility, the suspense of waiting for things to go wrong (or

2.13: Poem example – Why do I hurt myself?

It's anger that makes me do it
– anger I keep hidden away
and because it's inside me
I get angry with me in that way.

Sometimes it's revenge
– being angry with myself for not coping
I'm so stupid, I must be
but I can give up, I keep on hoping.

Usually it's a distraction.
The thoughts and feelings and flashbacks
are so upsetting, I'll do anything that
takes my mind off them –
like scratch and scratch and scratch.

I do wonder why I don't feel anything.
I didn't when he was doing it to me
– so I test myself with pain.
If I can feel that, then I'm not totally crazy!

And it's a relief.
A way of letting out the emotional pain
that gives me some hope that
all the chaos inside will wane.

Perhaps its a sort of hint
to the outside world: showing something
when all the inside pain is so invisible
and it's easy because I feel nothing.

And of course I hoped someone would ask why
and discover the abuse and stop it –
without me saying a word –
and then I could get on and forget it.

But it doesn't work well enough
so you either stop doing it
or you do it twice as often…

(A counsellor's words to express a
26-year-old mother's feelings, and approved by her.)

get even worse). They disappear into refuges, prison, care, hospital, convents, or just become a hermit at home.

Mixtures: Most survivors use a mixture. Using alcohol and drugs regularly brings a lifestyle that becomes all-important, so the result is that the survivor hides from the authorities, family and friends, and will suffer withdrawal symptoms later. Some people fight in a self-harming way – the fighting makes things worse and they feel more depressed, cheated and hopeless.

Using painkillers becomes a habit. It gets taken for granted, an ordinary part of life. Sometimes the habit has to get as horrible as the abuse before survivors feel desperate enough to stop. Stopping painkillers allows the pain back in. This is a concern for survivors starting counselling – will we insist they stop using the painkillers? No, we don't, but we do encourage them to change to a more healthy painkiller as soon as possible.

As people sort things out, their use of painkillers is likely to change. Some people need their painkillers more than ever when more memories start coming back, feelings get more raw and questions and circles get more intense. We find that the use of the painkillers drops after this 'Government Health Warning' (see page 110) period. It may rise again as various turning points are reached. For instance, telling a partner (more) about the abuse, showing (more) feelings about it or deciding to change a marriage or a relationship with an abuser or a child, and so on, can eventually give a lot of relief gained through anxious experiments. It is understandable that these would be difficult issues – most of us would find them difficult without any sexual abuse in our past!

People do not change their painkiller to a more unhealthy one during the programme. They are likely to use their usual one(s) more often or more strongly for short periods. A few people can suddenly quit their painkiller once their need for it has been explained to them. Most people cut down slowly, keeping it in reserve for a while. For some, there are extra questions: 'Can I use alcohol/sport/a hobby as well?' Can I work at a social/ sensible level?' All these issues are part of designing a new future.

REASONING

The reasoning is contained in the metaphor itself; the explanation is built in.

2.14: Case example – Doing without the painkillers

A woman in her mid-twenties asked questions about how people should re-act later in life to sexual abuse as a child. She was concerned that she seemed to have spent a lot of her life so far getting drunk and fighting. She would go to a pub and use an excuse to pick a fight with a man. And because she was smaller, she often got away with it too. She was worried because it seemed as though she had got into a habit of drinking and fighting. She felt that this was not a good thing for her young son.

She started to watch young children and told the Group one day: 'I realised they are born gentle and happy. So my anger and unhappiness was put in me by the abuse'. This allowed her to find the courage to report the abuse and gain some satisfaction from the discomfort the police investigations must have caused the abuser. The police could not find sufficient evidence to go to court. Even so, she felt better for having been true to herself.

USAGE

This metaphor becomes useful when survivors drop back into 'victim mode' and feel useless and helpless because of their coping methods. That is, they criticise themselves for being a drunk, an addict, a criminal, a fighter. This metaphor reminds them that there is a good reason – the Post Traumatic Stress responses. It is then a short step to remind them of The Trap, etc. In other words, the cause of the painkillers is traced back to the original abuse.

In the programme we do not insist that survivors 'give up' their painkillers before starting the counselling. This does mean that they occasionally arrive intoxicated, tranquillised, angry, starving, and so on. We avoid reacting forcefully unless there is an immediate danger to the survivor or someone else. We do ask – at a suitable moment and in a gentle way – what has made them use the painkiller just before the counselling. Is it the Government Health Warning, nerves at the thought of what we may discuss in the counselling, or has some crisis arrived and knocked them sideways?

Some people think about their Painkillers as an Escape Hatch: drink, drugs and pain, etc. Sometimes these don't work and they think about the ultimate Escape Hatch: suicide.

About Progress

It is often important to describe how the process of recovering actually happens. Although it is different for everyone in its details, there are some generalisations we can make. These can help by shedding a little light further down the path – it is the Guide's job to do this.

The Government Health Warning: Reassurance about feeling worse in counselling – at the beginning

Talking about how sexual abuse happens, and what it does to people, is likely to remind survivors about 'what actually happened' to them. The Government Health Warning is a metaphorical label that sums up the gentle warning that we should give early in the counselling. The warning is that the very fact of talking about it is likely to make you think about it, dream about it and, maybe, have flashbacks more often. We must emphasise that this is not a sign that you are finally going mad, nor that the counselling is making you worse. It is a temporary effect because the counselling is 'ringing bells' in the your past. It is waking up memories that you have probably been trying to push away (one of the Post Traumatic Stress responses, see page 72). So, if you start to feel worse, it is not because you are getting worse but because you are getting on with the spring-cleaning, sorting it all out.

REASONING

This 'ringing bells' effect is due to the intrusive memories of Post Traumatic Stress Disorder. It may have biological causes as stress affects the memory functions in the meeting place of the brain and mind. This increase in intrusive activity is often found in Critical Incident Debriefing and Post Traumatic Stress groups run for survivors of a wide range of traumas.

USAGE

The Government Health Warning is worth describing in the first session as part of the routine. I usually do it at the end of the meeting, along with setting a date and offering poems and leaflets. If and when it later proves to be relevant, it is easy to remind the survivor that this was half-expected. In this way it can be a safeguard against people getting too anxious about flashbacks and nightmares and dropping out of counselling.

Some people get an increase in feelings – like anger, sadness or anxiety. Others get more physical reactions–like stomach upsets, skin problems, aches and pains. Some get mental reactions – such as absentmindedness (leading to accident proneness and clumsiness) or concentration problems (which can lead to memory problems) as well as the flashbacks and nightmares, and so on.

We can deliberately divert survivors from their thoughts and feelings if they 'go inside' too much when distracted by intrusive memories and feelings. It can be important to check whether the counsellor reminds the survivor of the abuser in any way (see Giving Choice, page 150). We can remind them of what has happened to them and of the Storage Cupboard (see page 80). It is also very important to say that the way they have reacted to it is likely to be 'normal, considering what has happened to them'. (This is a very useful phrase.) Using the Post Traumatic Stress checklist will make this more concrete.

Note: 'What actually happened' is the most useful phrase to use as a general term. It places the abuse outside the survivor. Phrases like 'your abuse' bring an ownership, as though it is your property. This makes it sound like you bought the abuse, which means you must have wanted it (here is a Circle (see page 88)). These ideas may increase the survivor's feelings of guilt unnecessarily and unhelpfully.

The Compass: This allows us to measure progress

"One way we can check on your progress is to watch where your attention goes, what you have thoughts and feelings about. This is the usual direction of the your attention. Do you spend most time in the past, present or future? We can illustrate this by using an imaginary compass – the past points behind, the present is around you and the future lies ahead."

To begin with, survivors often focus their attention into the past for long periods of time. The memories and flashbacks (the 'intrusive memories' in the Post Traumatic Stress Disorder diagnosis) get in the way of ordinary life in a powerful way. When survivors start seeking counselling the Compass may have begun to swing to include the present more. This may be because of a sense of desperation coming from a growing realisation that the past is dominating the present and, probably, the future.

What we do in this counselling programme is to encourage survivors to understand their present in terms of the past. The impact of the trauma and the survivor's reactions to it have affected a great deal of her life. It is important to make this very clear in order to interrupt the circles of self-blame, guilt and depression (see Circles, page 88).

As the grip of the past reduces, and an increased confidence in the survivor's understanding of the present emerges, the tone of the counselling often gets lighter with increased humour and increasing self-awareness. A sense of curiosity replaces the reluctance to think about these feelings. Patience becomes possible (instead of apathy). In the later stages, The Compass begins to point forwards and survivors start to make plans with more thought and with more optimism. The size and duration of these plans grow, and the target dates involved, begin to move further and further into the future as the survivor finds more confidence and more clarity about what she wants. The Compass eventually points to the Horizon of Hope (see The Fogbank, page 91).

During this, the phrase 'I want...' becomes increasingly important. If you do not say what you want, you can't achieve it. Survivors who have avoided getting their hopes up because of the Monty Python Foot (see page 89) have to tackle this. They have to use Courage or Determination (see page 154) to get their hopes up a little. Then they need to recognise their achievements. This is often difficult too.

REASONING

Wartime studies on the psychology of morale, and later studies on trauma and post traumatic stress reactions, show that pessimism and the inability to see very far into the future are central reactions. Pessimism is one of the Post Traumatic Stress symptoms and 95 per cent of survivors are pessimistic in my experience. Therefore, it makes sense to have a means to describe these aspects of the survivor's experience, especially as it offers a positive suggestion of change. It is important to have indicators of change that do not re-focus attention back on the problems. Instead, we offer the idea that the start of something new is a better and more useful measure of change. The slow disappearance of things that have been inescapable – and therefore expected – for a long period of time is much more difficult to notice.

The Compass is a morality-free concept relating more directly to current personal position than causes of problems. It could be used with anyone with serious problems caused in any way.

USAGE

We can use this metaphor most usefully in the middle and later stages of the programme.

The Compass is useful in identifying progress. Clients often wish things would change but stay very pessimistic (in line with the Post Traumatic Stress symptom). We say: 'You daren't hope for what you really want (because you know you'll never get it), so you avoid any disappointments by avoiding any hopes'. This becomes especially important in the area of relationships, where so much is at stake. Relationships with children, partners, other children in the family, abusers, non-abusing carers and authorities may all be subject to this self-enforced passivity. Simple encouragement is unlikely to achieve much against such convictions.

But when we detect changes, whether planned or emerging freely, we draw attention to them: 'That seems different to the way you used to handle this sort of situation some months (or years) ago, doesn't it?' If the survivor agrees, it is then important to move rapidly on to ask 'Is it a better way? Is it difficult? Is it what you want?' Accepting that a new approach to certain problems may be more anxiety-provoking than the previous way can be reassuring. Here we have to link up with the survivor's experiences and the issues we know she is concerned about. Guessing the problems and consequences of a given choice or new action can help the survivor make reassuring comparisons. The survivor might say it isn't as bad as the counsellor expects or that there are some worries to consider. In either case, these answers are, in a way, reassuring – we are telling the survivor that she is not crazy to worry about these things, because anyone would.

Another way we can approach helping people become aware of changes is to discuss it as part of The Fogbank: 'Are you nearer the edge of The Fogbank? Do things seem a bit clearer? Can you see where these choices lead to?' Many survivors know when they feel they have 'taken a step', even though they may not know in which direction and with what consequences. It is very helpful to identify the gain of self-control with each step. Also, we encourage survivors to be gentle with themselves in case difficulties with the new reactions to the problems emerge. We encourage them to remember that they are coping with an extremely difficult situation that many other people wouldn't cope with at all.

At the beginning of counselling The Compass is unlikely to make very much impact and may reinforce the survivor's awareness of the past even more. We must discuss this area carefully, with sensitive awareness of the survivor's ups and downs. Any discussion in the early stages of the programme that focuses on the ways in which child sexual abuse actually happens is likely to have already brought back memories of it. It may also have triggered the more intrusive phenomena of Post Traumatic Stress responses. For example, talking over the process of seduction/entrapment may bring more nightmares, flashbacks, hallucinations and ghosts. We give reassurances about this (through The Government Health Warning, see page 112). However, this is in a general, statistical, research context rather than a personal individual and unique context. The next metaphor helps with this.

The Confusions: Sexual abuse is always confusing

When we hear the 'I must be stupid. I don't understand it all' theme, we have two ways to respond. We want to counteract this idea as quickly as possible.

One way is to say very simply that 'There's only one rule in this counselling: the word "stupid" is forbidden. There are better alternatives, such as "silly", "not at my best", "fed up", etc., or, in other situations, "ignorant", "mis-informed" or "cheated."' The word 'stupid' is such a great put-down that when clients use it about themselves, we allow ourselves quite a strong reaction. (See also Circles, page 88). Another way is to say: 'Sexual abuse is never easy to understand from the inside' or 'Part of the normal reaction to being abused is to be confused about it all'.

Survivors need reassurance about this. They will need plenty of reassurance and it often needs to be repeated. This is because we are contradicting a belief that the survivor will have had for many years, perhaps many decades. There are several issues that contribute to the confusion:

Social and moral complexity: Most of the metaphors say something about this. The ideas in Stealing A Pencil (see page 84) and The Impossible Jigsaw (see page 67) help to explain this. Because it's very easy to sexually abuse a child, the child is at the adult's mercy.

Tricked and Trapped: We can remind them of The Trap – the ways abusers keep children quiet: violence, threat of violence, bribery, confusion, emotional blackmail (see Stealing a Pencil, page 83). Of course, sometimes abusers use several means either at the same time or over a period of time, and the combinations can be confusing. If magic was brought into the situation, this automatically complicates things further – as it is probably intended to do.

Mind and body contradiction: We give survivors a chance to understand the confusions that are actually in the abuse. If a survivor is born with a normal healthy body, sexual stimulation will create a normal sexual response. This can happen well before puberty. If this normal sexual response happened at the age of 23 with a much loved wife or husband, everyone would say 'Great!, Wonderful!, We're happy for you!' If it happens in childhood, people might say 'This is too soon' and the child might say 'I don't understand this. I don't want to be here'. The result is that their body is saying 'This feels nice, it's a new sort of tickling game' and their mind is saying 'I don't like this'. This disagreement is easy to forget twenty years later. It is too easy to say 'Why did I stay there/go back there/again? I must have liked it/wanted it/started it'. And down that road are many, many circles and questions. Put like this, I hope it is clear that the abuse is confusing *in itself.* No wonder it's difficult to sort out later, with all the other problems from painkillers, difficult relationships and circles added on.

Anger at loved ones: There is another source of confusion to do with anger at the abuser. Some survivors feel anger, perhaps great anger, at the abuser. Others don't, and this often confuses them. They say 'Why don't I feel angry at him, everyone else does, what's wrong with me?' or 'But I liked him' or 'I loved him'. This is very confusing. Does this like or love mean that the survivor allowed the abuser to do the abuse or even wanted him to? These are awful questions to live with and very difficult to check with anyone else.

One reason why this source of confusion arises is because the abuser is often a grown-up relative whom the child is supposed to like or love – or at least, obey – or other people with a duty of care – professionals and people who look after children as a job or as an activity leader – whom the child is supposed to trust. Two pieces of research are useful here:

1. When a child is physically abused, he or she will often cling to the abuser. This used to confuse doctors and social workers who were looking for the signs of abuse because they expected to see fear and anxiety. Instead, they saw a clingy child who looked lovingly towards the abusing parent. It seems that the child tries to placate the abuser into being calmer and more loving. Inside the child's experience, there might even be loving feelings towards that parent while they try to placate him or her. In a sense, this would be in tune with the general idea of a family pulling together and helping one another.

2. Many years ago, in Stockholm, Sweden, a bank robbery went wrong and the police arrived while the robbers were inside. Some of the public using the bank at the time were held prisoner, which turned it into a siege. The siege went on for a long time and afterwards the

hostages were offered counselling. Many of them commented on what nice people the robbers were and how their motives were about desperation rather than greed. Some hostages refused to complain about the robbers and blamed the police for making the situation worse. Some didn't want to give evidence about it all. The authorities were surprised and asked the counsellors why this was happening.

The answer came back that over the period of the siege, the hostages got to know the robbers as people and understood their desperation. They stopped being 'dangerous robbers' and became 'sad, fed-up, poor people'. They had all talked together, eaten together, even laughed together. They had almost become friends, despite the unfairness of the situation. The hostages were trapped by the robbers and the robbers were trapped by the police. This fellow-feeling or comradeship complicated the situation for everyone. It was so confusing and surprising that it became known as the 'Stockholm Syndrome'. I think that this can often become a part of the relationship between abuser and victim.

We must also remember that some victims get angry with family members who did not abuse them. This usually applies to Mum and Dad because they didn't realise the abuse was happening and then immediately stop it. This is what dependent children want and expect, perhaps quite unrealistically. When it doesn't happen, they feel let down, abandoned, frightened and angry. Yet they may need their parents more than ever once the abuse is stopped, or disclosed once the victim is safe. So they may end up feeling guilty at their own normal feelings of anger. This complicates things: 'Am I allowed to feel angry? Poor old Mum was depressed, which was why Uncle Bert came round in the first place...'.

This same sort of process may be going on when, in later life, survivors turn their anger towards their partners in a relationship. It is almost as though they need some safe way of getting their anger out. Sometimes this is OK with their partner, especially if he or she understands it. But this can get violent – especially for men survivors, who often seem to have more anger in them.

Survivor guilt: There are times when people are rescued from terrible situations and instead of feeling safe and relieved, they feel guilty and depressed. They, and their relatives, are likely to find this difficult to understand as it seems to contradict what 'common sense' expects.

The reason may be that the victim is aware of another victim who has suffered worse or longer, or whom she had to ignore or abandon for her own survival. 'How can I feel happy when another suffered worse than I did? I should be ashamed of feeling relieved.' This guilt is likely to lead to depression because of the anger the victim turns on herself. This might make relatives try to cheer her up, but she could end up feeling even worse because she is letting them down too.

REASONING

There is not much to add to the reasoning here. The ideas are contained in the description. They are, very literally, relevant to most survivors – at least, some parts. This description could be accused of not really being a metaphor at all. All of these issues are good material for a wide variety of circles.

USAGE

Often, it is the word 'stupid' that prompts our use of The Confusions. Only the relevant parts are worth including – there is no need to confuse by bringing in too much.

In example 2.15 David shows us the confusion very well, especially how the death of his brother is so likely to lead to survivor guilt: why did he (David) not die instead? Also, we can see anger at the abuse coming out in crime. His feeling of helplessness may have led him to feel that if society didn't care about him, his crime was justified. He has used drugs, pain and work (scrubbing himself) as painkillers. He has tried to form loving relationships. He has tried to understand himself. He is not a criminal for the fun of it, out of laziness or because he was born bad. We can see that he was tricked and trapped several times by men who ignored his needs, his worth as a person and his place in the world.

Same, Different, Opposite: Judgments and comparisons

When people have been abused, they often make promises about how they are going to behave when they grow up. They say 'I am going to be a perfect mother', 'I will never row in front of the children', 'I will always be happy' and so on. Often, survivors make these promises to themselves or their

2.15: Case example – The confusions of the Rubik's Cube

David was in prison when I met him. He told me that he had run away from home and from a children's home to escape several abusers, one of whom was a church man. He had threatened to kill the first abuser with a gun and later his brother killed himself with that gun, in front of David. Since then he had collected guns. He had become a rent boy in London until he began to suffer from too many violent users. Eventually he turned to armed robbery to feed his family and his drug habit.

Drug abuse before and during prison had left him with liver disease and HIV. He had many haunting memories of the abuse and it effects. He sometimes had repeated nightmares and would wake up wanting to scrub himself clean endlessly or even cut himself until he saw blood. And when that didn't hurt – which it sometimes didn't – he felt very scared and would retreat into his own room and keep the light off and the door shut for several days at a time. He felt particularly bad when he felt the presence of abusers living near him in the prison.

When he tried to understand why he felt and behaved the way he did, he had always found confusions. Were his memories real? Were there worse memories he had blanked out? Why had it happened? Had he made it happen in some way? Was his judgement of people faulty in some way? Why couldn't he sort it all out? Why couldn't he be happy and normal?

David couldn't sort out all his feelings, memories and ideas about the abuse. He described it to me as being like a Rubik's Cube. No matter how he tried to twist and turn all the pieces, it still didn't make sense to him. He'd been twisting and turning it around in his head for over fifteen years, more or less every day. He felt it was impossible to sort out, considering how long and how often he had tried to. In prison he had far too much time to work on his Rubik's Cube and he felt he was getting worse – more upset, more despairing, more suicidal. He asked for counselling.

husbands-to-be. Sometimes they make these promises to 'the children I will have one day'. Even though they make these promises silently, they can have the strength of a spoken promise.

But because the world is not a perfect place, things go wrong and they are not perfect mothers, calm and controlled in front of the children and always happy. Then the survivor feels that she has broken the promise. This can feel like the end of the world and push people into depression. And because the promise was silent, other people may not realise what the problem is. More loneliness and isolation!

If there is something we like, we often search for the same again. When we see something we dislike, we often look for the opposite. However, same and opposite are only two possibilities. There is a third one: to be different. This is not really just one choice but many. If we think about this situation enough, there is a whole range of possibilities between same and opposite. Between black and white are all the colours. They just have to be described, searched for or, better still, noticed when they appear on their own.

Trying to be the opposite of a violent father, a depressed mother or a drunken sexually abusing grandfather can set you up for a fall. It is too difficult to be perfect. It is better – and easier in the long run – to aim for different.

REASONING

It is not unusual for hopeless people to get caught in the belief that there are only two possible courses of action – either black *or* white. This is an Illusion of Alternatives, the trap of logical thinking. Usually, there are several options. Edward de Bono has written many books on lateral thinking to show us ways of deliberately pushing our thinking away from the strictly logical and towards the creative. This metaphor allows us to interrupt the Circles of Hopelessness.

USAGE

In discussions about parents – the survivor's past (now or later) – the issue of comparison comes up. Given that most sexual abuse is committed by a father or stepfather and not prevented (or stopped quickly enough) by a mother, the question of 'How can I be a parent now?' comes up often. In those cases where the abuser was someone else, the child's parents often seem to have let them down in ways that slowed down the growth of confidence and made them more vulnerable to the abuse. This may have been caused by the parents having had depression, illness, absence, bereavement, emotional abuse, long hours at work, and so on.

These questions come up as:

'How can I learn to be a parent? – I was never shown how', 'How can I avoid being the same sort of parent as mine were?', 'If I can do it now, why couldn't (s)he/he/they do it then?', 'If they could do it for my sister/

daughter/friends, why didn't they do it for me then?'. Sometimes they are about sadness, other times about anger; both may be appropriate. Sometimes there is a complicated sense of a changing balance where babies and little children begin to restore the survivor's sense of worth and identity. But as they grow older and more independent they challenge, which can accidentally push their survivor parent's confidence back down again.

To survivors this feels like fate and inevitability forcing them back into a corner again. Having survived – or escaped – the abuse and the lack of care 'at home', they often have a period of respite from facing such demanding and taking-never-giving-back situations. Then, at some age, the children begin to feel as though they are demanding and taking all the time. This may be when they won't settle as a baby for some reason, as a self-centred five to nine-year-old who just wants to play all the time or as a teenager going through the difficulties of adolescence. The result is that the survivor parent feels back in The Trap again. It gets even more complicated because she can say: 'I know it's only my child, not my abuser'. It gets tempting to feel a little crazy – and very guilty.

When we ask about this, we often find survivors wishing to be perfect parents and bring up perfect children. Discussing it in this way, with these words, often brings a smile or a laugh and a 'Not really!', but, in a way, they *do* mean really. The wish to be as opposite as possible to their own parents becomes quite a passion, yet they can feel as though they are failing in this promise to themselves. This is because they can grow to resent the lack of help, care or respect they get from their children, and yet this makes them try harder to please their children. From the outside this may appear as though the parent is allowing or even encouraging the child's misbehaviour, but from the inside it often feels quite desperate because they are judging themselves (harshly) on their success as a parent by measuring themselves against their own parents.

We can help a discussion of this with the idea of three positions: Same, Opposite and Different. They want to avoid being the Same as their parents. They have tried to be the Opposite and have disappointed themselves. What would simply being Different be like? To show the three, we hold up three fingers and count out the three different positions.

We also need to remind people that we are not assuming that they haven't tried hard to sort things out. But they may have been distracted by the Opposite possibility before they discovered the Different ones. This needs to be opened up as a real area of possibility. We can illustrate the idea of there being many options within Different by holding up one hand as Same, one as Opposite and draw them apart to show a widening gap where all the Different possibilities are. Alternatively, we can say that where Same is black and Opposite is white, Different is all the colours in between.

Vertigo: Feeling confused while making progress

Sometimes progress is obvious – you can do something you couldn't do before or you stop doing something that has been a habit. Sometimes progress is very confusing and raises a lot of doubt and hesitation.

It is as though you are walking along a treacherous cliff path at the edge of the fogbank. While you concentrate on where to put your feet, you become aware of your surroundings out of the corner of your eye. You notice the cliff edge and the rocks and grass below that. Because you are concentrating on the path, a strange visual illusion starts. The rocks and grass seem to be moving forwards faster than you are. This only happens because you are noticing out of the corner of your eye. If you stopped and looked properly, you would see it is only an illusion. But the path can be so difficult in places that you daren't stop and look. The danger is that you feel this might put you off-balance and it distracts you, and then it really could unbalance you. This is like vertigo.

When things are changing, especially in your feelings, memories and thoughts, other people's behaviour can be confusing. Partners, children, other relatives, employers and even friends can seem to be doing things that throw you off balance. Their actions might be different to usual; or they might be the same as usual, but your attitude to them is different because you are changing. But you don't know how you are changing yet – if it is a good change or not – so it gets very easy to doubt yourself and even try to stop the changes.

REASONING

The path of progress is rarely smooth and easy. There are likely to be rough patches where people need support. Describing the reasons why change can be confusing is important. We would all like a magic wand that does it for us, nice and simple. But life's not like that!

This metaphor has links with The Government Health Warning and The Fogbank. However, we tend to use it later in the programme to encourage people who are discouraged or distressed about their progress.

The Garden Gate: Testing the water when changes start

2.16: Case example – A 40-year-old teenager!

After two marriages and three daughters, a woman who had depression and alcohol problems joined a counselling group. The early meetings were very difficult. However, a year or so later she began to argue with her teenage children, ask her relatives probing questions about the past, reconsider her employment and seek further education.

Of all this she said: 'I feel like a 40-year-old teenager!' She explained that she had become acutely aware of sorting out issues about her identity, aims for her life and hopes for her children. She felt quite odd about this – as though she was starting again or catching up with where she should be – but was very happy, despite her nervousness at the risks she had to take.

As people make progress, one of the things that changes is their assertiveness. They move from either passive (depressed) or aggressive (angry) towards being more assertive. This helps them solve problems, stand up for themselves, decide who has the problem, and so on.

This change rarely happens all in one go. Often, it is a process of change that takes months or years. Usually, it is a series of steps. Each step is aimed at sorting something out, usually different each time. Each step is often followed by a period of uncertainty and doubt or, perhaps, guilt and regret or nerves and Monty Python Foot self-blame for having taken risks previously avoided, and so on.

Other people – people who had a happy childhood – can be just the same sometimes. Doubt and nerves can slow down geniuses too!

The process works as though people start to pop out of their Garden Gate to set things right in the outside world. To begin with they remain behind their Wall. Then they will try quick 'popping out and returning home' visits. These journeys will get longer, go further and take on harder challenges with practice. This will be after they start to lower The Wall, move around in The Fogbank and get some confidence about their rights to say what they want. This continues and gets easier and easier.

REASONING

There are times when survivors slip back into victim mode and feel pessimistic. While we cannot give guarantees in any counselling work, we can give anonymous examples of the progress that others have made to give hope and open up possibilities. However, it is much more helpful to people in the middle of working (i.e. exploring The Fogbank) to hear about how other people got on rather than simply where they got to. Implicit and rarely-discussed metaphors covering much of this work are The Map and The (Personal) Journey (see The Fogbank, page 91). Survivors want to hear about other parts of the map and journeys other survivors have made – in other words, travelling information. In this, The Garden Gate joins ranks with The Crossroads, The Stepping Stones, The Wall, and so on.

2.17: Poem example – Don't be afraid – get help

Abused as a child, sexually and physically
What have these people done to me?

All my feelings deep down inside,
Tearing me apart but covered by pride.

But its getting worse, I just can't cope,
Counselling, my one ray of hope.

Today's the day,
What do I say?

The thought of me in that room,
Pouring out with all that gloom.

The first few sections were really heavy,
But finally life's becoming steady,

From always crying, worrying and hiding,
All these things are slowly subsiding.

After a long battle and this year has past,
I can hold my head up high and smile AT LAST!

Cheryl Gandy

USAGE

This idea can be brought up either at an early stage to discuss pessimism or later, when it's happening, to discuss progress. Pessimistic victims say 'What's the point? I'll never change' or 'They'll build another mile on the tunnel' (see The Trap, page 59) or 'I can't imagine ever feeling safe enough to tell my mother what I really think of her'. At the right time, in the right (gentle) way, it is important to challenge pessimism.

A paper on assertiveness, comparing assertive, aggressive and passive actions, is very useful for people to read at home. There is an example in the Appendix.

CHAPTER 3

How Counsellors Guide Recovery

This is book about a particular approach to a particular area of work. So far I have described the general outline of the programme and the details of the metaphors. While we use basic counselling practice in the programme, there are some specific areas brought in by the topic. For instance, it is much easier to empathise when you know about The Trap (see page 59) and The Impossible Jigsaw (see page 67). I have already described many areas through the metaphors. We start from 'where the patient is at' – that is, how they have reacted to the abuse at the time and later. This means that the counsellor must be sensitive to, and able to respond to, certain specific areas. The practice of counselling with this programme needs more than simply a knowledge of the metaphors.

Some Family Issues

The majority of counsellors have been trained in work with one person. This means that they tend to think about that person most. They may think about what has affected them and who has affected them. They may also think about how the 'client' has affected other people. However, there are times when it is important to think about how several people have affected each other, especially over long periods of time. This is where a 'family' focus becomes important.

Family of origin

Children live in families. The majority of sexual abusers live in the family where they commit the abuse, or did so at that stage even if they no longer do so. When the abuser lives in the same family, he has many opportunities to divide and conquer, camouflage activities and create confusion. The whole family will respond to these tactics, and the effects may last for years or tens of years.

Whether or not the abuser lives in the family, other family members will respond to the child's reactions to the abuse. These responses may not help the victim and this is more likely if the other family members do not know about the abuse. They will expect normal behaviour from a child even if the child is not in a normal situation. All sorts of misunderstandings and problems can start from this. It is important to recognise that these problems arise accidentally – no one in the family (apart from the abuser) intends things to get worse.

I heard about a brother and a sister who both knew about each other's abuse by the same family member. They couldn't talk to each other about it at the time, or afterwards, or even when the family found out years later. This was partly because they were quiet, private people and partly because of The Trap.

Children already vulnerable

I have found that many children who are sexually abused may have been emotionally abused or neglected previously. They may have been underachieving and slow in their growth of confidence. This marks them as vulnerable to the sexual abuse and it will continue to worsen during and after the sexual abuse.

Neil admits he developed a sharp instinct for potential victims, 'mostly middle-class kids who had no love or attention. I would say every single child I abused was emotionally deprived. I took notice of them, and forged deep, close relationships with them. Sex was just part of it. I was their friend. Of course, I used this as a means to an end. I totally abused their trust...'

(taken from The Personal Column, 5/3/95; *Night & Day, Mail on Sunday*, 'Neil's Story; a Child Sexual Abuse Perpetrator'

(Not his real name)

[There is more of this quote on page 88]

Other circumstances may have made some children vulnerable: illness, poverty, marital disharmony, single parenthood and so on. In these circumstances there will be the direct effects of the situation and the reduced support from the parent(s), who will also be struggling to cope. It can be worth untangling these bits of the history of what happened in order to get a better picture.

I was working with a very aggressive woman who could not understand why she kept accepting the sexual abuse. It turned out that poverty, overcrowding, a depressed mother and a violent alcoholic father made her vulnerable before the sexual abuse started. Then she learned to use sex to try to placate men if she couldn't fight her way out of trouble. This difference (fighting and seducing) confused her for many years and it was by unravelling these issues that it got clearer for her and allowed her to control whom and when she fought, and whom she seduced.

The Exception: When brother and sister sex is NOT abuse

Sometimes, an investigation or a disclosure brings out the suggestion that a brother and sister (for example) have had some sexual contact. There might be bad feelings, tears, fright or guilt whenever it is discussed. This does not automatically mean that the experience has been abuse. It may have been simple adolescent exploration or a younger child's curiosity. Even if it was more than exploration, and might have gone on for some time, it could still have been a protective and loving experience.

We must consider this situation very seriously. Other people's reactions could make things worse. The usual professional response could put a very different understanding on it all. This would make the 'help' much more destructive than the 'abuse'. It could lead to a tragedy – all the more since well-intentioned professionals could cause it.

For instance, let us think about a family where there has been emotional abuse and neglect. This may have been due to the parents' own problems with depression, alcohol or drugs – perhaps caused by a road traffic accident, experiences in war or even child abuse of one kind or another. If the children have to fend for themselves, they may become a team for their own protection. They may become a team against the outside world and see people outside the family as being dangerous and painful like their parents are already. In these circumstances, a hug could become a cuddle that could turn sexual, especially with teenagers. Although by normal psychological and legal standards this sex should not happen, it may be the only thing keeping these children sane, healthy and even alive.

If normal professional responses decide that the boy is an abuser and the girl is a victim, they are very likely to be separated by professional decisions. This could do more damage than good. There are now several histories of children from the same family who pair up against the world and come to a tragic end with one or both dying through suicide, self-neglect or an 'accident'.

In this book I can only say that if an adult's history emerges along these lines, we must consider our response very carefully. If it emerges during the assessment, we should ask the question 'Was it sexual abuse?' If not, other types of counselling might be useful because of problems from the other types of abuse. If this story comes out in a group, it may be necessary to ask that member to leave the group and talk it over in individual counselling. This may be more constructive for both survivor and group.

Responding to all this is very difficult. Very rare and complex circles are likely to have been created. They might be very difficult to recognise and difficult to interrupt. For instance: 'Was he wrong or was I wrong? It was illegal, so one of us must have been in the wrong, or were we both wrong? Was everything really OK until everyone else came along and told us we were wrong? Who did they think was wrong? What did they know about it, anyway! Perhaps they were wrong. But, it was illegal'. It may be better to understand and share the dilemmas than to agree with any of the options offered.

The Double Whammy

Another particularly tragic situation is that where the mother of a sexually abused child was sexually abused as a child herself. This is like being hit twice by the same bomb. It is probably the mother's worst nightmare. Most survivors make themselves a promise that they will make sure that their children's childhood is better than their own. They often make the promise to their child, silently, in their minds. These silent promises are then shattered when the mother hears of the daughter's abuse.

There is an irony at this stage. When the mother hears this news, her child is likely to be safe. As she suffers the shock and grief, the child is recovering and is, perhaps, already in the first stages of this.

It is often more difficult for a mother who is a survivor to comfort and protect her child than for one who is not. The survivor mother is very likely to feel enormous amounts of guilt at having 'failed' to spot the abuse and stop it immediately. In these circumstances it may be important to offer some support to the mother too. This is for two reasons: the mother is both a carer for a survivor and a survivor herself. (I imagine the issues are the same for any parent and child pair of survivors, so a father and son pair of survivors or a father and daughter or mother and son pair are just as likely to feel the complicated responses. I am assuming that the parents mentioned are not abusers.)

It is important that the child doesn't try to help the mother, at least for too long. She could try to become a parent to her mother, which would turn that relationship upside down. The child has already had too much responsibility in The Trap and The Jigsaw – responsibility from the abuser's life, freedom,

---

3.1: Case example – It was impossible to help her until...

I didn't address my own problems [relationships, kids, depression and suicidal thoughts, drinking and lack of confidence] till it happened to the kids. I'd completely pushed it aside, not even considered it, as I thought it was my fault – no one else to blame – I'd just buried it – or I thought I had.

I hated my youngest daughter when she told me because I thought 'how could she do it?'. How could *she* do it, because I blamed myself, then it had to be her fault too, not 'why did someone do it to her?'

Really, I never stopped feeling like that till I stopped feeling like that about myself. So it was impossible to help her until I got some help for myself. She was as guilty as I was – we were guilty!

Now I feel completely different, although I still don't know the truth of what happened to her as we've never ever discussed it. I don't think she's a naughty girl now. I don't know if we'll ever be comfortable to talk about it. I'd like to be, but...

I let her go [into care] because I couldn't deal with it.

My older daughter...also we don't talk about it...only once...I've never questioned that [in my own mind] either, sorted it out. I daren't because I'd have to confront my relationship with him [an older family member, different to the other alleged abuser]. It's another one I might have to dissolve. I'm not as close now. We don't see each other much. I just keep it like that.

It's more the pain that stops me talking about it with them. If neither of my girls had said anything, I'd never have done anything about my misconduct. Why do I still call it that?!!! – my experiences, I mean.

Sandy

marriage, etc. To take full responsibility for her mother too is a great burden. Yet the temptation is there, perhaps in feelings of guilt in the child (who might be an adult when she discloses the abuse) for not having stopped the abuse or told her mother earlier or having upset her mother by 'failing' to keep the secret. There are many complicated arguments and feelings here, too many to list and explain them all. We must take them individually. In the end it may require protection services for those still children, as well as the counselling services, to work with these issues.

A family therapy approach can involve both the mother and child, and, perhaps, other family members at times, in helping the whole family recover (assuming the abuser is not one of the family members). Where the abuser was a family member, we can work with the others to help them sort out how they are going to react to and deal with him.

All the above applies equally to the sexually abused boy who is now a father. Extra fear can grow when people realise that he might also be an abuser. Many mothers would be anxious about any possibility of this. Professionals also have to consider this if they become involved with the family. We have to hope they come to the right answer. It is worth remembering that even the man himself may have self-doubts along these same lines – 'It happened to me, so I know how to do it. Maybe I've caught the "disease". How can I be sure I'm safe to be a father?'

Current partner and family

There are several issues that can emerge in the new family. Health visitors are likely to see some of them, doctors and social workers may see others.

PROBLEMS WITH MARRIAGE AND RELATIONSHIPS

Sometimes, a girl leaves home to find a man large enough or powerful enough to keep the abuser away. Sometimes, the man knows this because she tells him. Other times, he gets only half the story or even none of it – a pretence that everything was OK in childhood.

Marriage difficulties can grow out of the confusions and contradictions that can follow from these different ways of reacting to the marriage. (Remember, the victim might be the man and the roles reversed.) More secrets are likely to follow – at least emotional secrets if not factual secrets. The distrust that abuse creates makes it difficult for victims to tell their partner everything because they would be extremely vulnerable if the partner then 'used' that information as a weapon in some way. Trust becomes a vital concern: 'Can I trust him (or her) enough to show my real feelings, even if they are complicated ones? If I can't, then the relationship is somehow empty, lonely and unreal. I need to tell him, but I daren't'. Too many relationships fail because of this fear of trying to trust. This is a direct result of the abuse.

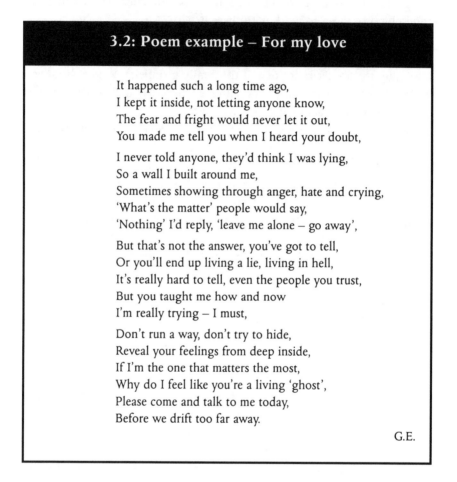

3.2: Poem example – For my love

It happened such a long time ago,
I kept it inside, not letting anyone know,
The fear and fright would never let it out,
You made me tell you when I heard your doubt,

I never told anyone, they'd think I was lying,
So a wall I built around me,
Sometimes showing through anger, hate and crying,
'What's the matter' people would say,
'Nothing' I'd reply, 'leave me alone – go away',

But that's not the answer, you've got to tell,
Or you'll end up living a lie, living in hell,
It's really hard to tell, even the people you trust,
But you taught me how and now
I'm really trying – I must,

Don't run a way, don't try to hide,
Reveal your feelings from deep inside,
If I'm the one that matters the most,
Why do I feel like you're a living 'ghost',
Please come and talk to me today,
Before we drift too far away.

G.E.

The girl's judgement might be impaired when she chooses a partner – that is, her ability to understand what other people are like behind their wall (we all have one) is low because of the abuse. A man who appears confident to begin with can emerge as having his own doubts and anxieties inside. This can rebound if he wants her to be the strong one in the partnership – after all, she has probably been pretending to be confident in exactly the same way! This can come out slowly or suddenly and create different questions about what to do next.

There is another possibility that grows from a different starting point. If the girl (or boy) victim looks for a partner who is soft and gentle, non-aggressive and caring, she may find that this goes wrong later. He may turn out to be too unassertive, unhelpful and absent. Patterns of behaviour can grow over years of marriage. What starts as 'He's wonderful, he gives me so much space and choice' can turn into 'He's a wimp, can't do anything for himself, always out fishing/drinking/working/etc.' Her disappointment can then grow to extremes.

As these difficulties involve The Crossroads (see page 103), other forms of relationship are sometimes explored and might be relevant in the counselling. For instance, homosexual relationships, either the committed long-term type or the very short-term, might grow out of a distrust of the opposite sex. Some survivors find themselves in a 'bisexual lifestyle' which allows them even more freedom to stay in control of relationship choices.

PROBLEMS WITH SEX

Sexual abuse mixes up love, sex and fear. It is not surprising that problems can follow in later life. Small events can trigger fear reactions about sex and during sex. Many survivors have sex because they feel it is a duty or out of generosity to their partner, rather than for pleasure for themselves. They often find they cannot have any pleasure in sex. Even when they do try, some of The Painkillers (see page 106) take over, for example counting bricks or wallpaper patterns, pretending to be someone or somewhere else or using drink or drugs to dull the Post Traumatic Stress responses.

It is worth pointing out that the after-effects of fright are likely to interfere with sex at a physical, biological level. When the fright causes a re-routing of our blood supply into those muscles we need to fight or escape, this takes blood away from genitals. So any situation that reminds us of the original fright is likely to cause the same reaction. This means that sex, or some aspect of it, may cause the same reduction of blood supply to the genitals and will interfere with the normal sexual response. In men, this will mean difficulties with erections. In women, it may mean difficulties in the vagina becoming 'ready for sex'.

We have not designed this programme to work with these problems in any detail. They often need more specialist help. In our counselling group we invite specialist speakers from time to time. We have invited a female psycho-sexual doctor to take the group on occasion. Individual counselling and marital and sexual counselling are other specialist areas of work that we can arrange outside the programme.

Sometimes, survivors can gain reassurance from general discussions of similar difficulties. Just hearing that the majority of the group members have some problems with sex can help some relaxation. Showing that the abuse has caused the problems – or at least some of them – can help with guilt, self-blame and self-disgust.

PROBLEMS WITH CHILDREN

Once a survivor has reached adulthood she may then become a parent. Various problems can follow this for quite a wide range of reasons.

One area concerns the responsibility of a parent: 'Can I keep my children safe?' Another issue, particularly with boys, is the question of 'Is he going to become an abuser?' Questions such as these can trigger off Post Traumatic Stress responses, feelings of helplessness, depression, and so on.

Breast feeding can evoke strong feelings for various reasons. One might be concern about sexual stimulation from the suckling. Another might be the repeated sight of a vulnerable baby highly dependent on a mother who is feeling far from strong and confident. On the other hand, the baby's gender can arouse worries. For instance, a girl could start off a concern in the mother about whether she can protect her daughter when she couldn't protect herself from the abuse, or the sight of a boy – or his penis – might cause the mother to wonder whether he will become an abuser too. 'Baby blues' or post-natal depression makes sense in this context.

We must remember the particular case where the baby's father is the abuser (or is thought to be) or claims some power over the baby. This power might be a continuation of previous trapping methods. Threats of taking the baby away (or organising the social services to do this) can have a specially depressing effect and, perhaps, prompt panicky or irresponsible behaviour. Tragically, these can then bring about the removal of the baby for the baby's sake. This might start a pattern of young women having a series of babies that are all removed, or heavily supervised, by professionals.

It is also worth going through the family life cycle to look out for 'danger spots'. A survivor might become anxious when she learns she is pregnant or even when she is planning a family, or it might be during the birth or shortly afterwards, or when the child is old enough to toddle out of sight or

3.3: Poem example – Secrets

Your child is born with squeals of fright,
Eyes clamped shut against the light.
A girl. She's so like you – her eyes, her face,
No. Forbidden fear, your secret pain,
You cannot live like that again.

You take her home – her Daddy's there,
His eyes, his voice all say he cares,
He's changing her – you scream inside,
You want to take your child and hide.

Long hours make days – and days make weeks,
Then 'Mum's the first word she speaks,
Daddy bathes her now – life's not the same,
Her joy has buried all your pain.
A girl.
She likes you so. Your eyes, your face.

M.

preparing to go to school. The child might be at the age the mother (or father) was when the abuse happened. Also, puberty, relationships, marriage or a grandchild could all bring back bad memories and feelings. We must also remember that sometimes it has nothing to do with age, perhaps it is when the survivor's abuser (e.g. granddad) visits the house.

Continuation of abuse

If the abuser is a family member, the victim's marriage will not necessarily stop the abuse. A girl might leave home to marry a man she feels is able to keep the abuser away. It doesn't always work. The abuser's power may not fade, he could force the abuse to continue.

If this does happen, the victim may keep it secret from her husband. This can only cause a lot of secret guilt – how can she tell anyone about this? It may be possible through prayer or in the confessional, but this is unlikely to help many who end up trapped yet again.

It is important to remember an extra source of confusion once the victim is an adult. The abuser can say – or the victim can think – 'Over the age of consent, so it's legal now'. This is very trapping, but it is not always true. In cases of incest, it remains illegal. In cases where the victim says 'NO' but is physically forced, a court of law would see this as rape.

If none of these apply to a particular survivor, the moral issues remain open for exploration. We feel that if the abuse continues over the age of consent date, it is morally no different. Free, informed and legal choice has not been possible. It remains, in effect, child abuse.

Gender Issues

There are important opinions and attitudes here and there in all this area about which sex of person we are talking about. Male or female victims, male or female abusers, male or female partners (or children) of survivors, male or female professionals.

I will only gather a few issues in this book as many of these important issues are mentioned in other books. The issues that are vital to this programme are already mentioned in the relevant places throughout the book so I will only summarise here.

The counsellor's gender is a very important consideration

Groups should usually have one counsellor of each gender to balance any sex bias that might creep into the discussion. It will also reassure group members that the two sexes *can* work together – the group leaders can demonstrate this by planning, discussing and disagreeing in front of the group. However, this does mean that one counsellor is likely to be the 'odd one out' and he or she must be a strong enough personality to take this on.

In individual counselling, the choice of gender of the counsellor should be given to the survivor where at all possible (see page 151).

The gender of the examples and case histories I have used in this book

I have put a warning note at the start of the book about calling victims 'her' and abusers 'him' (see page 9). The case histories are mainly women, but I am pleased to include a man too.

The gender of the abuser described by the survivor

When survivors describe women – or even girls – as abusers, we must be prepared to believe them. If we believe that survivors have very little reason to lie about the few facts that we do ask about in counselling, this is probably the least likely area for anyone to need to lie. Of course, they might delay telling the counsellor what the actual gender of the abuser was in case they are not believed, but that is different. That has more to do with the survivor checking on how much they trust the counsellor at that time.

The gender of abusers and victims in sexual abuse amongst brothers and sisters

This issue is given some more space on page 127, where I have discussed brother and sister abuse. More complicated is sister–sister and brother–brother abuse – or alleged abuse. Step-brothers and sisters, adopted or fostered brothers, cousins and other relatives can bring up similar issues in this area.

The different responses to sexual abuse in male and female survivors

As a generalisation, it seems to me that male survivors:

1. are less likely to tell anyone or talk about it in a counselling group

2. are more likely to drink heavily or use hard drugs

3. are more likely to become violent, lie, cheat and commit crimes

4. are more likely to have sex and relationship problems they try to hide.

Research may disagree with me and, in time, is sure to find more differences between the genders' reactions to the abuse. Even so, these factors are important to mention because they are very likely to alter the way a programme runs in real life.

The Realities of the Secret

One area of great importance to the survivor is the 'facts and figures' of what actually happened. Therefore, this is important to the counselling. Although it is difficult – and distressing – to ask about the history of people's behaviour, there are some very important aspects that are worth considering. How far any survivor or counsellor will want to go into these issues will probably depend more upon them and their progress than anything else.

I have put these issues as questions to be answered, as though from the counsellor's point of view. Even so, we are less concerned with chasing the truth in counselling. We are more interested in what the survivor believes. It may be important to repeat that this type of counselling rarely has proof of what did and did not happen years, perhaps decades, earlier. We have to rely on the survivor's word that she has clear enough memories of sexual abuse to be definite that it happened. We can accept some doubts and questions and memory gaps as well, as long as the basic belief is clear. We must also remember that public actions that a survivor takes – especially legal and financial – will rely very much on what various other people believe is the truth.

In line with this policy, all the quotes, poems and interviews in this book have been accepted as they are. They have not been investigated to find 'the truth' of what may have happened 20 to 50 years ago.

The trauma history

We do not necessarily structure the early interviews by 'taking a history' of the abuse. 'Taking a history' means asking lots of questions about the facts of what happened in the abuse and afterwards.

As well as being disrespectful to ask routine questions, it is too likely to endanger the counselling. The danger is that the survivor will assume that she must talk about all the secrets she has kept for years and is likely to avoid it. She will leave out parts, gloss over important bits and distort some aspects to reduce the anxieties she feels about this. She will be worried that she will be ignored, laughed at, told off or declared stupid or crazy or both. If she gets too anxious, she is likely finish the counselling before it gets even more painful.

To those counsellors who answer this by saying 'But I'm a professional, it's OK', I would continue to argue. Taking a history in a routine way is taking liberties. It ignores the impact of that history in that interview – the flashbacks and feelings triggered will often be too much to bear. There is no need. In a programme that is open and specific about what it does, non-survivors are unlikely to request help from it. Because we respond to the current results of the abuse, we need to know only a little about what actually happened during the abuse.

Survivors who are uncertain about the type of abuse they suffered appear occasionally. It is important to discuss the history in these cases.

We do ask some important questions and these are listed below. Some are only relevant to some survivors. The only way into these areas is to go slowly, at the survivor's pace or even slower. This is the process of untangling (see The Bowl of Spaghetti, page 95)

WAS THE ABUSER IN YOUR FAMILY OR NOT?

A vital question that makes a difference to the counselling is whether the abuser was in the family or not. In this we are including parents, brothers and sisters, step-parents and temporary partners of lone parents, step- and half-brothers and sisters, partners of older brothers and sisters, uncles and aunts, grandparents, and so on. We should also include adoptive families, but, perhaps, not foster families, unless they were very long-term ones.

If the abuser was not in the family, there is a chance that the rest of the early childhood experience was good for the survivor and can be built on. In other words, there are some good foundation stones, even if others are missing or shrunken. However, a problem can arise if the survivor feels guilty for not having been a 'good' child or for not having explained why he or she has had problems that were not the parents' fault.

All the same, there may have been other sorts of abuse from one or both parents that made the child more vulnerable to the sexual abuse.

If the abuser was in the family, it may be important to concentrate on the opportunities he or she had to discredit and demoralise the victim. We may need to untangle various forms of 'divide and conquer'.

WAS THERE ONE ABUSER OR SEVERAL?

If there was one abuser, this is bad enough. If there were several, the feelings of helplessness in The Trap are likely to be much worse. An important question is whether they did the abuse at the same time or at different times in the child's life. If it was during the same few years, the feeling of helplessness will have been very powerful.

This is especially true if the abusers knew about each other. If they did, they are likely to have told the child because of the benefits to them in building a trap. A child will feel even more trapped by several adults ganging up together. However, the level of co-operation amongst the adults may not have been as high as the survivor was led to believe at the time. This can be worth untangling. However, the opposite is true too. An organised gang may have wanted the child to believe that they were not organised and therefore encouraged the child to blame herself, as in the next point.

If there were several abusers who did the abuse at very different periods of the child's life, this is likely to have different effects. The most obvious result is an increase in frustration and helplessness because of the repeated 'just as I was recovering, it happened again' experience. Another is that the child (or, later, the adult) starts to wonder if they caused it to happen again? 'Did I like it? Did I make them do it?' are the questions in their circles. Here it is important to separate the sex from other needs that the child might have had at the time – love, affection, protection, and so on.

WERE YOU THE ONLY CHILD ABUSED OR WERE THERE SEVERAL?

If the survivor believes that all her other brothers and sisters (and cousins, etc) were untouched by the abuser(s), a question is likely to arrive: 'Why me and not them?' Sometimes it is worth challenging this idea – perhaps it was more than one of the children but each has hidden it from the other(s) (see the case example in the Introduction and also 'Why Me – The Answer', page 87).

3.4: Case example – The tragedy of a sister's sacrifice

An example is that of an older sister who had accepted continued abuse in order to honour a 'deal' with the abuser. He had promised that he wouldn't abuse her younger sister. But the young woman had been abused and when the older sister found out, she felt rage and depression and became a recluse and dangerously obese.

The younger sister felt a great deal of guilt that she hadn't made her elder sister's sacrifice worthwhile by somehow stopping the abuse. (We had to talk about how realistic this wish would have been.) Although the sisters have talked, they are not close, and do not support each other as 'sisters in adversity' could.

The tragedy is that the younger sister did not know of her sister's sacrifice until years later. The abuser had told her that her older sister wouldn't care if she found out about the abuse. (This is an example of the trap created by the methods described in Stealing a Pencil, page 84).

If there was more than one victim in the family, they may know about each other but be unhelpful or even antagonistic to each other. In these situations it is worth exploring the possibility that the abuser used a 'divide and conquer' approach to keeping them all silent. He might have done this by making each child jealous of the others. Sometimes a victim of this 'plot' will say 'But there was nothing to be jealous of. All I got was abuse!' The important thing to remember is what the other children believed – the abuser might have led them to believe that the victim was a favourite. Even more complicated is the situation where there was a favourite in the sexual sense. The abuser may have created a sexual performance 'league table' where he was, in effect, asking the children compete against each other.

All these possibilities rely on the counsellor's imagination and willingness to accept these possibilities as having been real. We are not searching for the truth though, we were not there at the time and we cannot prove anything. All we can do is settle on the explanation that makes most sense of the survivor's feelings, memories, thoughts and behaviour. That is what counselling is about. That is the start of change.

HAVE YOU BEEN FURTHER ABUSED AS AN ADULT?

There are two areas that can complicate the untangling process. If the survivor in the counselling is safe from abuse, there may still have been some abuse during adulthood.

The abuse that started in childhood may have continued past the survivor's eighteenth birthday. The suggestion that they did give legal consent becomes possible. Survivors may then argue to themselves that they had morally given consent before they were eighteen. This undermines the difference and starts a question about whether they had wanted – or even enjoyed – the abuse as a child. I feel this is such an unfair circle that it is worth us asking whether it is relevant if we find a few clues. Survivors are unlikely to mention it themselves, especially in the early meetings. It is an area where the informed Guide can forewarn and illuminate helpfully.

The counsellor's responses should include the fact that the abuser committed a crime (the abuse) when the survivor was a child. The abuser may have continued to abuse until stopped – the eighteenth birthday was not important to him in a legal sense. Alternatively, the abuser may have said something like 'It's OK now you're an adult' and suggested that the victim was more of an informed co-conspirator. This is still incest where there is a blood relationship between them and is against the law whether the people are adults or children. This does not apply when the abuser is a step-parent or a parent's cohabitee, so this may add to the confusion. It is morally wrong but is not illegal.

It is important to notice that these issues are slightly different for males in the UK – the age of consent may have been higher at the time. I feel that this situation will be very rare though. Many boy survivors get out of the situation in their teens by running away, becoming violent or turning to crime and being put into care or prison. It seems to me that men have much more anger towards the abuser than women do, as a generalisation. This may be because the abuse is homosexual rather than heterosexual and it raises questions about the survivor's sexual choices later in life. Abused boys can become heterosexual men, according to research.

The other situation worth mentioning is where the abuse has come from another person entirely, such as a husband (or wife). If the abuse within a marriage or similar relationship was at all like the child abuse, it will have felt like a continuation of it. This takes us to the issues resulting from abuse by several abusers discussed above.

IS THERE ANY ABUSE NOW?

In counselling we are trying to provide a safe space for the survivor to discuss important issues as freely as possible. This may be difficult enough if the discussion causes flashbacks or the counsellor's physical appearance triggers memories or feelings. But if the survivor is still in The Trap because abuse is continuing, the emotional forces resulting from the fright and fear are very likely to work against the aims of counselling. We must remember that this is exactly what they are intended to do. The survivor's misuse or avoidance of the counselling is not necessarily a personal criticism of us. It may be a habit of avoiding anything that threatens them or misusing anything that allows them an advantage.

In practice, this is an extremely difficult area to deal with. It can appear in several situations. The counsellor must be sensitive to the possibilities. For instance, a teenage survivor where the original abuse continues or a survivor in her twenties where the abuse has restarted (perhaps after a mother's illness, divorce or death) or where another person has commenced a sexual relationship in an abusive way more recently. I remember a woman who had been abused as a teenager and had become pregnant and the abuser had then been found, prosecuted and convicted. The court case details were published. Years later she married, but her father-in-law pressurised her into sex, saying, in effect, that she had done it before. Continued pressure had resulted in one sexual encounter that then provided blackmail ammunition and led to years of continued abuse.

In some cases the counsellor may not find out about current abuse until very late in the counselling process. In other cases the survivor may arrive with the current abuse as the presenting problem but describe it as a 'bad relationship' without mentioning the reason (the sexual abuse). In these situations the counselling will continue anyway until a clear statement does emerge.

Sometimes there may only be hints and clues and an unwillingness to discuss the issue of current safety – 'Oh, it doesn't matter, I'm used to it'. The question then is whether the counsellor feels able to accept this. For instance, the current abuse may be incest and, therefore, illegal or might lead to a divorce or leave children vulnerable to abuse. Without a clear statement from the survivor, and a willingness to tell others (police, social services, etc), the counsellor is left in a difficult situation. Intuition may be saying quite loudly that the survivor is still a Victim and is not free to deal with the emotional results of the abuse. The counsellor may feel that the counselling is unlikely to help – or it might even prompt the abuser to increase the pressure of The Trap to stop the counselling or, at least, prevent the current abuse being discussed. Obviously, this could lead to violence.

These are difficult issues for the counsellor to decide on. One possible reaction to remember is that the counsellor begins to feel that the counselling is being controlled by the abuser. This will feel like an intrusion and might flare up some feelings. These feelings must be considered very carefully. They may be real but they may not be helpful to the survivor. Sometimes, it might help to describe these feelings to give the survivor a chance to consider whether or not she feels similarly and, if not, why not. Occasionally, expressing the feelings by flaring up might be appropriate. Showing real feelings in a real way can offer a model for the survivor to copy (see Same, Different, Opposite, page 118). This area, where the counsellor can only suspect current abuse, is, perhaps, one of the most difficult to work with.

Particular issues

There are a few points that are particularly useful to discuss, although they may not always be relevant to each survivor. This can help with the untangling process. The counsellor will most often ask about these issues as survivors rarely wish to bring them out.

DID YOU EVER SAY 'NO'?

If they ever said 'No' (even in their minds) this can be useful in starting a new point in the conversation. Saying 'No!' means they knew they did not want it to happen. This might have been because of pain, moral reasoning, legal knowledge or whatever. It shows they did not want it to happen, even if the abuser ignored their wishes and they later said 'Yes' due to the pressures the abuser brought to bear.

It is easier to ask this question in a more general discussion of the issue of consent. Bearing in mind that it is easier for adults to understand what informed and legal consent is, we must expect some confusions. The abuser will have wanted to duck the issue, or muddle it up, to ensure he was not challenged by the child. So, as an adult, survivors usually have questions – often circles of questions – about whether they gave consent, whether they could give consent, whether they gave moral consent if not legal consent, and so on. This is probably less likely where violence was used to push the child into The Trap. The issues in The Confusions (see page 116) are relevant here.

WERE YOU INJURED DURING THE ABUSE?

If injuries occurred, this can also be used to show that it was wrong. It can be worth checking whether the injuries are still a problem and, if so, whether they have found suitable treatment. This may bring up the subject of telling medical professionals about the cause of the injury. This might be important physically or emotionally – for instance during child birth, hysterectomy, breast lump biopsy, and so on.

WAS MAGIC BROUGHT INTO IT IN SOME WAY?

Sometimes, abusers use 'magic' to trap children in their power more than the usual methods of The Trap (see page 59). I am only concerned about what seems like magic to children here, not whether there is such a thing in reality and what it might be. An abuser might use a number of 'tricks' to make an impression on the child. These might be party magic tricks (the disappearing coin, etc) or 'mind-reading' (very easy with children) or based on physical, biological or sexual knowledge, or the abuser might use 'props' to create the appearance of magical power – for instance, secret society passwords, clothes and property or friendships.

These uses of 'magic' might link in with the natural 'magical thinking' that young children have before they fully understand the way the world works (e.g. gravity, momentum, air resistance, etc). This could increase the power of persuasion the abuser gains through these tactics. An analysis of 'magic', the human activity, proposes that there are two basic types: power at a distance and power through touch. Power at a distance is the more obvious one for keeping children silent – 'I will know if you tell (or think of telling) behind my back through my magic'. Even as adults, survivors can still be frightened by this idea. It means they stay in The Trap and the emotional abuse continues beyond the sexual contact.

The area of 'magic' is a large and complex one, although it is rare to appear in counselling. It is an additional pressure in The Trap and the basic facts of the Trap are already sufficient to hold a child in silence for many years. It may be that abusers use 'magic' more often than we realise as it is more difficult for survivors to bring these aspects out in counselling – or anywhere else. It is possible that the use of 'magic' makes a breakdown of mental health more likely. It may be that people who have a serious mental illness continue to think, act and speak as though the 'magic' was true. Even though it may not be true, this would show that the 'magic' was powerful all the same.

DO YOU HAVE OTHER PROBLEMS THAT MIGHT BE CONNECTED TO THE ABUSE?

Survivors sometimes have additional problems that might be connected to the abuse. There are times, perhaps quite often, when they try to keep some of their problems quiet in case a professional gets cross with them. They might fear that they have 'too many problems' or that they talk about 'the wrong problems' in some way. It can be worth asking as survivors are sometimes very relieved to open up this new subject. In these situations, the connection to the abuse may seem tangled or trivial. Even so, it can be a worthwhile discussion.

3.5: Case example – That's why

'I went back in time again at the weekend. The bathroom, where my Dad put me in a tub of soda and bleach to get me clean and scrubbed me because I went with the boy next door. That's why the bathroom comes into it [terrors and fainting fits at night] and that's why I've got to keep clean'.

Practical Points

As well as using the metaphors, we are doing other things in the counselling process. It is not all just explaining. If it was, this would be a training course in 'Understanding the Effects of Sexual Abuse'.

Any counselling must take its theories seriously. It must be able to explain the way it works as well as get on with the work. Counselling must also take people seriously. It must accept that people have to make their own decisions – they can't be forced into a mould – so decisions about counselling, about the past, about the Law and about change all have to be taken carefully. The person must be considered.

One way to think about much of this is with the idea of empowerment. That is, the Counsellor and the counselling are giving personal power, control and responsibility to the survivor, instead of taking them away. This is done by actions as much as words. It happens in many ways. It must happen consistently. It is the opposite of abuse.

We can identify a number of ways this happens. There are likely to be more. Most of those listed below are likely to happen in the first few meetings. They set the tone and they address important issues that might affect whether the survivor comes back to the next meeting.

Giving quality time

BEING PERSONAL, INFORMAL, HUMAN

Within the limits of ethics, the working relationship should allow both counsellor and survivor to be human persons. This means allowing some humour, admitting to human frailties and keeping to 'I', 'you' and 'we'. If counselling becomes formal, impersonal or inhuman it isn't likely to work (25-year-old research tells us this: warmth, empathy and genuineness are vital). Worse, it may become a repetition of The Trap by reducing freedom, respect and individuality.

The list of metaphors must not be taken as the only correct set of descriptions of the issues. This would ignore the starting point of the survivor and the work they have already done. Counsellors should show their human side, a little humour, some small frailties and their good manners. This should not go too far. Large-scale personal disclosures could get too close to using the counselling for the counsellors' own needs and problems. Deciding on what is 'too far' depends on a combination of personal style, professional experience and the nature of this type of work. Each counsellor's own professional judgement is essential in this.

This issue is especially important in situations where survivors already have their own metaphors or unnamed understandings of the issues. We should allow them to keep ownership of their name or understanding. If the counselling is in a group, the members will have to agree about the names meaning the same thing. If the understanding is different, the counsellor should stop the line of explanation or challenge and rethink the issue. The counsellor's judgement must then decide how to react – whether to allow the difference, challenge it, add to it, etc. This is the counsellor's job.

GIVING OPPORTUNITY

The whole purpose of a counselling programme is to provide an opportunity for the survivor to make changes in his or her life. The way the survivor can use the opportunity depends a great deal on how it is given – that is, the information, the rules, the encouragement and so on will all influence the survivor's responses. Our job in the programme is to try to give the best possible opportunity to each survivor. In individual counselling meetings this can rely a lot on the counsellor to tailor the opportunity to what seems useful and appropriate. In group counselling the different survivors influence each other more. The job of the programme is to shape the process as much as possible to be helpful in both situations.

Giving information

In some ways, this is the easiest form of empowerment. However, we must remember that some of the important information is likely to be challenging to survivors. This is because we discuss areas that they are sensitive about, which is why we want to reassure them. Several of these issues are warnings to be cautious as much as reassurances. In bringing them up, we are inviting survivors to take control – which seems right. We must remember that this is an area in which they have had many bad experiences so we may be raising anxiety-provoking issues in our attempts to reassure. We may need to reassure survivors about our 'reassurances'. A motto for counsellors in this is 'take it slowly'.

'COUNSELLING CAN HELP'

I feel it is vital to give this message, both verbally and implicitly, early in the first meeting. This is a 'long-term investment'. If the survivor feels unable to continue the counselling at any stage, they may carry this message with them and find the courage to start again later. Because some survivors are not 'ready' for counselling when they make the enquiry, this is probably the most important message you can give in the short time you may have together.

THE GOVERNMENT HEALTH WARNING

Towards the end of the first meeting – or earlier if it arises – this issue is important to bring in. With this metaphor (see page 111) we are warning the survivor that counselling is not painless. We say that any discussion of things that have hurt and confused is likely to wake up a few feelings and memories. If the survivor has been trying to forget about them, these memories returning will be upsetting. But here is the opportunity to spring-clean these memories and feelings. This is what counselling is for.

'I WILL AVOID SAYING "YOU MUST TRUST ME"'

Although it can be tempting to try to reassure a nervous survivor in the first few meetings by suggesting they trust you, this is a bad idea. It is too close to the abuser's earlier behaviour when he was 'grooming' (beginning to flatter / bribe / frighten / confuse) the child. It is often too early in the counselling to say so like this and explain it.

It seems better simply to accept that at that stage the counsellor is a stranger to the survivor and that trust has to be earned over a period of time. At this stage it is easier to repeat that the programme is designed to allow survivors to listen. This will let them judge for themselves about how much sense we make and how fair we are being.

'NO GUARANTEES, NO MAGIC WANDS'

At the same time as the trust issue arises, so does the issue of the counsellor's power to help. I think we can forgive survivors if they arrive in counselling half-hoping for a miracle. Most of us want that if we are in great pain.

I feel it is important to take a few moments to talk about this openly. Counsellors do not have a guarantee of total change and we should say so, but the counselling programme can bring changes. In our introductory meetings we describe the progress of survivors we have known – always anonymously.

PLAIN LANGUAGE, CLEAR PLANNING

It is important to reassure survivors about what they are getting into. Many will worry that counselling might backfire in some way.

For instance, the statistical link between being abused and becoming an abuser is quoted by some organisations as a reason why abuse should be stopped and victims helped. Unfortunately, one effect of this is to put victims off counselling because they don't want anyone to think of them as potential abusers. If they did, that would just double up The Trap. And we must remember the survivors themselves – they do not want to think of themselves as potential abusers either! Unless publicity is very clear about the small percentage that this applies to, survivors will jump to the conclusion that their children will be taken away, they may be locked up and that, in the end, there will be no help for them. They are then likely to hide away even more. This is too much of a danger for us to ignore it.

We should do all the planning about the counselling clearly, out loud and in plain language. This is not patronising. It is essential that survivors should understand the process. The process of counselling may be complicated but we should keep the description of the process as simple as possible. We should avoid professional jargon. If the counsellor works for 'the authorities' (such as the social or psychiatric services), the rules should be set out clearly about all the possible consequences. This is ethical and cannot be ignored.

Written records of the plan, confidentiality rules, organisation's policies and Constitutions, etc, should all be available to the survivor. They should not have to ask.

EXPLAINING WHERE METAPHORS COME FROM

While we hope that the metaphors are simple to understand, we still need to explain why we use them. We hope that the metaphors are reasonably self-explanatory, although it can be useful to explain how we found each metaphor. We built some from a sentence or an idea from a survivor and some came from a counsellor's grappling with a way to explain an idea. We try to be open about the method we use and to allow doubts and criticisms from survivors.

EXPLAINING PROFESSIONAL AND MANAGEMENT DECISIONS

When we have to make decisions that affect the whole programme, we must explain these fully. These policy decisions may affect ethical, financial or practical issues. Wherever they affect the security – and feeling of security –

of the survivors in the programme, we must reassure and explain. Some of these decisions may be unpopular and we must allow survivors to express their disappointments and displeasures.

Giving choice

Again, this is an important area, but a possibly challenging one for many survivors. These questions get to the centre of the survivor's choice and control over counselling. Therefore, we must be prepared to accept their decisions. This means that we, the counsellors, need to know whether we have the flexibility, the permission from our employers and the resources to provide what survivors ask for. If we don't, we must say so clearly and offer the choice of finishing the counselling there (and provide some ideas about a 'next step' for them).

'THIS COUNSELLING IS VOLUNTARY. YOU CAN INTERRUPT IT, SLOW IT DOWN OR EVEN STOP IT AT ANY TIME'.

We should try to say this in the first meeting, if at all possible. It is important for the survivor to know this quickly. It must be true. Even if the survivor's parents, partner, children, doctor, social worker or psychiatrist has pushed for the counselling, we must allow the survivor to stop it if they want to. Very few do want to stop once they've started.

'IS THERE ANYTHING ABOUT ME THAT REMINDS YOU OF THE ABUSER?'

We must keep the counsellor's age and gender in mind. For myself, I must remember that I am probably the same age and the same sex as the perpetrator was when the abuse happened. Very small triggers can set off the Post Traumatic Stress response flashbacks and memories, and this applies to the counselling situation as much as to 'real life'. The counsellor's own person may trigger responses. If this is something that triggers memories too often and too distressingly, finding a new counsellor might be the best answer. But the first, and relatively easy, step to take is to ask directly.

I have had various 'Yes, there is' answers. Sometimes it is too vague to pin down – 'something about your eyes', which leaves you with little response other than 'please tell me if/when it is getting in the way'. Often, the answers are more precise. One woman said that the colour of my shirt was too similar to the uniform shirt worn by the perpetrator. It was easy to remember to wear a different colour shirt. Another example was 'It's your moustache, it's a different colour, but the same shape'. We had to agree to remember whose moustache it was and to accept that it might be off-putting. I apologised and said I would not be shaving it off.

It might be an item of furniture, pattern of wallpaper or the smell of the room that can trigger PTSR responses. This is not a frequent problem, however. The usual response is 'No, there's nothing that worries me'.

'WOULD YOU PREFER TO TALK TO A MAN OR A WOMAN COUNSELLOR?'

It is worth discussing the issue of counsellor gender here. Some people have said that men should not do counselling with women sexual abuse survivors because of the obvious gender problems involved, but there are several points to think about.

One point to remember is that some perpetrators are women. Occasionally, this is by a woman alone. Research says that more often the woman is encouraged, or even forced to abuse, by a man who also abuses (both the child and woman). In the first case, the survivor may prefer a counsellor of different gender because she feels she cannot trust a woman. In the second case, it may be that women survivors are more hurt and angry at the woman than at the man. These are rare situations though.

Another point is that recent research is showing that boys are abused too – by men and by women. Nothing in this book has been written exclusively about women survivors (except where female biology and health is mentioned). The same approaches can be used with men survivors, although the emphasis will be different on certain points. (In this book the survivor is assumed to be a woman and the perpetrator a man to keep the him/her/he/she grammar simple, see Notes on page 8).

Also – most importantly – we have to remember that many women survivors prefer to talk to male counsellors. There are various reasons. We must hear them and respond to them supportively.

One reason is that they may be more embarrassed about talking to a woman. This is probably because they will assume that the woman counsellor has not been sexually abused and that this must have been because she said 'No' to a man when the survivor couldn't, so the counsellor might criticise the survivor or be disgusted. Or she might even be angry at the man *for* the survivor, but this should be avoided by any counsellor – it is not counselling. (There may be an ethical or legal requirement to notify the authorities but this should not be done angrily.)

Other women have said that they simply feel more comfortable talking to men. Some feel their challenge is to face a man and talk about it all. I have met a few who said that 'men don't count, so it's not so embarrassing to talk to them'. There are those women who say 'It is what you know, and how you understand me that is important', especially where other professionals have let them down in some way.

Yet another reason I have heard is that the survivor's mother was an emotional abuse perpetrator and left the survivor isolated, depressed and, therefore, more vulnerable before, during or after the second abuse. In this situation it is easy to understand a survivor's anger at her mother and her distrust of other people in a mothering role.

The result of all these issues is to make us avoid taking decisions about the counsellor's gender on generalisations. We must ask the survivor what she wants. We must give choice, not take it away.

In this counselling programme we rarely talk about the sexual abuse itself (what actually happened). We talk about feelings, memories, ideas, reactions and change. There are a few issues that make a difference: how many perpetrators, what type of silencing method the abuser used, did the survivor ever say 'No' – even in her mind? We should take these issues into account in understanding a survivor's reactions – even though they tend to be rare – so we reduce the normal embarrassment that people might have in talking about sex to someone of the other gender as much as possible.

'CHOOSE YOUR OWN GOALS'

We suggest that survivors try to think about where they want to get to with the counselling. There is a difference between getting away from the problems and moving towards a better sort of life. It is much easier to plan to go forwards and then it is much easier to notice when you are getting somewhere.

This area of work tends to arrive in the early to middle part of the programme. The later parts are then aimed at helping people work towards their goals. This can take a long time – months or years – because survivors have a great deal of rebuilding to do to catch up on life. After all, they have put their life on hold since the abuse, because of the abuse.

'DO YOU WANT TO TALK ABOUT WHAT ACTUALLY HAPPENED OR NOT?'

Only occasionally, we find survivors want to discuss the events of the abuse. Usually they are happy to accept the suggestion that we talk about The Trap and the after-effects. We prefer not to talk about the details. We assume that it would be more embarrassing than worthwhile. Even so, we do not assume that we should *never* talk about the sexual contact.

Technical Note

This point is where my programme differs from some other approaches to counselling for adult survivors. The previous experience of professionals working in Post Traumatic Stress Disorder counselling is that the service should be

1. as soon after the incident as possible

2. as near to the area as possible

3. as optimistic as possible

and there is a strong belief in

4. encouraging the victim to re-live the experience in detail.

These ideas are very similar to the way in which people are encouraged to get back onto a bicycle or a horse after a fall. In many cases they seem to work well, but I feel there are important differences that we should pay attention to.

Previous ideas about this area of counselling arose from the military setting, where much of the early research was done. This produced the approach known as Critical Incident Debriefing, which had the benefit that it can be thought of as a brief form of psychotherapy which works rapidly and is therefore useful for both the patient and the funding body. But sexual abuse is a different type of trauma to those that soldiers usually suffer. Abuse often lasts longer, is more confusing and is more secretive. I believe that this sort of approach is inappropriate for use with adult victims of child abuse on three of the four requirements above:

Point 1: Counselling often commences years – even decades – after the abuse. This is usually as soon as practical because the victim has kept away from helping services. The Trap has caused this, just as it is intended to by the abuser. With the vast majority of adult survivors who come forward for help, this requirement cannot be met.

Point 2: Victims will often travel many hundreds of miles to get away from the geographical area in which the abuse occurred. This is one of the seventeen possible Post Traumatic Stress symptoms: the avoidance of reminders. In many cases this can leave them vulnerable to financial, housing and social pressures. Attempts to encourage them to return 'home' are likely to fail.

Point 3: We can support this point wholeheartedly.

Point 4: The idea of encouraging victims to remember the details of the abuse is based on a belief that this will force the victim to re-organise her attitudes about the experiences. This comes from the fact that victims can create distorted attitudes about their experiences. The unexpected nature of the 'Stockholm Syndrome' (see page 219) in kidnap victims is a good example of this. Equally, 'Survivor Guilt' amongst disaster survivors is another.

Where the events have taken place recently and relatively nearby, this is quite possible. Where they took place distant in time and geography, this is not so easy. The value of such recovered memories is placed under so much doubt by the justice system that the alleged 'False Memory syndrome' is a great worry to all victims, whether they appear in court or not. Such criticism of memories does not happen to victims of other trauma, such as disasters, car crashes or accidents. There are usually witnesses and forensic evidence to help sort these out. For abuse, there is usually no such assistance because it happens in secret. This has become a very daunting business for survivors.

The most simple argument is that re-living the abuse is a frightening experience which some survivors will try to avoid. They may want to avoid it so much that they refuse to come to the counselling. The comments about this in one of the case histories show this clearly (The Wasted Years, page 170).

Overall, we can see that the basic ideas do not fit well enough. We need a better method if we hope to work successfully with adult survivors.

CHAPTER 4

More Guidelines for Counsellors

More Metaphors

Because we talk about so much of life's experience, we often cover issues and areas outside those I have described as metaphors so far. There are some descriptions of parts of the person that we use to talk about change. Because they are already in normal use in the language, we cannot really call them metaphors. They describe invisible but important parts of the person and we need to include them here to complete the explanation of how we work in this programme. Bandler and Grinder (1982) explored the usefulness of giving names to these parts of people in detail.

'Parts of people'

COURAGE

Courage is that part of us that helps us to take risks, experiment, do things we are nervous about.

When we need to face frightening situations, we need to be brave. This is partly about willpower and partly about believing in our strength of character. Many survivors have more courage than they think they have. We find this despite the effects of the abuse. We could expect that repeatedly being frightened in powerless situations would squash any courage. Sometimes it does, but at other times it seems to nurture more quiet courage.

A difficulty with coping through courage is the few occasions when it disappears. This is very scary! When those parts of yourself that you rely on fail you, it can feel like the end of the world. To other people it can appear that a surprisingly small difficulty has completely thrown the survivor. The survivor is likely to feel very foolish and try to cover it up in some way. We aim to encourage a survivor's courage through the programme.

DETERMINATION

Determination is that part of us that helps us to do difficult things, stay in tiring situations, keep on going. Those survivors who feel they have little or no courage often have lots of determination. This gets them through the problems and crises.

The downside of coping through determination is that it can be exhausting. There can be a danger of wearing it out. In these situations a survivor can suddenly appear to crack before people realised they were under stress. This is due to the accumulation of tiredness. Even more surprising is when people crack after the crisis is over – the determination held them together throughout it but suddenly vanished afterwards when everyone else would be celebrating! This feels totally crazy to people and they are very tempted to hide it as much as possible. We aim to support a survivor's determination through the programme.

CONFIDENCE

Confidence is that part of us that helps us to relax, be assertive, be clear with other people. Most victims have their confidence squashed by the abuse. The whole aim of The Trap is to ensure that victims do not have the confidence to tell anyone else. We aim to boost a survivor's confidence and help regain the level it would have developed to if the abuse had not knocked it off course in childhood (see The Monty Python Foot, page 89).

HOPE

Hope is that part of us that helps us to do new things, change things, improve ourselves. I feel that hope is a well-spring of human life. I feel that it is automatically in all of us, although there might be exceptions in cases of severe brain damage by accident or in birth. For the great majority of people, we all hope for better, nicer, happier, healthier, richer times (and so on down what might be an enormous list!).

Human intelligence makes predictions about the future all the time. This starts as babies – we watch a ball roll behind the chair and look to see if it emerges on the other side. As adults, we predict and anticipate the smallest things – such as where our foot will land when we walk. We predict the most significant things too – about life, relationships, health and so on. Most people are aware of predicting significant things with some hope. Pessimists are aware of predicting and countering with 'It'll go wrong'. Survivors are often so certain that things will go wrong that they forget they are predicting.

Alcoholics Anonymous recognises this in saying 'Live a day at a time. Avoid predicting disasters – they may not happen, so give yourself a chance'.

If we are trained to believe that things go wrong, we start to damp down our hope. We force ourselves to avoid hoping for what we really want, to avoid the disappointment we expect (often quite wrongly). It is important to remember that Post Traumatic Stress symptoms are relevant here. Most trauma victims feel like this, regardless of the type of trauma, it shows that enough bad luck can affect humans in this way. We explore this issue with survivors with the Unhealthy Childhood Questionnaire (see page 223). We aim to feed hope to survivors through this programme.

JUDGEMENT

Judgement is that part of us that examines other people – their motives and capacities – to understand the social world we live in. It is a very important aspect of protecting ourselves. Abuse makes survivors distrust and ignore their judgement. They can sometimes end up with a blind spot where they do not see danger signals. This is probably because although they want to be safe and keep their children safe, they also want to avoid seeing, thinking or feeling anything that might remind them of their own abuse, so they can fail to protect themselves or their children from the very thing they so want to ensure never happens. This is a tragedy.

Yet survivors may also be very acute observers of people and intuitively 'see' more than most others. Their experiences made it much more important to understand and 'read' people than most other children, and this practice accumulates into adulthood. All the same, they may not give themselves credit for this. They may make mistakes a few times and then they can get (more) pessimistic. The fatalism that comes from their lack of hope makes them likely to get more cross with themselves – for instance if they find out too late that the first impressions they ignored were right, they are likely to blame themselves harshly. We aim to help survivors believe and refine their judgement about people, relationships and themselves.

Using these 'Metaphors'

We use these names for parts of the human being when we are talking about changes that are wanted, planned, happening, avoided or achieved. For instance:

'Do you think you have enough courage to tell your children?'

'Now you are changing your pattern of drinking, is it mainly by determination and will-power or is it getting easier as you go?'

'Where did you find the confidence to be so assertive?'

'You must have started to hope you can change after all those years of being stuck in the circle. You have suddenly started talking to your husband.'

These are positive examples, identifying the start of something new, emphasising change and building confidence. Sometimes, we discuss a planned change or an obstacle or a longed-for-but-impossible ideal:

'Will it take more determination to do that or more courage?'

'Are you the sort of person who works more on courage or more on determination?'

Mottoes

In a working pattern that can last for 12 to 24 months, various themes begin to stand out as repeated sayings. While describing them is not essential, they give an important background flavour to the programme. We often talk about mottoes – those short phrases or sayings that summarise a belief, reason for action or goal. There are two sorts of mottoes in our programme – those that we supply and those that survivors choose.

Mottoes we suggest

"BE GENTLE WITH YOURSELF'

This is a reminder that the symptoms of the abuse come from the abuse, not from birth (see Serious Frights, 'Flu and Bruised Knees, pages 73, 69 and 71). I wrote this in large letters on the Information Sheet about Frights (see page 220).

We also say:

'You have been doing the best you could in extremely difficult circumstances.'

'You have not failed to live a normal life – you have succeeded at coping with abnormal experiences.'

'AVOID USING THE WORD "SHOULD" ON YOURSELF'

Take the 'should' out of your sentences about yourself and your future. Put in the word 'want' instead. The idea is to reduce the amount of self-criticism and increase self-respect. It also points in a forwards direction and allows planning about how to get what you want.

We also notice words like 'just', 'only' and 'simply' as versions of 'should': 'I just can't tell her…' 'Always' and 'never' are as worrying for us; they make things seem totally true when they may be partly, or sometimes, true. Sorting these out can let some hope shine through. Although these are 'just words' (notice the example), it is through words that we express ourselves and also hear ourselves. If we tell ourselves off, put ourselves down or give ourselves unreasonable targets, we are squashing ourselves with The Monty Python Foot (see page 89).

'SAY "I WANT" MORE OFTEN'

During the Future-focused Stage (see page 8), the questions of 'where to aim for, how to hope for, what to plan for' are very important. They can feel pretty impossible, especially as The Government Health Warning will make The Bruise more sensitive to The Monty Python Foot.

'PAT YOURSELF ON THE BACK'

Get into the habit of making a point of recognising and acknowledging your successes. This might be easiest if you start with the small ones. At night, try to summarise the day's achievements – every day – and sleep on a success instead of a problem. This will help your confidence.

Mottoes survivors choose

We sometimes encourage survivors to choose a motto for the foreseeable future. This is often to help them get through a particularly difficult stage. Making it a personal motto helps to focus the survivor on it. They construct it, we do not force it on them. The idea is simple. Think of a motto to hang over your fireplace on the chimney breast. Write it down. Remember it. Use it. Put the motto in your purse, on the wardrobe door or on the chimney breast.

We suggest three guidelines:

Keep it quick – it is best if it is short, straight to the point and easy to remember.

Go for action – it is most helpful if it is about action, things to do leading to achievements to remember (action needs plans and is about going forwards into the future rather than staying caught by the past).

Keep it positive – it is most useful if it is positive and about starting new things, easier to do and more noticeable when successful (it would be a pity to achieve your targets and not notice).

There are three more useful guidelines that other counsellors have suggested:

Stay safe – the action must be safe, or at least as safe as possible, if there are risks.

Be responsible – the plan must be responsible to you and to others. It's no good making progress and holding others back or harming them. 'Do as you would wish to be done to', even if this wasn't true in the past.

Keep it cheap – the help you need must not be so expensive that you can't afford it. Plan to work within your budget. 'Cheap' can mean 'better' if it achieves good results.

These are some examples of the mottoes chosen by survivors in the interviews of survivors later (see Chapter 5). This was a meeting to talk about how things have been before during and after counselling. I organised the meeting by designing some questions to be used in all the interviews. They were agreed beforehand and one of them was about mottoes.

Hope and Humour

These two aspects are central components of the programme. They appear to be essential parts of any counselling or psychotherapy, although different approaches work differently with them.

Encouraging hope

I have mentioned hope many times already. It is a continual theme that spreads through the whole programme. It is essential. Hope and optimism are basic building blocks for counselling. Some forms of psychotherapy might work differently, perhaps aiming to make the client discover her own hope and optimism. This does not suit this programme. We want to be direct and positive. We constantly try to give hope to bolster the survivor's hope. This is essential because survivors often dare not hope for anything to go well. The most obvious way to do this is to tell survivors about others we know who are making progress. These stories do not have to be about total success, just about courage and achievement in difficult circumstances. After many ups and downs, one single mother with three teenagers told me:

4.1: Case example – I can now

'After what I've been through over the summer, I know that if it had happened a year ago I would have gone to the mental hospital. I couldn't take all these problems in the family. Now, I'd rather take a couple of anti-depressants and get on with it. I can do that now.'

This little quote, with a few anonymous details, is a useful story to keep ready. It can be reassuring to survivors whose doubts are growing and whose courage is failing. Another is the story of a young man in his twenties who told me that he had considered suicide but had decided to 'do it the hard way!' – that is, he decided to live.

Encouraging humour

Humour is another aspect that I have often mentioned already. It is a continual theme and is essential. Rather than go into detail, I will talk about three aspects that come to mind.

4.2: Case example – Humour helped a great deal

'Counselling has opened up channels at home with my husband and, even more so, with my sister (another victim of the same abuser within the family) and we talk almost weekly. We remind each other of the nitty-gritty details, the horrible things that happened.

My husband doesn't really want to know, so it's nice to able to open up and talk to my sister. She's been so good. She lets me ramble on and there's times when we actually laugh.

Like when we used to hear the front door go [close] when Mum and Dad went out. We had to be quiet as mice and hide under the bedclothes. (It made no difference because he lifted us out and took us downstairs.)

And about the time when we trapped him in the kitchen. My sister lured him in there and skipped out and we jammed the door with a chair.

Things like that have brought us humour which has helped a great deal.'

THE SURVIVOR'S HUMOUR

Example 4.2 is a Survivor's story, from a position well down the path on her way to a new future.

Humour seems to be important to survivors. It is often part of their hopes for their future. When they are Designing a New Future (see page 99), they say 'I want to laugh more'. Figure 1.8 on page 44 shows this. And it comes true.

The direction of the Compass (see page 112) depends on the survivor's sense of humour. As the survivor makes progress, the humour comes out more and gets less giggly or aggressive, more sophisticated. The programme can start quite tense and later becomes quite fun between the serious bits.

THE COUNSELLORS' OWN HUMOUR

Humour is important in keeping us alive and sensitive to the intricacies of the counselling. Humour is about understanding double meanings and collisions of meaning. These are often very relevant to the complicated twists and turns of reality in a survivor's experience.

Humour also helps us show our human side. We want to help survivors relax and trust us as much as they possibly can – survivors will not work very well in a distrusting atmosphere. This is a complicated issue. We must not say 'Trust me': we must leave it to the survivor to decide how much they can trust us. We can help by showing our human side rather than being overly professional, straight-faced and distant (see Giving Quality Time, page 147).

If we, the counsellors, run out of humour, our ability to work is reduced. We need to be aware of this danger, especially in such a difficult area of work.

'SERIOUS BUT NOT SOLEMN'

When we start in the first session we say that the counselling programme is 'serious but not solemn'. We explain that we will be talking about very serious issues but we will not get solemn about them because that would be off-putting. We avoid disrespectful humour. Usually, we are laughing at ourselves – quite often it is about momentary lapses, losing words, slips of the tongue and so on. Occasionally, we are laughing at a complicated situation the survivor may have talked about – the situation, not the survivor.

CHAPTER 5

Five Survivors' Histories

Here I have gathered five survivors' histories to show how real people experience the abuse and the following years. I think it is important to know how real survivors think and feel about their situations. Before I understood these things, I felt difficult about responding to survivors when I was counselling them. It was tempting to stick to the first problem they mentioned – depression, alcohol misuse or relationship problems. As I began to understand how sexual abuse happens and what it does to people, I became more and more convinced that counselling had to talk about it all, not just parts of it. This means it is essential to understand a lot about the survivors' experiences.

Without this knowledge, it is difficult for a counsellor to convey a sense of willingness to believe survivors. This is really important to the success of any counselling with survivors. If they feel disbelieved, they are likely to say as little as possible in the counselling, or even leave it altogether. They do this to limit their pain – which, if we understand how great their pain is, makes a lot of sense. Anyone would do the same.

One problem for any counsellor newly starting in the area is the question of how to get relevant experience before counselling survivors. Reading and listening to first-hand accounts is really the only way.

Similarly, for survivors to come out of their isolation, they need to get a real, strong feeling of being believed and understood. Hearing professionals describe issues they have found in textbooks is not really enough. Counsellors can repeat things they have learned without understanding the complex emotional implications. If they do this, the danger is that survivors will not feel understood as a person in their own right. They will feel as though they are being compared to a textbook. No one would like this and no one would feel safe enough to take the enormous risks of starting to talk about such vitally important issues. I think survivors need to hear about other survivors' experiences. This is why group counselling is so central to *ASCSA's* work. This is why we have a library of poems. This is why I have included so many snippets of real-life examples in this book. This is why I have included five longer histories here.

The Interview Project

These survivors have all volunteered to tell me about their lives in an interview roughly an hour to ninety minutes long. My idea was to use one questionnaire (see Appendix) with all of them. I hoped this would show the differences between them better than me asking questions about their lives. Briefly, the sections deal with the interview, the abuse, before counselling, during counselling and nowadays. You will see that they responded quite differently to these sections. This shows the different personalities as well as the different childhood and adult experiences they have had.

The interviews took place over a two-week period towards the end of my writing this book. This means that the survivors are of different ages (though they are all in their late 30s to early 50s). They have had different types of abuse from different types of abusers. They are at different stages in their recovery. They have had different lengths of counselling and different types of counselling – that is, some went to a group, some had individual counselling and some had both. They have coped in different ways and with different amounts of success. Some of them have other contributions in the book (examples or poems) and others have only been invited to help through the interview.

In the event, some of the similarities are just as interesting as the differences. I will leave my comments about them until after the histories to let you think about the similarities and differences without me swaying your imagination.

I have used the survivor's own words, checked by them before publication, and have shown the name of their choice. The few alterations I have made I show by using square brackets round them [like this] – see Notes on page 8 for details.

I have also been careful to keep confidentiality with their names. I am pleased and grateful that they have given me actual christian names rather than codes like 'Number One' or initials like 'A.L.' or even 'Anonymous' – although I offered them the choice. Case examples feel much more real with a name.

Deni: Working hard – getting nowhere

Deni sits and listens to questions read out to her, with a copy in front of her.

THE INTERVIEW

Are you willing to be interviewed with the questions shown? – Yes.

Are you willing to allow this interview to be published? – D'ya know I was quite flattered that you asked me – that you'd want to include my experiences.

If I do publish who should I put as a name? – I want you to put 'Deni'. No one will know but me and some of the group members.

THE ABUSE

The abuse, can you say what happened, briefly? – I've never really talked about it yet, haven't had the guts to bring it out in the group yet, I was just getting there…there's things trapped in my mind, I can't recall them yet.

But you remember some bits? – Yes, little bits.

Can you say anything about these now? – Nobody else knew about the abuse when it was happening, as far as I am aware. I had all the physical symptoms like wetting the bed, funny behaviour, my sister tucking me in tight in the bed every night and so on. These are the bits I can remember: retreating into a fantasy land, creating my own idea of what life should really be. One thing springs to mind: I was aware of my sexuality, or of sex should I say, before my time, before I should of done. I remember being sat in a tin bath with my sister, horrified when my uncle looked in at the window! Aged three, I tried to cover myself up! Also, horrified to see my sister in bed [playing] with father. I was scared because it seemed wrong. I'm still not sure how it started [the abuse], or when, but I do remember being about eight and a stranger touched me in the passageway between the houses further up the road.

OK… Let's move on – Yes!

BEFORE THE COUNSELLING

What was life like before the counselling? – I was a wreck living in a big black void. I felt as if I was stark raving mad; literally. I spent most of the time under the influence of tranquillisers, anti-depressants mixed with brandy, whisky – which didn't mean to say I was drunk, just helped me stop thinking, put me to sleep. Having half to three-quarters or a bit less of a bottle per day.

It must have been about a half, I'd have been legless if it was more and I couldn't afford it anyway at the height of my drinking.

Did you have problems? – I was a single mother, depressed, plus having rows with the kids. Can't blame them because they didn't really know what was wrong, neither did I. Well, I *did* but didn't want to acknowledge it at this stage. I was working hard but getting nowhere, trying to do everything but getting nowhere. Still have days like that! [laughs].

DURING THE COUNSELLING

What was it like to start the counselling? – Starting counselling... I remember trying to think, when I saw your leaflet, one of my daughters was so fed up that she said if I didn't get help she would move out. I was on holiday and there was a pervert there and I had gone to the solicitor because I was freaked out and one of my daughters was putting pressure on me to do something about it. He wanted to get my youngest daughter to take her swimming costume off. She was 12 or 13. I saw a leaflet about the group [*ASCSA*] while I was waiting to see the solicitor. I took it and read it at home and called you about three days later. The first time was horrendous. Had to be half-cut to get to the group!

Do you remember the first meeting before the group? – I was quite calm. I felt it clarified some of the things, for instance the post traumatic stress reactions. I knew it would be difficult but I knew there was light at the end of the tunnel [pause]. The second meeting was much more difficult. I'd had time to think, stirred things up, wanted you to be there while I talked to my mother. I think I was half hitting back at everyone, half wanting her sympathy and love and wanting her to understand. And using half a tumbler of whisky in the process!

Do you remember any turning points in counselling? – Understanding the post traumatic stress bit was one. Recognising that I wasn't the only person feeling as lousy. Not feeling so ashamed about the props I'd used because other people had used them as well. We all felt that men were bastards. We all had this in common in the group and that was the right feeling for then [3 years ago]. I feel different now. I can see a time when my last daughter leaves home – soon! [laughs]. The house is too big and I would be interested in Mr Right, but it would have to be a long slow relationship.

Do you remember your changes? – It was slow and difficult and a bit at a time, chaotic. I'd think I got it right and then I'd go down [into depression] again! It was very confusing and nerve-wracking but I'm getting more calm and sensible these days. The ups and downs were surprising to start with. Then I got used to them as long as someone reaffirmed that it was normal to go up and down. None of my changes were planned but sometimes I came away from the group not having talked about what I had planned to talk about because somebody else's issues were more alarming or more useful. Then you'd take those home and help you look at things in a different perspective, comparing with other people's reactions. It was scary but sometimes exciting though, especially if people noticed some sort of change in me. It was more confidence building but sometimes you really had to look at yourself so deep. There were some things I learnt about myself, like if I haven't managed to say anything because I was full of self pity, but if someone else who found it difficult to talk *had* managed to, I felt that I'd let the group down because I hadn't talked. Maybe something I could have said would have helped somebody, but I couldn't!

What did you use to get through the changes? – Lots of painkillers, alcohol and anti-depressants and the group's support, which gave me confidence to move forwards and keep going to the group. One particular member inspired me – she'd stopped drinking and smoking but still used anti-depressants. The group helped right from the start. The second or third meeting really opened my eyes. It helped a little bit at a time with no hindering – don't think so – it became like a fix, it was making me feel a little bit better each time. I always came away with something – even something awful – to think about. It was like Pandora's box – once you'd fished it out you couldn't put it back!

Did you need more than the group? – Sometimes I needed to talk outside the group, family and personal things [a house fire, a mugging and trouble with a daughter].

What helped most? – I don't feel ended, completed yet. I haven't had enough of my fix yet, Dave! At the beginning, listening to the others who were brave enough to say something, my admiration for them was enormous. I felt that I should be more courageous. It's not fair to expect anyone else to do the work for you. In the middle, it was like a jigsaw. I got the outside frame, it's how I always do jigsaws.

The jigsaw puzzle is you? – Yeah.

Is there anything that we didn't do that helped? – You'd have put me off trying if you'd pushed me too hard, but you always knew how to, when to. You seemed to know how much to push when necessary and when to stop – when the warning signs were given, I suppose. I never found that you pushed me so far that I said right I'm never going to speak again. I was once sent by a GP to a man at their unit, a psychiatric day unit. It didn't work because he seemed like one of the 'dirty mac' brigade – he just seemed to want to know the nitty-gritty. He pushed me too much so I spent most of the time in tears, clammed up, never went back. Wrong attitude! It felt like being victimised again. Like this morning, you let it go and backed off. You didn't say 'I want to know' [in a commanding sort of voice], you're not pressurising.

Is there anything that we did or didn't do that was crucial do you think?

– No, you were always there at the end of the phone if I got to a really crucial stage. Even if I left a message I knew someone was out there listening and would be there for me between the group meetings.

Is there anything we didn't do that would have helped? – What, other than a 24-hour phone line! I suppose we don't ask for the help we need, don't want to feel a nuisance, feel ashamed of asking for help. Sometimes I felt in the group my problems were trivial compared to someone else's, although they were important to me.

Is there anything we could have done better? – No, I don't think so, Dave.

NOWADAYS

And nowadays, about your memories, how much do you remember about what happened to you? – I can remember every bit of the one incident, more than I used to be able to remember. I can remember a little about one other incident before that. There are some things that happened afterwards in my teens and my marriage which were all symptoms of what happened earlier. I know there is something I still can't remember that happened when I was very young and I need to forgive myself for that before I can sort out my feelings about the incidents that I *can* remember.

How do you know there was a first instance? – Gut instinct, I suppose, feelings, because I remember the tin bath and other examples and I can't explain why, something caused it. My uncle at the window was only playing. I loved him, but I was terrified. Why?! I've shied away from men ever since, even the uncles I love so much. I have a fear of men.

Why? – I remember more these days, but they all trouble me less. I get the odd nightmare and the odd flashback. I wake up shouting NO! I'm not as worried about this because I'm sure it's that first incident's memories trying to tap, but I'd wish it would hurry up and get it over and done with! My feelings, yes, my anger's gone off a bit a lot. I feel I'm a very angry person at the moment, but I'm able to express it a bit different now. I don't take it out on *me* so much. Before, I beat myself up, hurt myself. Now I can direct my anger at the right situation earlier so I don't blow it out of all proportion. Which is better than in the past when I could only direct it at myself and I bruised myself, hit myself with whatever I'd got in my hand at the time.

Like what? – Well, for instance, the edge of a book or a long-handled screwdriver I remember, or I dug holes in the kitchen work surface with cutlery knives! [laughs] I haven't done that for a long time.

Your behaviour, has that changed? – I still drink in times of stress, due to other factors [the fire and the mugging, etc.] I drink less and share it to...not lone drinking now, it's now a pleasure. Occasionally I have a drink before bed to help me get off to bed. I'm shattered at the moment because the GP's given me sleeping tablets which aren't working. I'm still using anti-depressants, but more because of the fire and the mugging than the abuse. I'll be able to stop again once I'm over this hurdle. My depression is different and for different reasons. I hope!

Suicidal thoughts? – I know what I'd do if I needed to. I planned it years ago but I don't think I'll need to. I hope I'll never feel as lousy, so that in a way I suppose feel better. Men, well, none, and I've fallen out with the two men friends I did have! One's my brother! Because I stood up for myself! I'm rather hurt and angry because one's just sulking but perhaps he wasn't that much of a friend but I can live with it [laughs]. I've given myself a pat on the back for sorting out the kitchen repairs but two black points for not handling them [the men who were trying to 'help' in the first place]. Sex, no none, I feel the same, not interested at all. With my children I'm different. And they are actually listening to me now. My youngest actually thanked me for some advice the other day. One of the others came back for a second hug this time before going off to Spain. Last time we didn't even speak! My old family? Yes, got that in perspective, which is amazing. I'm less worried about keeping the family together. I'm more protective about my mum because she's standing up for me more. My sister and I are more open. I can say things without worrying about losing her love. There's no eggshells any more. We're more light-hearted with each other – we don't take things to heart so much if it's a small criticism. My brother, well, I think he was trying to make some money on the side over my kitchen fire and the repairs so...

I'm angry at the Job Centre for forcing me off a re-training course. They told me the wrong advice a year ago and I could have completed the course but they said I couldn't so they have put me back by a year. I've applied for an occupational therapy assistant job which might lead onto other things. I was a dinner lady six years ago but because of the depression, well, going down hill fast, I was ill and then emotionally starting the second breakdown. My health? Well, I've had my first tetanus course because of the mugging. I've totally avoided it previously for years. Personal things [for instance smear tests], no, I'm not over that hurdle yet. I know I'm due, but... I'm making excuses! Professionals, mmm! I'm less involved but could go back if I need to. I hope I don't need to go back.

What are your plans now? – My plans? I'm in limbo at the moment, too busy sorting out the house and kids. But that's easier than it used to be. I've no immediate plans for me...but maybe I'm still putting everyone else first anyway! That's a mask, I want to concentrate on me for a while. I shouldn't laugh. It still feels that I'm not allowed time for myself. Life's unfair, someone else always clamouring for my attention and my time. My time is getting more precious now, partly because I'm getting older and partly because if I get a fresh start there might not be enough time to enjoy it.

Do you have a motto? – My motto? [smiles] I had several but can't remember all of them now! I hate that, when your brain shuts off! 'Smile more real smiles' I suppose. Surprising what you get back from people if you smile. Good things, but not when you have the mask on!

What helped most? – *ASCSA*! That's it in a nutshell. You think of all the things I went through that we put in that newssheet article and now look at me!

When we first met, Deni had 15 out of 17 of the Post Traumatic Stress responses. Deni has some poems in this book – check through the List of Survivors, page 244.

Jenny: The wasted years
Jenny sits with the list of questions in her lap, going through them.

THE INTERVIEW

Are you willing to be interviewed with the questions shown? – Yeah.
    Are you willing to allow this interview to be published? – Yes.

THE ABUSE

The abuse, can you say what happened briefly? What age you were and who did what. You say what you want to say. – Yeah, what!

How about starting with 'When I was such and such age' – Seven.

Was it physical abuse, sexual abuse, emotional abuse or neglect? What happened? Any of those? – Yeah. Have I got to say it? You know what 'appened. [pause] How about my father had me away. How's that sound?

OK. [pause] Also there was physical abuse, wasn't there? – He was always beltin' me, threatenin'.

And emotional abuse, being let down, promises broken? – Well, he never…never, uh, what should you say, he always used to promise to buy me things, and he never did, in place for his favours.

Right, and emotional blackmail and stuff? – Well he knew nobody would 'ave believed us. That's the hold they have on you.

It started when you were seven, how long did it go on for? – Till I left when I was fourteen.

And as far as you know the same was happening to your sisters? – I don't know, I don't speak to them. [pause] My brother used to get beat up, really bad, [pause] that was the one what abused me as well.

How did you cope with that? – Huh! Drink, and take drugs, and went and earned a living.

What do you mean by that? – Well, if 'e was getting it for free, I might as well get paid for it by other people, mightn't I?

Was that a way of coping with it, a bit of fun for you, or really earning a living or something else? – [pause] Uh, get back at 'im, that n'all.

BEFORE THE COUNSELLING

Since you left home, before you started the Counselling, what was life like? – Um, well, I dunno, tried to commit suicide several times [pause] I used to think of suicide and I went down the river several times with pills and a kitchen knife, determined to walk in. Pity I didn't like the cold water! Just as well really! Um, I used to drink, I used to take drugs. You do everything to keep your mind occupied so you don't have to think about things like that.

You had a hard life early on, didn't you? – Well, yeah, in Borstals and Approved Schools and running away from them. Never went to prison though!

But you did end up doing various crimes though – Never hurt nobody, only ourselves. Stole from shops and factories, we was on the run, no one to help us. They had something you wanted, so you took it.

How would you describe those years? – Wasted years, that's 'ow I think of them.

That's thinking about it now. How did you think of it at the time? – I thought that's normal. I thought that's how it's s'posed to be.

So you thought you were doing the best you could? – Well, yeah. I brought up a family. I made sure they was all taken care of.

And fought anyone who tried to interfere? – Yeah, still will! [pause] I've calmed down a lot now, but I didn't believe in things like social workers. Who are they?

And teachers as well? – Well, they're in authority as well, aren't they? They're nothing! [pause, looks abashed] Well, they didn't do nothing for me when I was younger, did they? So why should they take over now?

But some of them were so young then, they couldn't have helped even if they'd wanted to! – Yeah, well they're figures in authority aren't they, they're people higher up than you that has the last say – on your life, in other words. What did they ever do for me?

Thinking back now, how did you cope with it all? – [pause] In today's thinking, I think I've wasted a lot of years and I should never 'ave... Well I dunno, I often think...how should I put it?...if my father didn't start it in the beginning, I would never wasted all them years. But today, I think I'm as good as anybody else if not better in many places.

Why did you decide to start counselling? – Because my eldest daughter was put into care and the social worker pushed me into it.

DURING COUNSELLING

What was it like to start counselling? – My old man [husband] said to the social workers: 'If they'd lived anything like I 'ad they'd understand why I was like I was'. The counselling started with six sessions...and then there was a gap of over a year because I didn't like you. Then we met, oooh, what was it, for about three years. It was my decision to go back to counselling, my decision that was important. Thought it was about time I done something about it. Several idle thoughts prompted the decision and I saw the social worker for a while, first. I still write to her, she was a friend.

How do you remember the changes you went through? – Things were worse before they got better, seemed a total waste. I was hearing him and seeing him when I was sober and I started to panic. The changes were slow and difficult and I kept going back down the ladder. Three steps up one back. It was nerve-wracking and scary. But my confidence built up.

How did you cope? – To get through these changes I used drink and drugs for three-and-a-half years. And the determination.

Did you use a group? – I said no to the group. 'Don't like people' I said, 'it's not private in a group' you know.

Of the various things we did, what helped most? – Knowing you were there to listen, there was somebody there for *me*.

Was there anything crucial that we did? – No crucial thing.

Was there anything that we didn't do that would have helped? – No.

Is there anything we could have done better? – Another six months of counselling on top! [laughs!]

NOWADAYS

Nowadays, how much do you remember about what happened to you? – I still remember – but I try not to.

How much do you get strong feelings about what happened to you? – I have feelings now. I had anger before and suffering before, that was all, but nobody cared. Nowadays I got lots of feelings, other sorts of feelings. I don't often have strong [violent] feelings now, I'm placid. It's OK, my behaviour has changed.

What's different in your behaviour? – Nowadays I only have three-quarters of a bottle of whisky a week...um, usually just Saturday night and if I have any crises. Before it used to be one bottle every night. A whole bottle. I've been avoiding my GP. I still take the headache pills but only a quarter as much and the tummy pills – for gallstones – same as before but less.

Are you still avoiding the doctor for other things too? – I've been for a smear, and I'm proud of myself. I've only ever had three and I'm 50! And those have only been in recent years. I do still get depressed sometimes now and again, but I cope without any anti-depressant pills. I have too much time for thinking sometimes.

How are your relationships? – My husband and I are still together. Sort of. We have less arguments. We don't have sex. That's better for me but he doesn't like it. And I'm good these days, I mean I'm not earning a living [i.e. being a prostitute]. It's OK.

Kids? Well, I don't see my son [who abused the eldest daughter]. I haven't seen my eldest daughter since January [It's now May]. She's leaving us alone. The other daughter I'm very close to, closer than before. She's now 18. She's got difficulties with accommodation. She stayed with us for a week which turned into three months! And her baby is the centre of my life, I have him once a week. My youngest son is studying for University now. He's got brains and I'll support him. He's doing philosophy and art and design and things.

Yes, I know, I used to keep them off school. I would argue with the teachers, even hit them, anything to protect my kids. Now I'm nagging him if he's not doing his homework, but he wants to. He's really interested.

With my old family, I miss my sister, the one who died [of cancer about a year before this interview]. And I've been writing to my brother, the one who's in prison for life. He was affected by mum and dad, perhaps more than the rest of us. The others, I don't miss them.

What about the brother you were closest to? – Well, yes, I still see him. Not so often, he's poorly now.

Have you been employed since the counselling? – I've been for a few jobs, voluntary work for the hospital baby unit and for the handicapped school. Working in their shops. I applied for a couple of jobs as a shop assistant but they want me to wear a skirt. Yuck, ugg! I do enjoy meeting people more now, so working in shops is OK.

How are your relationships with professionals these days? – My health care is the same as before. And the kids, well I let them look after themselves, they're old enough themselves. With professionals I'm much more polite, health visitors, cops, teachers, I'm better. I give them what they give me, so if they give me nice then I give nice. It's OK. Still see Pete [drug and alcohol counsellor] every week, he's nice, he helps with lifts for the animals to the vets.

Do you have any plans? – My plans are for myself. I just existed before. Now I like to see the little-un grow up, I enjoy taking him out.

Do you have a motto these days? – [pause] If it's anything it's 'enjoy life while you can'. It used to be 'look after number one!' [laughs]. I still sleep with the light on quite often. My husband asks every night: 'light on or light off?'. I'm very jumpy with the light off but when my grandson is there it's OK. I can do it.

What helped you most? – Seeing you lot, you an' Pete [myself and the drug and alcohol counsellor]. Alright, I'm still seeing Pete, 'e must be doing some good, I don't drink so much! I'm using grass much less and I don't take as much speed. Life's much cheaper now! [pause] Well, seeing you, I mean, I don't think I would have coped if I kept it bottled up. Well that's the way I see it anyway. Most prob'ly I wouldn't 'ave been 'ere. Nobody knows your feelings till you…until its too late, really. Then they think 'Oooo, I wish I'd done that, I wish I'd listened'.

Well, that's the tragedy of child abuse isn't it? – In this day 'n age you shouldn't have to 'ave tragedies like that. There again, we should've, I always maintained it, we should've 'ad you lot then. Where the 'ell were ya, not born most prob'ly! [laughs].

Any comments? – Nah!

The abuse started at around seven years and continued until Jenny was about 14. In her early 20s she had three marriages and, in the third marriage, four kids. She started counselling at *ASCSA* and CODA at 45. She had 12 out of the 17 Post Traumatic Stress responses. When we met for this interview she had 3 out of 17 responses. She is now 50. Jenny has some poems in this book – check through the List of Survivors, page 244.

Anna: Living with hatred – wishing my life away

Anna sits with the questionnaire, occasionally glancing at it, discussing the issues before we have started the tape recorder: '…I think there's no easy answer to the cruelness that has happened in the past, you just have to try and live with it and cope the best you can'.

THE INTERVIEW

Can I ask you about the interview, are you willing to be interviewed with the questions that I've shown you here? – Yes.

Are you willing to allow this interview to be published if I show you what I've written before it actually goes? – Yes.

THE ABUSE

Can I ask you about the abuse? What happened, can you say briefly? – Briefly, the abuse, mmm, was perpetrated by my father from a very early age up until my teenage years. After then I left home and it stopped.

OK. Can you say what the actual abuse was, as much as you are prepared to say? – The abuse was sexual abuse, mmm, of various sorts, it was actual sexual intercourse and other sorts of sexual abuse.

OK. All right. From what age? – Six.

While it was happening, what did you do to cope? – Well, I think I just became very reclusive because I was frightened. I couldn't talk to anybody about it so I just became very withdrawn, and I was afraid that if I did talk to people that they might suspect and then I would get into trouble. So I just shut off really and went into myself and shut myself away. That's all I did and I didn't, in the end, I didn't cope with being around people at all.

OK. Do you remember using alcohol, drugs, work, school work for instance, hobbies or anything like that before you left home, that is, while it was happening as ways of shutting off? – Well, in my later years at home when sort of 15-ish I started, mmm, having drinks that were in the house and experimenting with them and I discovered then that it was a good way of helping me to shut off and numb the pain, yes.

BEFORE THE COUNSELLING

OK. So can I ask you about life after you left home but before counselling started, what was life like generally? – A lot of the time it was a nightmare. Sometimes I could cope. Things carried on happening to me that I didn't want to happen. Mmm, I just felt like a victim really. All my life I walked into situations where I put myself into a victim's situation, mmm, I found it very, very difficult to cope with ordinary situations. I drank a lot, took drugs, mmm, pretended a lot about things, found it hard to relate to people, found it hard to go to public places. Mmm, it was very, very difficult and painful and I just used a lot of painkillers really, to get by.

What sort of painkillers? – Well, mainly pills that you could get hold of in the 60s because I was in my twenties then, mmm, and LSD I used.

How did you decide to start counselling? – I joined the local volunteers association and, mmm, met quite a few people in the sort of counselling, mmm, circles. Also, I was dealing with people who were receiving counselling so it gave me a chance think about myself and whether I could have counselling myself. Before, I hadn't really thought, that counselling – although I knew counselling was available – I hadn't really believed that it would help me so I didn't bother. But then, you know, it took a long time before I began to feel that it may be of help.

Since you left home at 16 or so, what sort of age were you when you thought of counselling? – About 49 or 50 I can't remember now, 3 or 4 years ago.

A long time to wait? – Yeah.

DURING COUNSELLING

What did it feel like when you actually started the counselling? – Well, it felt terrible because it made me go back and sort of remember lots of things and re-live things. It was very, very painful at first. In fact, I thought it was going to make things a lot worse and several times I nearly stopped. It was hard to carry on. I had to persevere with it once I'd started.

Do you remember turning points in the counselling? – It kept offering me hope. I can't really remember any particular turning points but it was just a gradual process that happened over a period of time, a longish period I would say.

Continuous or bit at a time? – It was up and down but, mmm, because I gave a lot more thought to it when I was outside of the counselling. When I went home it was on my mind a lot so therefore I looked forward to going to the counselling as a way of, mmm, release really. I was able to talk about things rather than just think about things, and I think that I found that was helping, where as in the past, all my life, I'd only ever thought about it, never talked about it. So it was talking about it that helped me over a period of time.

Can I ask you a few detailed questions about that period and how the change felt. Was it easy or difficult? – It was difficult.

Was it nerve-racking or calm and sensible, or understandable from when it happened? – It was calm and sensible, sometimes it was bit nerve-racking because all my feelings would well up and I would feel, you know, angry about things and upset about things, but most of the time it was calm and sensible.

Was it sort of planned stages where you said I must look at this and then I must look at that or was it a series of surprises or things that you just had to deal with? – It wasn't structured in my mind. It was a series of surprises really and just a process really. Things would come up that would possibly make more sense of things.

Would these happen slowly, or would they happen faster and faster, or was it all chaotic? – No I think it, it... things seemed to get better. And then after about 2 years things seemed to get worse again. I think what happened was a lot more of my anger was coming up to the surface and I was just getting really angry inside and angry that the counselling hadn't worked as well as I'd hoped. I was getting angry about lots of things and I thought 'well this is a waste of time, I'm not going to bother any more'. But once I'd realised that it was deep rooted anger that was coming up for the first time, I realised that I needed to go on, get through it.

So when you were 6, 7, 8 you were shutting off all this anger by being reclusive. It was all that anger from those times that was finally coming out? – Yeah, I think it was anger from years and years and years. Actually it had to wait because I was never ever able to express those feelings in front of anybody.

You were married for some part and had kids. Was there any anger from that bit as well? – Yes. I married somebody who didn't allow me to show my feelings so it was the same right the way through. I couldn't show my feelings at all, so everything got bottled up all the way along the line.

So over 2 or 3 years of counselling you have had something like 40 years worth of anger to deal with? – Yes. I lived with hatred, really, hatred against my parents.

Did you build up your confidence in the end or was it confidence draining as you went through? – I think it did build up my confidence, yes, because I was talking about it in the counselling room and I think that helped me build my confidence. I didn't feel... I was beginning to feel different about myself.

What did you use to get through these changes – courage, confidence, determination, more painkillers? – You mean during the counselling. I didn't use painkillers. I think that I was just able to see things in a more rational fashion. Mmm, and basically I was feeling better about myself so therefore I wasn't on self-destruct anymore. Because that's what I had been doing all my life and, mmm, and I was beginning to feel that I had more purpose in life.

You went to the group and I think had a few counselling sessions outside of the group. Did the group help at first or in the middle or towards the end? Or was it a lot or a little or did it even get in the way, the group? – I found that it was being in the group that helped me. The counselling sessions I had outside the group, I didn't feel, didn't help me at all. So it was counselling in the group that helped me, yes.

So of all the things that we did do what would you say helped most at the beginning? – Well, I think it was just basically, mmm, listening to other people talking about their experiences and their thoughts and feelings. It, mmm, put things into perspective for me and the counsellors helped the way they sort of very gently handled the whole situation. You didn't feel as though you were being analysed, or looked at in an odd fashion. You didn't feel that there was something wrong with you like you do when you are in a one-to-one counselling situation. I think that was important for me that I needed to feel equal and, mmm, I could easily relate with other people in the group.

Was it the same all the way through or were there different things in the middle and towards the end? – I think it was the same all the way through, yeah.

Was there anything that we didn't do that you think would have been helpful? – No, not really, no. I think we covered a lot of things that were important.

Could you say whether there was any one crucial thing that we did do that helped? – I think the times when we were able to talk about our feelings were very good. We did a brain storm once about feelings and I think that was helpful.

Right. Was there anything we didn't do that would have helped? – I can't think of anything, no.

OK. Is there anything we could have done better? – No, I don't think so.

NOWADAYS

Talking about nowadays, I'll ask you about memories. How much do you remember about what happened to you? – Not a lot, considering it happened over a long period of time and often. I don't remember a lot of details. The things I remember most of all was just how I felt about my own childhood.

Do you remember more or less than you did before the counselling? – More.

Does it affect you more or less than it did before the counselling? – Well, I'm able to remember things more now, or rather I am able to allow myself to remember things, whereas before the counselling I didn't want to remember anything, so I was able to shut it out and refuse to remember because it was just painful to remember anything, whereas now I can let myself remember things and it's not painful, although I still feel pretty bad about what happened.

Can I ask you about feelings, do you get strong feelings about what happened to you? – Things trigger it sometimes. If I see things on the television or hear other people talking about things, it triggers my feelings off.

Is that more or less than before the counselling? – Well, I'm more able to cope when things do get triggered off, yes.

Do you think you get triggered off more or less often than before counselling? – Well, I think I'm more able to understand things now, so I don't feel so frustrated. And, you know, I'm more able to work things out when things get triggered off, rather than just have a lot of feelings about it and feel awful.

I just wondered whether the triggers were more often or less often? – Well, I think I'm much more aware of sexual abuse and what goes on than I was before because I don't think I wanted to know before.

Does that mean the triggers are more often and that they don't hurt so much? – Well, the triggers are more often but I'm more able to express my anger about it now, rather than just hurt about it.

OK. And that's better? – That's better, yes, because I can express myself and it's like a release when you, it's like fighting back, really, against it.

OK. Your behaviour. I'm wondering what has changed there. Use of alcohol, other drugs, doctors, medicines, is that different to how it was before the counselling? – No, because I'd already given everything up before the counselling.

Depression. Were you depressed before? – Yes, I would say that. Mmm, I get depressed less now and for shorter periods of time.

OK. Suicidal thoughts or suicidal attempts or hurting yourself? – No. I don't get those anymore, I used to get them a lot, yes.

Did you do any of them? – Yes, I did attempt to take my life on several occasions.

Did you ever harm yourself? – Yes, I did several things to hurt myself. I would do… I would also do reckless things, not caring whether I killed myself.

Has that changed now? – Yes, it has changed, although I still have feelings that I want to get my life over and done with quickly. I don't actually do anything about it, but I still feel that I want the time to go by quickly.

Wishing your life away? – Yeah, I still do that, yeah, I don't know why but I do.

Habit? – It could be habit, maybe there is still [pause]… Deep down, there's still a feeling of no self-worth. Maybe it's just left the permanent impression that I wasn't really worth anything and still aren't.

But I think you are happier these days. You've got new relationships which seem to be going well? – Yes. I've recently got married again. And, mmm, and I'm very happy in my marriage. And I'm married to somebody who says that he loves me and shows a lot of love to me.

He allows you to show your feelings in your relationship? – Well, I still hold back on lots of my feelings because it frightens me that it might be a nasty side that my husband might not like, so I don't show all of my feelings.

And you haven't told him about the abuse? – No, I couldn't do that because…in case he would feel different about me. I don't want to take the risk.

Can I ask you, in this relationship, is your sexual relationship better or worse than it was in previous relationships? – I would say it's better, mmm, because there's no pressure on me, there's no pressure put on me to do anything I don't want to do and it's all very sort of, I don't know really, there's no pressure.

So does that mean you've changed? That you could find, or say yes to, a man so different to the men that you used to go out with before? – Yes, I think I'm able to judge men individually more now than I used to because I used to think basically men were all the same and they were just, you know, out for what they could get for themselves. And that they disregarded what I wanted. But I can see people in a different light and I can see men in a different light and I think that I don't expect as much now. I don't… I put myself on more of an equal basis with people so therefore I'm not expecting something from them. I'm able to give as much as I expect and I think that's helped me a lot to look at people differently and… I think the group helped me to do that quite a lot and also I think I'm more able, if things did go wrong, I think I'd be more able to cope with things going wrong now. So therefore it's enabled me to take the risk of having a relationship.

Are things different between you and your children these days? – Well yes, since they've grown up, we are able to relate as grown-ups.

Is that just because they are grown up or because you are different or both? – It's both, a bit of both, mmm, yeah.

What about other people in your family, is there anything different? – Well, my relationship with my mother wasn't very good for a lot of years, mmm, but again, I can… I can cope with her better now, although I don't see her very often. Mmm, it doesn't upset me just thinking about her like she used to. I can just put her to one side and just, you know, not let her affect me as much now. Although, having said that, when I think of her and my father – when I really think of what they were like together when I was younger – I find that hard to cope with. I don't want to think about it at all and it's something that I still bury.

Are there any changes in your education, have you been on courses lately or got any new employment, change of job? – No. Although I have given up working for somebody that I was working for and I'm sort of working for myself more now.

So you've become self-employed? – Mmm, well I was self-employed before, but the bulk of my work came from the shop and I've packed that in now because I felt a slave to him and I'm not going to be shoved around by anybody.

You must need a lot of courage to believe that you'll get more work from different sources instead of one source? – Yeah, I don't feel trapped in the situation that I was in. Now, I don't feel as trapped, I feel free and more able to make up my mind about things.

Positive move? – Very positive move yeah [smiles happily].

Is there any difference in your health care of yourself, medically? – Possibly, I'm, yes, I think I'm looking after myself better and not driving myself as much as I used to do, thinking that I just had to carry on slaving away. I do give myself more time off and rest now yes.

Any checks and that? – I really haven't needed to have any health checks lately, no.

Can I ask whether you used to have a problem with smear tests and things like that? – Yeah, definitely had a problem with smear tests.

And nowadays? – Well, I don't have to go for smear tests now because I've had a hysterectomy so that doesn't happen any more.

Relationships with professionals, is that the same or is it different? – Yes, I am able to relate with professional people better now. I feel more equal to them and not inferior.

Did you have a problem with professions at all in the past? – Very much so, I hated having to deal with professional people of any sort.

Were there any particular reasons for this? – Yes, because my father was a professional person and all his friends were and, mmm, I'd only ever had very bad experiences from those sort of people, being used and abused by them.

You said that in the period between leaving home and the counselling starting there had been a number of incidents. Were any of those with professionals? – Yes.

Do you want to say any more or would you rather not? – Well, I have experienced sexual abuse from a doctor when I was in my early 20s and I never did anything about it because I was frightened and didn't think I had any rights. I thought that I would be the one that would end up in trouble through it. I've had occasions where professional people have made advances in sexual ways and I think it's because I was in a vulnerable situation, because I was never able to stand up for myself or have anybody around me who would stand up for me.

Can I just check? These professionals, were they actually meeting you because of their jobs or was it casual friendly neighbourhood meetings? How did these things happen? – I think it was both...both situations at different sorts of times. And especially at work, yeah...yes, managers and people in high positions would target me, yes.

Can I ask you a bit more about the future? Do you have plans, new plans, for yourself, your children, your marriage? – I haven't got specific plans, no, I'm just getting on with my life in a happier way.

Does that mean you don't actually need very many plans or does it mean the plan to have a new relationship has actually worked? – Yeah, the plan... Yes, I think I did plan to have a new relationship which is working very well at the moment and I am relating in a much different way, yes and I'm very determined to make it work.

So does that mean the plan is to keep on going because its good? – Yeah, I think the biggest change is that I am able to give out a lot more than I did. In other words, I've got the confidence to give without worrying about being rejected and I just feel a lot more confident about things. I feel more like a human being now.

OK. What about hobbies these days? – Fishing, I have really got interested in. Before I was a workaholic, though I didn't really understand it at the time, I was just glad I didn't have to think about things [abuse] so much... And I recently had a pleasure flight, which was wonderful. I'd do it once a week if I could afford it! Freedom! Floating around without a care in the world.

Do you have a motto these days? – What, for anybody?

For you? – Mmm, for myself? Well, I've always had to tell myself to be very, very determined, very determined to battle on.

Do you still have to say that to yourself these days? – Sometimes, yes, sometimes.

No reclusiveness? – No. I don't think the battle is quite so hard as it used to be, but I still do have to be determined about certain things. The poem [Hidden (written about two years before this interview) see page 232] sums me up as a child. No one knew me, at school or at home. No one knew anything about me. Writing it was very difficult. It frustrated me at first because I couldn't write it properly. It was the first one I'd done about abuse. It ended up with short lines, a short poem. My other ones had longer lines and were longer length too. Dreadful, my mind went wild trying to think of long lines, but my memories are in snippets, so… No, I'm not a recluse anymore!

So you are using your old motto not so often? – Yeah, I'd say so, yes.

Can you say what helped you most through your life? – Well I think I was always grateful that I was able to read very well and learn things because I was able to get more of an understanding about things through books and, you know, ferreting things out.

And as far as the counselling went, can you put a finger on what helped most? – I think it was just being allowed to talk about things, even if they were just trivial things, and talk about the way things are now with family and friends and, you know, parents and children. To relate – as from being a child to having children and being a parent, all that sort of thing – to the group helped me a lot really. I used to feel terribly mixed up in my mind about all these things, parents, and children, and all that. I found it hard to put myself in a parent situation when I didn't want to think about my own parents, but now the group has helped me to get all that into perspective. It was helpful to hear the other members saying the same things and having similar problems with their own children and husbands.

Any last comments you want to add? – Well, I'm very glad that I did start counselling because that was something that I had never believed in for myself. I thought it was just for other people, and I just didn't think it would help me at all. But it has helped a lot and I think it is…goes a long way to being the answer to a problem that doesn't look as though it has any answers at all.

Thank you very much. Last check, has this interview been OK? – Feel free to edit it just how you want.

Anna had only 2 out of the 17 Post Traumatic Stress responses when we did this interview. Anna has some poems in this book – check through the List of Survivors, page 244.

Cheryl: Always the question 'Why?'

Cheryl waits to be asked without referring to the questionnaire.

THE INTERVIEW

Are you willing to be interviewed with the questions shown? – Yeah.

Are you willing to allow this interview to be published? – Yeah.

THE ABUSE

The abuse, can you say what happened, briefly? – The quickest way to say it is that my grandfather interfered with me when I was eight and the last time he tried it was when I was 19 and had my first baby. It started slowly and was once a week when we moved nearer. When I was 14, I was living with him and Nan and it was worse – worse in two ways because he would do it when he wanted to and because it was hidden from my Nan.

What did he actually do? – It was touching, watching me, coming into my bedroom at night and sex in the morning and after school.

How did you cope with that? – I blanked it, knew it was happening, but didn't acknowledge it. I put a wall up.

BEFORE THE COUNSELLING

Before the counselling, what was life like? – Up and down, hard to cope, unexplained. There was always 'why?' [pause] dodging interfering busybodies like social workers, stone-walling them and later using them for what I wanted.

What did you do to cope? – Everything was there getting on top of me. I would sink into depression and couldn't climb out. Not all down to him. The whole situation and the build-up inside…confusion…

What do you mean by 'everything'? – Well, the abuse, homelessness, physical and emotional abuse from my mother. Shouldn't call it emotional abuse because she wasn't that loving in the first place. I nearly didn't cope. I did overdose and have my stomach pumped and I cut my wrists once, a case of causing pain to forget pain.

Did you drink or use any drugs? – No, I've never done them. Still don't drink…it's not really me!

How did you decide to start counselling? – I was pushed into it. Everything was bottled up. I needed to release. The attack by my mother was the last straw, the bottle was full and starting to overflow.

DURING COUNSELLING

What was it like to start counselling? – Nervous, shaky, scared, wanting to do it but not wanting to do it.

Do you remember any turning points in the counselling? – The first one was the first step of asking for counselling and keeping appointments. It took courage to walk into that room with you sat there and talk about it all.

How do you remember your changes? – Nerve-racking…you hitting the nail on the head. You used to come out with something and I would go 'There you go again!' [pause] Scary renewing memories, making me think about it, emotional. The change was gradual, things just got easier in life and coping as the counselling went on, being able to speak about it, let it out rather than keep it in.

What did you use to get through the changes? – Courage and determination, and the counselling built up confidence then. There was a time I wouldn't be able to sit here and do this with you.

Did you use a group counselling? – No, individual counselling. You kept on at me 'would I join the group?' No! It took enough to stay there talking on its own.

Why not? – Needed to get myself sorted out first before going to others.

Was there one crucial thing that helped? – Comes back to hitting the nail on the head all the time, dunnit.

Was there anything that we didn't do that would have helped? – Not really.

Was there anything we could have done better? – Don't think so.

NOWADAYS

Nowadays, how much do you remember about what happened to you? – Don't think I'll ever forget it, but it's easier to remember now. It's not as painful being able to talk about it, cope better. It's not as sharp.

Do memories get in the way, the way they used to? – No.

Do you remember these things nowadays? – Not very often. Before, there were things my boyfriend would do that would trigger memories of things that he [the abuser] would do.

Is it more or less than before any counselling? – Less, I should imagine. I react less to triggers, probably still there, I just don't see them any more.

Does it affect you more or less differently than before any counselling? – No, I am still the same person but calmer, able to cope.

How much do you get strong feelings about what happened to you? – Since he's died there's been there's still that [question] 'why?' But as for remembering it, it's not that strong anymore. I s'pose that you could say I have control over it now, it doesn't run wild like it used to.

How often do you get strong feelings nowadays? – Not very often.

Is this more or less than before the counselling? – Yes, less.

Does it affect you more or less or differently than before any counselling? – Same again, able to cope better is important.

Have other things changed your behaviour? – Less depressions [pause] still get them but not because of that, usually money problems, children problems, normal life things.

Have your relationships changed? – My boyfriend is now my husband! I've got a calmer relationship, used to have a lot of rows, still have some, but not very often. They're not 'get out of my house', 'I don't want to see you again' like they used to be. Not as intense and built up. They're not triggered by memories of him [the abuser].

Is it easier to make up afterwards? – Oh yeah! With the kids I take a different approach. I can accept their behaviour, I can cope and understand them better. There is a definite 'don't want to be like my mother' feeling, don't want to give physical abuse like she did. I'd rather send them to their bedrooms than beat their heads through the wall.

Are there any changes with how you are with your old family? – They all know but they don't mention it. The abuser's dead. Ha!

Is there anything different with education, any course or anything? – No.

What about employment? – Abuse never got in the way of work. Now I have one child who gets disability living allowance and I get carers allowance.

Health care? – That's the same [i.e. unchanged].

Relationships with professionals? – One daughter is in trouble at school and they are sending her to a psychologist again. It didn't work last time. A broken record repeating itself! Didn't get anywhere with psychology before.

What are your plans nowadays? – To be a normal family, just to cope. Mmm…that word 'normal' there is important. To make sure it doesn't happen to my children, obviously.

Do you have a motto now? – To take each day as it comes, take each day as it comes. Even with my husband, I get a great expanse of affection then a row. Each day is different, could be weeks before the next row but you don't know which day, and with the moods of the kids and myself, I don't know what to expect.

Can you say what helped you most? – Just being able to talk about it, to know I wasn't the only one. It wasn't just me. And as the poem *Why?* says, it was just because I was there at the time. [This poem had been written about a fortnight before the interview and is not included in this book.]

Do you have any comments about this? – Don't ever ask me to do this list of questions again! [laughs!] [pause] The depressions I have nowadays, they're not a tunnel like they used to be. Do you remember the tunnel always had another mile added on the end just when I thought I was getting somewhere! [pause, smiles broadly] I'm a spoilt brat at the moment, I'm getting my patio, and all paid for and legal too!

Now that we have finished is it OK for me to publish this interview? – Yeah.

This counselling lasted for about one-and-a-half years and finished about five years before this interview. Cheryl has several poems in this book – check through the List of Survivors, page 244.

Adrian: *I still feel like killing him, but...*

Adrian sits with the questionnaire but waits to be asked questions.

THE INTERVIEW

Are you willing to be interviewed with the questions shown? – Yes I am.

Are you willing to allow this interview to be published if it goes OK and I show you what I actually want to put in the book when I've written it and given you the chance to cross things out and change things? – Yeah, there's no problems with that.

THE ABUSE

About the abuse, can you say what happened, in your own words, as brief as you like? – There was a babysitter that used to come round several times, male, he used to come upstairs after I had gone to bed and mess about with me.

What sort of age were you when that started? – I was about 12 or 13.

And how long did it go on for? – Um... went on for about 2 years altogether.

Can you say what you mean by 'mess about' or would you rather not? – Yeah, he used to come up and when I was in bed he used to [pause] usually what used to happen was he'd, puttin' it bluntly, give us a blow job, um...he used to stick his finger up me arse and generally mess about like that.

OK. What did you do to... Did you use any of the things that I call painkillers like alcohol, drugs, sport, aggression, violence, theft, any of those things in those two years when it was happening? – During the two years it started when it was really goin' on I started to get involved in the drugs scene, eventually it led on to me gettin' heavily involved in it.

BEFORE THE COUNSELLING

Moving on to the time between the abuse and the counselling starting, which must have been quite a lot of years, roughly how many? – I think it must have been a good 20 years I suppose in between.

So what was life like in those 20 years generally? – Very hard, I mean I went from bein' a drug addict, which I eventually became, um... I went for counselling and treatment on that in a rehab unit. Eventually I became an alcoholic.

DURING COUNSELLING

OK. How did you decide to start this particular counselling? I know you've been to counselling before but what made you start this particular one? – It just seemed the right time in me life to try an' get things sorted out and straightened out and maybe straighten meself out, perhaps I could live a normal life.

Can I remind you that the doctor's letter that came with you actually mentioned accidents and dangerous situations at work you had had, rather than abuse? Anything you can say about that? – As the counselling progressed and more seemed to come out, um...it just seemed the right time to bring out what had happened years before, um...it was, it just seemed right somehow. I don't know, maybe it's because I actually had trust in you Dave, this time, rather than the other people that I've seen over the years, um...and it didn't take long to work out that I could trust you whereas before I've never had any trust in any of the counsellors.

OK, thank you. With other people that I've interviewed I've asked them what was it like to start counselling. Perhaps with you I should ask what was it like to start when talking about the abuse rather than before about the accidents and stuff? – It was hard to start with. I spent a lot of sleepless nights just before I told you wonderin' whether I was doin' the right thing, even though deep down I suppose I thought I was doin' the right thing. But when I made a conscious decision, it seemed the right thing to do and then it was hard. It was hard to talk about it but I'm glad I did.

During the counselling can you remember any particular turning points? – I think the hardest part all together was actually bringin' it out in to the open, especially talkin' to another male about it. That was the hard part, but as we progressed it seemed to get easier.

OK. As a matter of interest, would it have been easier if the counsellor had been a woman and you'd had the same amount of trust, would it have actually been easier to continue the counselling once you'd said it? – I couldn't really give you an honest answer on that. I don't know.

OK. Thank you. I'd like to go through what you think now of the changes that you've been through in the counselling, do you think it was quick or slow or middling? – Middlin', right, OK.

Easy or difficult? – I would just have said it was hard to start but got a lot easier as we went along.

Were the changes continuous or were they a bit at a time, step at a time? – It was just one step at a time, I think, to start with.

And then did it become a smooth climb, or was it faster and faster, or was it all over the place? – I think it was all over the pace to start with, um…but then it just all seemed to come out in one go.

OK. Was it understandable or confusing, at the time I mean? – Very confusin' with a lot of feelings.

Nerve-racking, or very calm and straight forward and sensible? – Very nerve-rackin', I suppose, it was. It was sort of dealin' with a whole new set of feelings. Although they had been there for years and years, it was openin' them up and just like steppin' into a dark room, frightened, yeah, frightened. I didn't know what to do.

OK. Would you say that you got used to all these changes or is it still always surprising every time something new changes in your feelings and thoughts or when you find a new way of doing things? – Still surprisin' me every day, um… I got different feelings on the abuse now to what I had at the start of it, um… I feel in me own mind a little bit better than I was and that I was dealing with it, how I was dealin' with it.

OK. So has it been exciting or scary or bit of both at different times, or what? – Both. It's been frightening, it's…it's… I've still had a lot of sleepless nights over it but I'm pleased it's out, it's come out, yeah, so it's a relief in some ways.

Did it build up your confidence or did it make you lose confidence? – Uh, a bit of both really. I lost a bit of confidence in meself to start with but then I sort of feel more confident within meself now that it's come out.

Getting through all the difficult times of those changes did you use, did you lean on your confidence, determination, courage, painkillers, alcohol, drugs, etc? – No, I made a conscious effort that, a conscious decision that there was no way I was goin' to go back to the booze or the drugs. I was just goin' to fight this, um… So far, touch wood, I've done it.

We haven't talked about a group because we haven't had one for men so we need to go straight on to the various things we did. Can you say at the beginning, in the middle and towards the end what helped you most, thinking back? – Thinkin' back on it, I suppose the middle was, when I built up enough confidence in meself to actually bring it out, um…over the several sessions that we had had leadin' up to it. There was a bit of wariness as to how I went about bringin' it to…and it was… I suppose I was scared to start with, but as me confidence started to build up and I got more and more trust with you it was easier to come out with…talk about. I think that made the big difference.

Can you say what it was that made you think that I could be trusted, was there any one thing, can you put a finger on any one thing? – I don't know. In some ways I suppose I felt safe talkin' about things to you which I'd never ever experienced before with any of the other counsellors that I had seen. I mean that when I went to the [Drug and Alcohol Service] and places like that, they were more interested in the weather and the traffic and crazy things like that. They weren't really gettin' to the bottom of it and therefore I wasn't openin' up to them like I should have been and I wasn't gettin' results that either of us was after. Really it was just wastin' their time.

Were there any things that that you think we didn't do that actually helped, anything we avoided doing? – The main problem I've got is the fella that done it, um…as I've explained to you several times I still feel like killin' him but, uh, due to, down to your advice like you told me to lay off and yeah I mean I have. I still want me revenge on him, but I suppose I'll have to do it in a different way now.

Is there any one thing that we did or didn't do that you could say was really crucial? – No.

Is there anything that we didn't do that we should have done that would have helped? – No. In some stages I came out of our sessions and I was physically drained. Then I'd start thinkin' about it, like, and, like, maybe half-way through the week I just needed to talk to somebody and, like, I felt at a loss at that particular time but then once I'd got through it seemed to be all right.

Is there anything that we could have done better do you think? – No. The main thing is that it came out and you gave me the confidence, which I will forever be grateful for.

NOWADAYS

Coming on to nowadays, if we think separately about memories, feelings, and behaviour, thinking about memories, how much do you remember about what happened to you nowadays? – I can remember every single detail.

How often do you remember these things nowadays? – Not as much. I mean, I didn't used to think about them very often before, basically because I was either too drugged out of me head or too drunk, um…but now I sit here some nights thinkin' about them, but not that often.

And when you do think about it does it affect you more or less than it would have done before? – I suppose I get a bit irritable and down about it but I'm beginnin' to come to terms with it.

Do you get strong feelings about what's happened to you? – Yeah, very strong feelings. I'd love to… I would dearly love to see that man pay [pause] dearly love to see it.

Do you get those sort of feelings often these days? – I suppose they're more often now than before, um… I still get the strong feelings like, but like, later [pause] 20 years it's been sat there, um…it was goin' on in me head I suppose another couple of years won't make a lot of difference.

And your behaviour. Have you noticed other things changing? You've got a list there in front of you. Do you want to go through it or pick out the ones that…? – I'm not drinkin' any more, not usin' other drugs, um… I'm still takin' some of the pills that the doctor gave me, um… I don't get depressed quite so often, there's no thoughts of toppin' meself or anythin' like that, um…yeah, I mean I've had two goes at it over the years, um… I've had one accidental overdose it wasn't intentional, um… I done me wrists a good few years ago but that was all partly down to it [the abuse].

OK. What about relationships with men, with your partner, kids, old family? – Well, I'm now on me fourth marriage so that must tell you somethin' about it, um…well this one's not goin' exactly too strong now – it's hard. The kids that we've got, yeah, no problems. I still get a bit tense and upset when they come. They seem to be round most of the time, like, but that's only to be expected, I suppose, um…now they are all in their 20s and 30s, um…me adoptive parents I don't have a great deal to do with. The abuser, who's not in the family, uh, I think I've said enough about him, could get meself into trouble! Employment, I used to be a merchant seaman so I'd stay out of the way for most of the year, um...basically 'cos he still lives in the village where me parents live. I don't suppose I could be trusted if I ever saw him, but there we go. Health care, of meself, I've started lookin' after meself a bit better, um...but how much of that is down to what happened or how much of it is down to me not takin' any drugs or alcohol anymore, um... I don't know. Relationships with professionals, um... I've always had trouble with authority, rebellious by nature I suppose! But I get on with the people I have to, but that's about it. Plans for the future, um...keep goin' as I am at the moment, try an' get through it, try an' forget about it if I can, but not let meself get down.

OK. Have you got any plans for changing job, getting re-trained or anything like that? Sort of start a fresh life in that sort of way, work or education or anything? – I just got meself a job a little while ago doin' up a pub, renovatin' it, um... I, um...the ongoin' plan's to stay there once it's opened up. I can't see that there'll be any problems with the drink and everythin' so everythin' is lookin' up at the moment. No temptations.

Say that one again about the temptation? – The temptation's not there. Drinks, cans of drink come into the house every day, uh, 'cos the wife still likes a drink. Um... I walk down the shop and even buy it for her, I've had a bottle of wine in the fridge for over a week now, that's still there, it's still got the cork in it, so there's no problems.

OK. Do you have a motto these days, an idea of how you want to get on? – Yeah, I've got me dreams but I just take one day at a time. Like if I get through to midnight tonight without havin' any trouble I'll be happy.

So 'day at a time' is your motto? – OK.

Is there any one thing you can say that helped you most? – Gettin' the confidence to talk about, I suppose. Well I'd kept it hidden for so many years and tried dealin' with it by meself, that was the hardest thing and I just keep thinkin' if only I'd opened me mouth all them years ago somethin' might have happened and me life might have been a little bit different.

OK. Anything else you want to add? – In the middle of all this I've managed to trace me natural mother and this has given me a big boost. And we are in frequent communication and it feels good.

OK. Now we've done this, gone through all the questions and that, how do you feel about me publishing it? – OK. No problems at all.

What do you want me to call you by way of a name, the other people have got a Christian name? – Yeah, just use me Christian name, whatever.

Your actual one? – Yeah, whatever.

Adrian was only funded for twelve sessions of counselling. The abuse had happened over three years, finishing twenty years before the counselling started. After the sessions finished, all his relationships collapsed and his temptation to drink got worse. His previous lifestyle meant that he had few friends to support him. His family didn't know whether to believe him when he told them about the abuse. Life got lonely and tough.

Thoughts About These Histories

I have gathered these interviews together to show as much as possible about how abuse affects real people and real lives. I think the idea of the questionnaires was reasonably successful. The interviews did not produce all the information I would have liked from the survivors. This was partly because I couldn't say it for them and ask them to agree. Although I could tell them what I wanted the book to say, I couldn't prompt them too much about their own personal details. But let me draw some points out of these real-life situations. I want these examples to show several things.

The tragedy of sexual abuse

The titles 'The Wasted Years' and 'Wishing my Life Away' say this very clearly. Each of the survivors' stories tells of the tragedy from their point of view. People who do not know about the abuse (or do not care about it) might just see 'drunks and druggies', layabouts and spongers, delinquents and criminals, liars and fighters, and so on, but these histories show the damage that child sexual abuse does to individuals and the consequences for society. Each individual tragedy must cost enormous amounts of money in health and social services, unemployment and other social security benefits, policing, legal aid, court and prison costs, educational costs, and so on, perhaps over the survivor's whole life – and this is in addition to their own personal struggles with the initial symptoms and the longer term consequences of the abuse.

The need for painkillers, like it or not

Four out of five survivors have used these for long periods, feeling they had no choice. Jenny took alcohol, prescribed medicines and street drugs. Adrian took hard drugs and then, later, alcohol. Anna took street drugs, including

LSD. Deni used whiskey and antidepressants. They all knew they were using these drugs (alcohol is a drug), and prescribed drugs from doctors, to blur the haunting ghosts of the past. Any hope of stopping the substance misuse needs to have the Post Traumatic Stress responses and the Circles of Confusion stopped first. This was why they started drinking and taking drugs in the first place. If these were going to come back again, perhaps worse, how could they even start to think about stopping their painkiller without some other painkiller to sort it out? Perhaps counselling can be a painkiller in its own way – hopefully with a permanent effect, not just a few hours at a time.

Drugs are not the only painkillers. Jenny's large number of animals (kept partly for pets, partly for breeding) was, in a way, a workaholic painkiller. Cheryl says 'I cut my wrists once, a case of causing pain to forget pain' – very much as mentioned in the poem *Why do I hurt myself?* (see page 108).

The anger and frustration

The titles 'Still Feel Like Killing Him' and 'Living With Hatred' show this clearly. Adrian speaks about revenge and refuses to hide his feelings about the abuser. Anna mentions 'it was deep rooted anger that was coming up for the first time…anger from years and years and years'. She also uses the word 'hatred', which is a stronger feeling than anger, to me. Jenny says that the only feelings she used to have were 'anger and suffering'. Now she has many more types of feelings. Deni talks about hitting herself with books or tools in the past. Deni also talked about feeling angry with her mother, about feeling like 'hitting back' at her. Cheryl seemed angry at her mother – though also frightened, originally, of her mother.

The depression and suicidal temptations

All five survivors had depression problems and suicidal thoughts at least once. Jenny and Adrian both say very clearly that they had thought about, or even tried, suicide. They had done this during depressions, with anger and frustration and pain all pushing them into such lonely misery that they couldn't see any point in life. Deni talks about being 'a wreck living in a big black void'. She also discusses suicide and an important point that she mentions briefly is that once she'd planned it, she didn't need to think about it, just decide to do it if she felt too miserable. Anna says that she tried several times and also did reckless and risky things without any care about whether she lived or not. Cheryl mentions an overdose and cutting her wrists.

The fears and confusions

Deni talks clearly about having a fear of men. Anna mentions being frightened several times – originally when it happened, when sexually assaulted as an adult, and even nowadays, in case she does something to make her new marriage go wrong. She tended to shut off and become a recluse (a hermit). Adrian repeats that he was frightened in the counselling in case it was a mistake and went wrong. Deni is clear that she has memory problems. Part of her doesn't want to remember because its all so frightening, another part desperately wants to understand what happened. Cheryl mentions confusion and tension 'build-up inside' her.

The distrust of professionals

Professionals are mentioned as being limited in how much they are usually able to help. This is often because these professionals did not seem to know how to recognise or react to the abuse. The help they did offer tended to be seen as failing to get to the bottom of the problem and a temporary thing, even as a bit of a nuisance. This was partly caused by the survivor's pessimism. The limited success of the help kept the survivor's pessimism alive. We do have to make some allowances for progress, however. Professionals were only beginning to take the battered baby research seriously twelve to fifteen years ago. Catching up with the research on sexual abuse only really started seven to ten years ago. So, before that it was true that professionals really didn't know how it happened and how bad it could be.

In her interview, Jenny hints at her previous attitude about professionals – which had been quite condemning. Adrian suggests that any counselling that does not have the abuse being a central issue will not get far. Deni says that her first counsellor used exactly the wrong approach. Anna points out that her parents were professionals, which prejudiced her against those she met later. She goes on to say that she met one, a doctor, who abused her even though she was an adult.

Each survivor shows different individual points of interest

Deni talks a bit about her relationship difficulties with her children. Cheryl mentions her work to Break the Chain. Anna talks about Triggers, and Cheryl mentions them briefly. Adrian talks about revenge and violence, though he hasn't done it. Jenny talks about crime and prostitution, which is useful because these issues do not appear anywhere else in this book. What is also useful is that Anna gives a good example of the Government Health Warning. In her case she gets more and more angry for a while until she realises that she should be angry and that, in a way, calms her down. Other people might get more and more sad or depressed or anxious.

Relationship issues

After the counselling Anna, Cheryl and Jenny all commented on relationship improvements. Anna feels 'more able to judge men individually' and puts herself on an equal footing. Cheryl has got married and the relationship is calmer. Jenny's marriage is a bit better, for her. Deni and Adrian, both feeling the need to continue counselling, still have relationship problems. Deni still wants no relationship and Adrian foresees the end of his fourth.

Intrusive memories

Cheryl, Jenny and Anna all report that they are less troubled by memories these days: 'It's not as sharp... I'm more able to cope and understand... I'm placid.' Jenny has a wider range of feelings, which she is pleased about. Deni remembers more but is less worried about it. For Adrian, it is all still very strong: 'twenty years it's been sat there – in me head... I would dearly love to see that man pay'.

The hope and humour on the horizon

It is also nice to see the little bits of hope and humour that creep into these interviews. The survivors were nervous, although they all knew me quite well. They were unsure how their words, feelings and lives would appear in print – a natural concern, I think. Even so, they made small jokes, smiled proudly, gave credit to the counselling for the help they had received and spoke hopefully about the future.

CHAPTER 6

Setting Up this Programme

In this book I am suggesting that we can collect a relatively small number of sensible descriptions (metaphors), in a 'plain language' manner (see page 49) and that these can be useful in guiding both counsellor and survivor in counselling (see The Guide in The Fogbank, page 91) through the confusion of thoughts and feelings and decisions that survivors of child sexual abuse meet on the road to recovery.

The metaphors are not a set of fixed regulations but a foundation of stepping stones for a pathway to health and happiness. The pathway is 'client-tailored' – it will be different for each survivor because their starting point, their personality, the problems and their goals are all different. However, most survivors will have more in common with each other – and other sorts of survivors – than they will with people who are not survivors of a major fright.

All the metaphors cover a definite issue, a particular area of the Fogbank we could say. Therefore, they are like fixed-shape stepping stones. This means they are easily recognised and reliable. This helps to make the process of counselling friendly and familiar. This is important to keep the counselling away from re-traumatising the survivor by unnecessarily amplifying their pain and uncertainty. We all get nervous about an unfamiliar treatment, even if we are convinced it is for our own good. This seems natural. Very few of us doubt how normal it is to feel nervous before a visit to the dentist! We all appreciate reassurance from the familiar in such situations.

These tools may also reduce the counsellors' uncertainties about helping abuse victims. Counsellors can get nervous about making things worse and letting the survivor down. They can worry about getting upset if their own feelings and responses get too strong. These metaphors will help counsellors familiarise themselves with the issues involved in counselling adult survivors of child sexual abuse.

Programme Development

Getting this programme running takes a lot of effort, it is not a straight-forward project. It concerns what is still an unpopular subject. It requires a lot of support. It needs staff, finance, time, effort and survivors willing to join. It is a large project if all the components are used. Setting this up has some practical implications that are worth mentioning. It makes sense to start with the core components and then add on the other bits when the time/funds/staff/need is appropriate.

It seems to be important to consider the sorts of locations where this sort of programme can be developed. It may sit better in some settings than in others. I feel an important factor is the way survivors will view the programme, especially whether it is safe. Safety often depends on independence from any forces that survivors think might make things get more painful and more difficult. This might include the abuser, family and spouse and even professionals.

Statutory organisations

Statutory organisations are those that the government has said must be provided by law: such as the health services, social services and the probation service. Setting up this sort of programme in a social services or mental health setting is likely to put some people off. Many think that a social worker will interfere with their relationship with their children. We have to remember that this is (currently) one of their jobs, where necessary. We also need to remember that a social worker (or equivalent, NSPCC or police officer) may have failed them in childhood. This may not be fair – these professionals may not have had a chance to help. But survivors may have strong feelings about them all the same. Also, many survivors are worried by the thought of seeing a psychiatrist. They may already be convinced enough that they are going crazy (because of the Post Traumatic Stress symptoms) and try to keep away in case they get locked up. *In other words, they will actively avoid those services that have psychiatrists or social workers involved.*

For survivors with other problems that already involve the social or psychiatric services, it may help to have services within these organisations.

They may be 'closer' and more accessible than those provided by an entirely separate organisation.

Statutory organisations receive funds to do their work. Much of this money goes into paying for professionals to work with those who need the help. Although there is no law that says that survivors of child sexual abuse should be given all the treatment they want, few organisations would admit to refusing to help. However, most organisations are very stretched and have little money to go round. If survivors don't ask loudly for help, they are not likely to get much help. Statutory organisations do not search for people to help unless they are forced to by law. Often, the result of all these issues is that statutory organisations could and should help, but often don't help more than a few survivors – although they would like to do more, they have not got the time, money, professional training or experience.

Voluntary organisations

Voluntary organisations are created by choice, not by law. They can also offer help to various people, usually in different ways to the statutory organisations. Most are specialist organisations concentrating on small areas of problem, for example particular diseases, alcohol abuse, suicidal thoughts, debts and housing problems, marriage and relationship problems, etc. We set up our first full programme in the voluntary sector. That is, we started off a whole new organisation for it and applied successfully for charity status as a non-profit making organisation. We then looked to take referrals of survivors from social services and health services as well as from survivors making their own enquiries after seeing a poster, leaflet or newspaper article.

Voluntary organisations usually have funding problems because they have to search for financial support to do everything. They have to make their own income, somehow. This can lead to a lot of insecurity among the staff and survivors about the safety of the organisation. This slows down trust building and adds to the financial and emotional costs. In a perfect world, we might set up several programmes in different settings to make it accessible to different sets of survivors and to take advantage of the different funding possibilities.

Development Difficulties

There are some areas in the development of a real-life programme that can often be difficult. I thought it was best to offer some ideas and answers here.

Difficulties starting the counselling

There are some difficulties for the counsellor.

ENCOURAGING ENQUIRIES FROM SURVIVORS

This stage needs publicity if you are to encourage enquiries from the public. Leaflets, newssheets, adverts, posters, publicity stunts, newspaper articles, and so on, all contribute to attracting the attention of survivors (and fund donors too). A different way to organise this is to arrange referrals through other sources – doctors, phone helplines, colleague organisations, and so on – then publicity is not necessarily needed. Helping survivors get from enquiring to a first meeting is an important step to work on. Giving choice and control is vital.

ENCOURAGING HOPE IN THE SURVIVOR

Also important in these early stages is giving hope. This can be difficult as survivors are usually very aware of the Monty Python Foot (see page 89) so it can be a good idea to discuss this over the phone, or by letter if they prefer that method of communication. It is sometimes worth admitting that 'Keep your hopes up' is potentially dangerous advice (see The Bruise, The Boomerang and The Monty Python Foot, pages 85, 105 and 89), like 'Trust me' (see page 148).

ENCOURAGING PROFESSIONAL COMMITMENT

Some survivors have powerful professionals involved with them by the time they make contact with the programme. Also, the organisation's funding structure may require contact with professionals. Describing the organisation and meeting professionals' doubts (especially if the organisation is in the voluntary sector) will be important. It is worth telling professionals wishing to run this sort of programme that they will not always get co-operation – many statutory workers are suspicious of 'cowboy outfits' they do not know already. This area needs short- and long-term work.

Difficulties during the counselling

In a programme of this length there is plenty of time for things to go wrong that will affect the counselling.

Sometimes, survivors have been hanging on for grim death by their fingertips. Then, as they enter the programme, the discussions open up so much feeling and confusion that they feel very much worse and can get extremely anxious about this. This can then make their professional supporters anxious too, which can lead to a withdrawal of their support and even the survivor giving up on the programme.

It is important to mention the Government Health Warning (see page 110) to professionals to prepare them for this possibility. Plain and simple reasoning for it must be offered to ensure the 'worsening' is not taken out of context, especially over painkillers.

PARTNER AND FAMILY DISTRESS

Most survivors have a current partner or a family, very few live completely alone. A few still live with their parents – some of whom might have been abusers, some might not. Let us leave current and old abusers aside for the moment. The people who live with the survivor may go through some 'ups and downs' as the survivor finds her way around The Fogbank. These ups and downs can occasionally stress the family a great deal and the difficulties can grow to serious sizes.

Sometimes this is because the survivor is more busy with sorting out personal things than she used to be and partners and children can feel ignored; or she gets more assertive and this can rock the relationship.

Support for the family is an important area to consider. Perhaps the most important thing to say to them is that most of the new problems are related to times in the survivor's past before she met her partner or had the children. In other words, her moods or problems are often not personal – even if they feel that they are. (We must check this before getting too far into this discussion.) This can make it easier for all of them. The survivor may feel less guilty about being snappy or moody. Partners and children know they do not have any major mistakes to apologise for. People can stop guessing what's wrong and what to do about it. It is easier to see it as a temporary rough patch caused by the counselling waking up unhappy memories that had been asleep but still uncomfortable – like an arm with pins and needles in the middle of the night.

Supporting the family means that the programme has to be able to work with people beyond the survivor. This needs time and funds, travel and skills. It needs to be built into the programme. *ASCSA* has considered running a quarterly 'families meeting' to give a little support on a more regular basis.

This would be more of a foundation to build on when a crisis happens in a family than meeting relatives for the first time when things have got very difficult.

RETURN OF THE REALITY OF THE ABUSE

There are times when the abuse returns in significant events from the 'outside world'. For instance, a court action may force a survivor to be a witness about something, or someone, connected to the abuse (even if the abuse is not the issue in the court). The survivor may decide to try to take the abuser to court to 'restore the balance of fairness' as part of their progress in sorting it all out. A parent (abuser or other) may become elderly and start to relive parts of the past. For instance, I heard a woman say that the hardest thing she had to do was to listen to her elderly mother recount the beatings she had had from her husband (the abuser) without telling her mother that he had sexually abused her. Another woman visited her senile mother regularly and was frightened rigid when her mother shouted 'Stop fidgeting!' in exactly the same way she had done 45 years earlier.

These 'invasions' have to be weathered. Some might be easier to get through if nature or illness is clearly the cause. Even so, these 'invasions' can feel as though they are sending the survivor back a few steps in the progress they have made. But, having got through these setbacks, we should encourage the survivor to take some extra pride in that achievement.

Difficulties finishing the counselling

Finishing off counselling after a year or two is probably similar to completing any other counselling relationship. However, it is important to take extra care over it because of the great importance survivors put on the counselling. To lose it before they feel ready could bring back a lot of helplessness originally caused by the abuse.

FEAR OF HELPLESSNESS

It is right that they should feel vulnerable and dependent upon the counselling in the middle stages. This is true for most people going through counselling anyway. We hope they will not feel this at the end. Sorting out the ending may take some weeks of discussion. Sometimes, some individual time is useful. I mentioned other methods of staying in contact earlier.

FEAR OF FAILING (AGAIN!)

The degree of half-hidden dependency that the survivor may feel during the counselling programme may echo the abusive relationship in some ways. It is the process of letting The Wall down (slowly, a bit at a time). This dependency is a necessary stage, it allows survivors to re-discover trust and develop confidence in their opinions and judgements of other people. However, it is a high-vulnerability time when survivors feel they are taking enormous risks. We also have to remember that it was at precisely such a vulnerable and trusting stage that the abuse trap took hold so the finishing period will have echoes of this and will shake the confidence they have developed so far. 'Have I done the right thing?', 'Can I trust the counsellor?', 'Will I make a fool of myself, again?' are all too familiar questions (Circles) for the survivor. Poem A2 on page 24 in the Introduction shows this well. This dependency may make this counselling a bit more difficult to bring to a close than other types of counselling.

FEAR OF ISOLATION

I think it is useful to avoid a sharp cut-off from the self-exploration and relationship-changing process. It is important to suggest ways in which Survivors can continue to grow and develop like other people. Writing poems and short autobiographical stories can be therapeutic, either by clearing the air, or simply confirming the person. They can then be 'sent' to other sufferers, perhaps through the counsellor or through a support network or newsheet. These poems can then help others build up the courage to start their own counselling path. They can get through The Fogbank and let in a little sunlight – Hope.

Aftercare becomes an important issue. Occasional contact with the counsellor or group will reassure them. They can see that the continued counselling activity means the ideas and the work are still worthwhile. This idea will seem unusual and even wrong to some counsellors. The usual aim for counselling is to encourage complete independence. It is ours here too. The issue is the speed at which survivors can be 'launched into the real world'. It is almost as though this is their first time on their own two feet. A woman half way through her recovery said 'I think I'm a forty-year-old teenager' (see the Case Example on page 123). Later, she asked 'Am I trying to run before I can walk?' as her doctor signed her as unable to work because of depression. The depression had been lifting, things had been changing, confidence, interest and excitement about life had been building. She wanted to start a vocational training course but the paperwork the state needed to allow her to do this eventually defeated her. The doctor heard the distress in her voice and responded. The voice had been the 'little girl again'. She was distressed to hear herself return to this voice.

Skill Development

The process of getting used to doing counselling by this programme takes effort and time. It is likely to be more difficult for the better-trained and/or longer-experienced counsellors simply because it is new learning. For the less-trained, the temptation to rote-learn the metaphors must be avoided. Survivors are people. People feel more cared for if the explanation is thought about while discussed. Mechanically reciting the metaphors will put people off too much, too fast. A programme might never recover.

It may be important to say that some people who are training or trained as counsellors find it too difficult to use these metaphors. This may be because they are too used to other methods of work and the metaphors they use (e.g. The Unconscious, The Conditioning Process, The Relaxation Method, etc) or it might be because they are too used to facts and figures and feel uncomfortable with approaches using empathy (but facts and figures are metaphors too) or it might be that they feel the metaphors given above are in some way wrong for them. Whatever seems wrong, it is better to admit it and decide not to use this programme than to misuse it.

These metaphors are not a replacement for counselling training. They are intended to help experienced counsellors familiarise themselves with the issues relevant to this area of work. This use of the metaphors takes confidence as a counsellor as well as creativity and experimentation. It does not come easily to everyone.

There are some other issues that will concern most counsellors trying this approach that we can identify reasonably easily.

Recognising relevant metaphors

Survivors often talk in hints and clues. They are understandably nervous about committing themselves openly to the thoughts and feelings about the abuse and their responses to it. They are frightened of the consequences: this is The Trap. Counsellors have to learn to 'tune in' to the issues that the metaphors describe. They are best used in the flow of discussion – in response to, and in confirmation of, the survivor's interest in that area. The discussion is not forced into a series of steps, each with it's own metaphor, unless this is completely necessary. One time when it might be necessary is in the first few introductory meetings if the survivor is unable to talk. Listening is then OK.

The metaphors used should always be related to something a client has said, hinted at or appears to feel. In this last case, counsellors should mention that they are guessing. It is OK to say it is an informed guess based on what other survivors have said about the subject. We can say something like: 'I am guessing that you feel like…and I'm going to talk about it because it is an important area to understand. Please tell me if I'm guessing wrong'. This keeps the work in a 'client-paced' approach.

Timing the use of the metaphors

When a survivor starts to talk about something we recognise and have a metaphor for, it is important not to crash over the point they wanted to make just because *we* know what we're talking about. This is a danger when we are new to the programme and want to use the metaphors. Equally, it is a danger when we are tired and thoughtless or when we are in danger of getting bored because we have worked the programme for too many years. Apologising for having so much to say can be useful in restoring the empowerment balance. It is especially important to explain why we use the metaphors in the earliest meetings. This is simply done: 'I want to reassure you as quickly as I can that nowadays we know quite a lot about how sexual abuse happens and what it does to people'.

Using any spontaneous humour helps us avoid the approach becoming mechanical and allowing slightly off-subject remarks from time to time also helps. Adapting the metaphors to fit the survivor's circumstances is also important, making them as personally relevant as possible. Another way to stop the counselling session sound like primary school is by offering a small degree of personal disclosure about non-sexual matters. For example, the counsellor's own creativity problems or ability to laugh at him/herself and so on may make the situation more familiar and reassuringly human.

AMENDING AND CREATING NEW METAPHORS

Each new survivor in counselling is unique and each programme is newly constructed with him or her. What is most important is that the metaphors make sense to the survivor and use her language if appropriate. It is no good fighting over whose metaphor is 'right'! They both become 'wrong' and the fight is damaging to the counselling relationship. It can be OK to agree that when one uses a particular name for a metaphor, the other remembers that he/she calls the same metaphor by a different name. In individual counselling the survivor's name should be used. In group counselling the counsellor's name should provide more common ground for all members.

METAPHORS FOR THE HERE-AND-NOW

While many of the metaphors describe events in the past, we can adapt them to situations in the present. As someone is considering a relationship we can use The Compass (see page 112) to point forward rather than back, The Crossroads (see page 103) to decide what sort of relationship they want and The Garden Gate (see page 122) to remind them that they may still be testing the water for a while.

Further Developments

Wider uses for metaphors

Often, we use the metaphors for descriptions of the abuse and the normal human response to it. They can help for current complications too.

For example, an area that often comes up is that of marital and parenting relationships. The Same/Different/Opposite metaphor helps here and leads on to 'Designing a New Future'. We can respond to crises of faith, creativity or identity with The Crossroads metaphor if this is relevant. When people seem to be testing the water with some area of change, The Garden Gate can lay a basis for a lot of work.

Sometimes, the context of the counselling itself can be important to discuss as well. The Fogbank is a useful one to return to as a reminder of where the survivor started. The idea of the counsellor as The Guide can lead into talking over the survivor's current need for a guide and whether it is less than it was before.

We could use many of the metaphors for other forms of child abuse. Feeling trapped is a common theme and we should remember that sexual abuse contains an element of emotional abuse – as do neglect and physical abuse.

6.1: Case example – Metaphors and poems can help with other abuse

One father in his mid-forties was brought to counselling by his wife, who was fed up with losing her temper at their children. As she talked about what made her lose her temper, it became clearer that her husband's emotional problems prevented him from asserting himself over discipline issues and prompted him to undermine her efforts. He came to the counselling, accepted what his wife felt and asked if it could all stem from childhood physical and emotional abuse by his step-father. We explored this using the relevant metaphors and some poems that focused on non-sexual aspects of rejection, isolation, violence and pain. It rapidly made a difference to him, the marriage and the children.

Wider implications for professionals

This programme has implications for all professionals who help people who might be survivors. It raises questions like:

do professionals ask about it often enough?

do they know how to ask in encouraging ways?

do they know what to do next?

Child abuse is still a difficult subject for many professionals. Because it is so disturbing and so difficult to help with, many professionals delay their training in this subject. In the past, training has often been about statistics and photographs of physically abused children. These may shock professionals into being aware but it can make them more worried about the subject. It can also lead to arguments about statistics, politics, sexism and so on, which get in the way of helping professionals, trying to deal with the practicalities in their real working world.

This programme can be used to train professionals for the practical world where they may meet survivors and try to help them. It can help to explain how sexual abuse happens and what it does to children, in just the same way as it helps with survivors and their relatives. That level of understanding makes helping a lot easier. Different professionals have to help in different ways: some refer patients to specialists, some do a little general counselling and others can do more.

Still growing

As the years go by and we continue to use the method, it does not lie still. Because it is usually going on in a group of people, its various parts get used in different amounts at different times. Some metaphors are only used occasionally, some often. Some may be used so rarely that they become an endangered species. I have wondered whether those ones should be taken out of circulation. Does their rare use mean they aren't effective or they aren't relevant any more? Perhaps.

And new metaphors come into being. Someone says something that triggers off a thought that gets put into words as a story. The story has a start, middle and finish that make it different from the usual free-flowing conversation and sharing of opinion. This usually happens when someone is trying to explain something that they are not clear about (or when someone else isn't understanding well).

BLACK FOREST GATEAU

A new metaphor, developing as the book's writing is developing: 'Imagine being given a large slice of Black Forest Gateau, just when you were ready and interested and hungry. Wonderful! But compare that with being ordered to eat a whole cake in double-quick time when you really didn't want to. It was too much at the wrong time, in the wrong way...'

STEPPING-STONES IN THE BOG

In discussing the idea of making progress (and for most survivors it is an idea, not a fact), various metaphors come up for discussion. One that we've found useful is the idea of stepping-stones toward wherever they want to be. When they are starting out all they can see is the bog. Later, when they have made some progress, they can look back and see the stepping-stones they've been on.

In a given group, the members will have preferences as to which version or alternative of a given metaphor they like. So, The Fogbank becomes The Pit and the Wall becomes The Plastic Coffin. In some way the group will become a little different to previous ones, and yet I think it will still be tackling the same issues, the same human difficulties.

This ebb and flow of use makes this method a living and growing one. It will never stay still for long. It will alter and change bit by bit and this is right. There is no one fixed set of metaphors that are 'the only right ones'. While the central ideas are unlikely to go out of use, the precise nature of the metaphors explaining them is very likely to change.

APPENDIX I

Questions For Case Histories

This interview

Are you willing to be interviewed with the questions shown?

Are you willing to allow this interview to be published?

The abuse

What happened? (briefly)

What did you do to cope? – use painkillers? (which?)

Before the counselling

What was life like?

What did you do to cope? – use painkillers (which?)

How did you decide to start counselling?

During counselling

What was it like to start counselling?

What were your turning points?

How do you remember your changes?

    quick/slow

    easy/difficult

    continuous/bit at a time

    step-wise/smooth climb/faster and faster/chaotic/chaotic steps

    understandable/confusing at the time

    nerve-racking/calm and sensible

    got used to it/always surprised

    planned stages/a series of surprises

    exciting/scary

    confidence building/confidence draining

What did you use to get through the changes?

    confidence/determination/courage/painkillers

Did you use an *ASCSA* Group/*ASCSA* counselling?

Did the Group help?

    at first/in the middle/towards the end

    a lot/a little

or hinder your progress?

Was the group enough or did you need more?

If you didn't use the group, why not?

Of the various things we did, what helped most?

at the beginning
in the middle
toward the end

Of the various things we did not do, what helped most?

at the beginning
in the middle
toward the end

Is there one thing that we did or did not do you could say was crucial?
Is there anything we didn't do that would have helped?
Is there anything we could have done better?

Nowadays

MEMORIES

How much do you remember about what happened to you?
How often do you remember these things nowadays?
Is this more or less than before any counselling?
Does this effect you more or less or differently than before any counselling?

FEELINGS

How much do you get strong feelings about what happened to you?
How often do you get strong feelings nowadays?
Is this more or less than before any counselling?
Does this effect you more or less or differently than before any counselling?

BEHAVIOUR

Have other things changed?

Use of alcohol/other drugs/doctors medications
Depressions/self-harm/suicidal thoughts/suicide attempts
Relationship with husband/men in general, wife/women in general, generally, sexually,
Your children,
Your old family (non-abusing),your old family (abuser(s)), abuser(s) not in the family.
Education
Employment
Health care of yourself, of your children
Relationship with professionals: doctor, social worker, psychiatric nurse, health visitor, psychologist/other counsellors
Your plans for yourself, for your children, for your marriage/relationship
Your motto

What helped you most?

Leaflet 1

WHAT IT REALLY MEANS AND HOW TO SPOT IT

Being assertive means:	*It means avoiding:*
Deciding what we want	Beating about the bush
Asking for things clearly	Being a bully
Taking risks	Calling people names
Being calm and relaxed	Bottling up feelings
Expressing feelings openly	Being a doormat
Giving and taking compliments easily	Being over-suspicious
Giving and taking fair criticism	Going behind backs

TO SPOT ASSERTIVENESS, WATCH OUT FOR...

Aggressive	Passive	Assertive
Shouting	Whining	Calm & controlled
Loud voice	Soft voice	Clear & distinct
Clenched hands	Wringing hands	Relaxed posture
Pointing finger	Shuffling feet	Still & steady
Glaring eyes	Downcast eyes	Direct interested eyes
Folded arms	Stooped back	Upright posture
"You'd better...	"Would you mind if...	"How can we sort this?
"Stupid!	"Sorry...very sorry...	"What do you think?
Nagging & prying	Expecting failure	Interested & hopeful

So Practice these!

BEING ASSERTIVE

There are 3 main ways to behave when facing people in difficult situations:

Passive   This is when you allow someone else to shout you down, boss you about, tell you off - even when they have no right to, its only their temper, you haven't done anything wrong.

Aggressive   This is when you shout back louder, quicker, and more often, or use physical force when faced with a difficult situation - even if someone else started it.

Assertive   This is when you stay calm, remember you have nothing to be ashamed of, say what you want, keep out of rows you don't want to get into, walk away from a situation that's getting nowhere.

Being Assertive is between passive and aggressive, it is not passive or aggressive.

Being Assertive is most likely to solve problems and calm people down.

Being Assertive at work comes from knowing your job, knowing you have authority to command or instruct, being confident that you are doing your best.

Being assertive at home comes from knowing what you want, knowing you have the right to ask for it, being sure you are doing your best, even in difficult circumstances!

Being assertive will help when you are facing anger, unfairness, disappointment, anxiety, fear, depression. It will help you look after yourself and make a happier and healthier future.

Practice will help.

Try it out when you can. Pat yourself on the back when some of it works.

Remember the bits that work: use them again.

TO PRACTICE THIS, TRY TO:

BE CLEAR: KNOW WHAT YOU WANT BEFORE YOU ASK.
BE SPECIFIC: SAY EXACTLY WHAT YOU WANT, AND ONLY THAT.
BE DIRECT: USE DEFINITE WORDS, LIKE "WANT, WILL, TOGETHER".
BE CONFIDENT: YOU CAN ACT PROPERLY AT HOME AND IN YOUR JOB.

ASCSA
ADULT SURVIVORS
OF
CHILD SEXUAL ABUSE
AN INDEPENDENT ORGANISATION FOR
SUPPORT

c/o 4 West Street, Ryde, Isle of Wight, P033 2NN
Registered Charity 1043154

CONSTITUTION, POLICY AND AIMS

Introduction

This organisation has been set up because it is likely that there are many adult survivors on the Island who do not receive any help with emotional problems they may have.

National research suggests that most adult survivors do have emotional problems, which get in the way of ordinary life. This can make happy and healthy relationships with their original family, partners, and children very difficult.

Local research suggests that there may be hundreds of adult survivors on the Isle of Wight who have not yet received any help. This is not unusual: most adult survivors try to hide their emotional problems as much as possible. This is a normal reaction coming from embarrassment and fear of the consequences.

ASCSA is for Island people who were sexually abused who want help with it all.

ASCSA is independent and confidential.

ASCSA Philosophy

Adult survivors deserve help with the emotional problems that can often come from their abuse as a child. This should be offered in as open and approachable a way as possible, and without making additional worries.

The help should be offered in as simple and reassuring way as possible. It is important to avoid making anyone feel worse about themselves for seeking help.

Aims and Objectives

ASCSA aims to offer a counselling service through a discussion group for adult women survivors to help them recover, and through them to help keep their family as happy and healthy as possible.

ASCSA hopes to offer a supportive community network service to adult male survivors where possible, and may be able to do more in the future.

ASCSA also provides leaflets, quarterly Newsheets, professional articles, lectures and seminars about its work.

Constitution of the Group

The group has a written constitution which is agreed by all members when they join. This is intended to help all members start from an equal place, to ensure their safety within the group, and encourage them to make best use of the group.

The Aim of the Group

To provide safe place for survivors to share their feelings, seek and offer support, and help each other through life's difficulties.

Group Rules

Briefly these include:

1. The group is voluntary,
2. the group is confidential,
3. the group will protect the vulnerable,
4. the group will choose its own character,
5. the group will encourage members to apply for compensation,
6. the group will contribute to an evaluation of its usefulness.

We hope that *ASCSA* helps: we want it to.

As a charity, the group is provided free to all group members and there is no charge for enquiries. *ASCSA* is totally dependent on grants.

Dave Simon, Director, 12/1/95

HOW COUNSELLING CAN HELP AFTER SEXUAL ABUSE

A SHORT LEAFLET TO EXPLAIN HOW TALKING ABOUT FEELINGS CAN HELP

This leaflet is intended for people over the age of 10 or so. It may also help people caring for younger children.

CONTENTS:
WHAT SEXUAL ABUSE DOES TO PEOPLE
WHAT DOES THIS LEAD ON TO?
HOW DOES TALKING HELP?
WHAT ACTUALLY HAPPENS IN COUNSELLING?
WHERE TO GET COUNSELLING

WHAT SEXUAL ABUSE DOES TO PEOPLE

One of the difficult things that sexual abuse does to people is to make them feel as though they are the odd one out. They think they are the only one who feels so bad and so confused about it all. This is partly because they don't know anyone else who has been abused, so they can't compare their reactions.

When a child or teenager is abused, they are stuck in a frightening situation. The results of this fright are very similar to those of anyone else who has had too much to cope with. After wards, car crashes, muggings, and kidnaps, people of all ages and both sexes end up with the same reactions, considering what has happened.

Nightmares, memories, sudden tears or tempers; avoiding the person or place; sleeping, eating, relaxation problems; can't concentrate, too jumpy, feeling hopeless; lose interest in school or work, hobbies or pets.

WHAT DOES THIS LEAD ON TO?

As well as feeling lonely, miserable and confused, people who have been abused spend a lot of time trying to understand it all. But sexual abuse is almost always difficult to sort out. Sometimes the normal reactions make this more difficult and lead on to feeling hopeless about understanding it.

These things can make people feel worse: it gets tempting to doubt memories and wonder if it really happened that way. Many people doubt themselves so much they begin to think they must be stupid or even mad.

With these feelings they usually hide it all away as much as possible. They might start to drink or smoke too much, eat too much (or not enough), feel so desperate they hurt themselves, give up on relationships with their friends, partners, family and children.

When these things go wrong too, they are often tempted to say "I knew it would all go wrong – it's no good trying, I'm useless". So the next time they try to sort things out, they only try halfheartedly... and it doesn't work...

They begin to think that life is like that... and they hate it.

These are also NORMAL reactions.

HOW DOES TALKING HELP?

Sexual abuse can only be done in a few ways, and nowadays counsellors know about these. This knowledge has grown over the past 5 to 10 years. Before that, it was not really understood very well.

Knowing how it usually happens makes it possible for us to know what it does to people. With this information, we can reassure people who have been abused, and their families and carers, about their reactions. We can reassure them that they are not alone – there are many others who have very similar feelings.

WHAT ACTUALLY HAPPENS IN COUNSELLING?

It is useful to separate three stages of talking:

1. How it usually happens and what it does to people – at the time and later.

2. What people actually want to sort out.

3. Helping people get to grips with these changes.

There is no magic wand for all this: it takes time. It needs the courage and determination that people who have survived sexual abuse have, even if they are low in confidence. We rarely talk about what actually happened during the abuse. We go slowly and gently. In a way, there's no rush. It's better to get it right. So we go step by step, when people are ready, at their pace.

What we do is guide people around the tangles that need to be sorted out, and help them find answers. We can give hope that it is possible to change things. We can give moral support to say that victims of child abuse have not done wrong. We can help people sort out where the confusions have come from.

One of the difficult things that sexual abuse does to people is to make them feel as though they are the odd one out. They think they must be the only one who feels so bad. Sometimes, it helps to introduce people to others who have been through similar experiences, by letter or in a group, so that they can reassure themselves that they have reacted to it all in the normal way. They can also listen to each other's answers to problems and help each other with new ideas too.

Counselling is always as confidential as possible: we make as much privacy as we can. Sometimes we have to stop and consider any children who might be being abused nowadays. If we hear of any, we have to make sure they get help: they need to be protected.

WHERE TO GET COUNSELLING

Ask for a list from Social Services, Doctors, or the CAB.

ASCSA: Adult Survivors of Child Sexual Abuse

This is an island charity which holds weekly group counselling meetings in Newport. It is free, independent and confidential.

Contact Dave Simon & Veronica Temple 614795 to ask questions, request leaflets, or arrange an appointment to hear more details.

APPENDIX IV

Reactions to a Fright

After any fright people often react in similar ways. The fright could be from bad news, an accident or an assault, or a sudden family crisis. Frightening situations affect us greatly.

Sometimes people worry about the way they are reacting, and become concerned by their normal reactions to fright. Occasionally, they expect to recover quicker than they do and get upset because of this disappointment. Other times people worry about another member of the family, if they are reacting differently, or seem 'out of character', or seem not to be reacting at all. Recovery is not something that can be easily rushed. This information sheet will help you recognise the normal reactions.

SHOCK

This is almost always the first reaction: you can't believe it's happened, you think it's all a dream, you feel numb. It can go on for quite a while: from hours to weeks or months. People can sometimes mistake this shock for calmness, and continue to expect you to cope well from then on. Other people may tell you to "wake up" and "get a grip".

The good thing about this stage is it gets you through the ordinary day without too much upset to begin with. It slows down your reaction, gives you a bit of time to adjust.

ANGER

This stage often comes second, but may come after SADNESS. It can range from anger towards the person who caused the fright, to anger at yourself, relatives or friends, – or even towards the professionals helping you. This can push you towards fighting for your rights, or for someone else. It can make you a bit rash, or seem to act out of character if you are usually shy or quiet. During this time you might find yourself a bit accident prone because you are distracted by it all.

This anger is normal and comes at some stage for almost everyone.

SADNESS

This often comes after the ANGER, but can come before it, or together, or swapping over – first one then the other, perhaps changing quickly, which can be very confusing. The sadness is very understandable, but is not always welcome as people sometimes want to be getting on with life and looking forward instead of back. Tears let the pain out and start you adjusting to the new situation.

The sadness can last a long time, on and off, depending on what started it and how you feel about it. Sometimes the sadness comes back out of the blue and feels just as bad as the first time, but this usually happens less often in time. You may become prone to illness.

GETTING USED TO IT

After a time, people get used to the new way their life is to be. If it was a small fright, you may be able to forget about it. When it's been a big fright, or went on for a long time, many people say that they never "get over it", but they do get used to it. Even while things are settling down, the ANGER or SADNESS might sometimes suddenly pop up unexpectedly. If the fright was fairly small for you, you should feel more-or-less yourself within 4 weeks.

Different people have these different feelings in different orders. There is no right way: only what is OK for you. It is usual to be unsure quite how you will cope.

You may go through them in a step-by-step way, or chopping and changing all the time, which can be very confusing. While this may be especially worrying to many people, it is the way some people get changing quickly.

You may have different lengths of time in the different sorts of feelings and this may depend on your usual personality – whether you are used to showing anger and sadness, and which you prefer – or people around you and how they react to the fright, or to your reactions.

You might even miss out any of the first three "stages": this does not usually matter.

Remember, family members might react in different ways too. Don't be surprised if some get on other's nerves about "not caring enough" or "not getting on with things soon enough". You can expect more family rows than usual. Changes of routine are normal for a while. Young children may get more aggressive than usual, or may go very quiet to try and protect adults from upset. Elderly people may get very confused, or may suddenly "come alive".

If the fright was especially serious for you, there might be some other reactions as well. For instance, you might not be able to sleep properly, feel very tense and jumpy, or unable to concentrate. You might have bad dreams or day dreams that come out of the blue about the upsetting events. You become very sensitive to hearing other people's problems – more so if they are similar to your own. You might worry that you have forgotten some aspects of what happened, or keep wanting to avoid places and people that remind you of it. Recent frights sometimes bring back old ones: memories or feelings can return and complicate things.

These reactions will usually fade away in time. The more serious it was for you, regardless of how you think anyone else would react, the longer it might take. Different people react differently: there is no correct pattern of reactions, or time it should take.

REMEMBER: EVERYONE RECOVERS IN THEIR OWN WAY
BE GENTLE WITH YOURSELF

APPENDIX V

Questionnaires and Statistics

Post Traumatic Stress Questionnaire

This questionnaire is usually printed on one side of A4 paper. It is smaller here so it may be difficult to read and it would seem awkward to write comments and notes on it.

POST TRAUMATIC STRESS RESPONSES

Name;   Date:

A.   Traumatic event(s)

B.   RE-EXPERIENCING

1.   Distressing memories *repeatedly* getting in the way of ordinary life

2.   Distressing dreams *repeatedly* waking you up - nightmares

3.   Flashbacks; suddenly finding yourself back there as though it was happening again

4.   Intense distress when meeting or seeing something similar, or meaning the same

C.   PERSISTENT AVOIDANCE

1. Trying hard to avoid thoughts & feelings about it all

2. Trying hard to avoid situations or activities or people or places that remind you of it

3. Getting upset because you can't remember some important aspect of what happened

4. Serious/sudden loosing interest in important activities (work, hobbies, skills, pets, etc.)

5. Feeling separate from the rest of the world, being isolated and lonely, even in a crowd

6. Unable to have some feelings; they disappear, feel blunt or stuck in a vice

7. Unable to see far into the future, expecting things to go wrong more that usual

D. PERSISTENT NERVOUSNESS

1. Difficulty in falling asleep, or staying asleep

2. More irritable, or having more outbursts of anger

3. More difficulty in concentrating

4. Always watching or listening out for someone or something

5. Very easily startled; much more jumpy than usual

6. Bodily feelings and reactions to similar events (shakes, butterflies, headaches, pains)

E. DURATION

Less than one month   6 months or more delay; delayed onset

More than one month   6 months or more presence; long term

OTHER REACTIONS

Post Traumatic Stress Statistics

The chart below shows the percentages of how often I found each symptom in 89 survivors I have asked using the questionnaire.

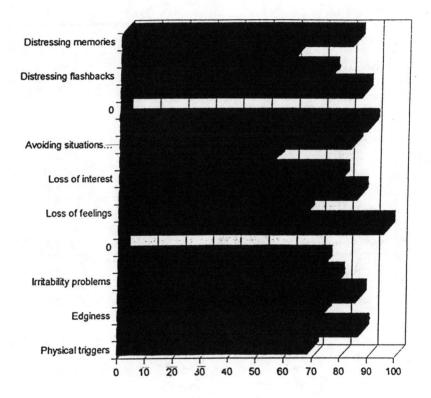

Figure B.1: PTSR Statistics – Symptoms from the questionnaire

The table of figures shows the percentage of each symptom in the order of the most often found at the top and the least often found at the bottom. Although these are statistics (a dirty word for many people) they can show us some interesting things. This table gives a better picture than the previous chart as we can see that pessimism (that is, hopelessness) is the most frequent and forgetting is the least frequent. So, the biggest reaction is an attitude problem and the smallest concerns memories.

Symptom	%
Pessimism	95
Avoiding thoughts	88
Mental distress triggers	86
Jumpiness	86
Feelings of isolation	85
Concentration problems	85
Distressing memories	84
Avoiding situations	83
Loss of interest	79
Irritability problems	77
Distressing flashbacks	73
Sleep problems	72
Edginess	71
Physical triggers	69
Loss of feelings	65
Distressing nightmares	60
Forgetting aspects	52

Figure B.2: PTSR Statistics — In order of frequency

This shows the percentage of survivors who have each overall number of symptoms. We can see that quite a percentage have all seventeen symptoms, none have less than nine and the mathematical average is thirteen. In a little more detail, we can look at the percentages having one, two, three or four of the first group of responses – the memory problems and 'intrusive phenomena'.

In each category we can see a few survivors who had no symptoms. But in each category we see that the majority had most of the symptoms. All the seventeen

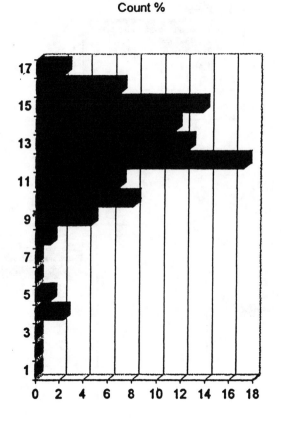

Figure B.3: PTSR Statistics – Number of symptoms per survivor

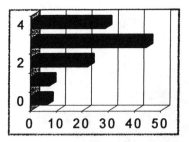

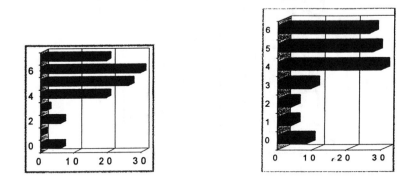

Figure B.4: PTSR Statistics – Three categories

different responses can be seen in the group of survivors. All the different combinations can be seen too. Some survivors have more memory symptoms, others are bothered more by avoidance behaviours and others have more nervousness problems. The variety is endless, very few people have the same pattern. Everyone has their own set of responses. There is no one combination that everyone should have.

Some of the other problems associated with the Post Traumatic Stress responses are shown here. They are a mixture of problems and painkillers (remember that some painkillers bring their own problems too!).

We can see that depression is the highest at 81 per cent, followed by sexual and relationship problems, then alcohol misuse and suicide attempts.

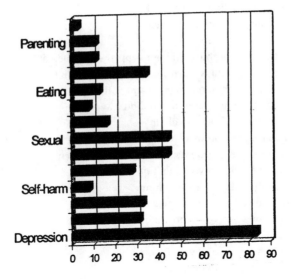

Figure B.5: PTSR Statistics – Associated problems

Unhealthy Family Questionnaires

These are a pair of questionnaires about 25 bad experiences, each related to childhood and adulthood. They work alongside the Post Traumatic Stress responses questionnaire. Perhaps they should be called Unhealthy Childhood Questionnaires.

The experience of living in an unhealthy family

Thinking about your childhood – from birth to leaving home – did any of the following things apply to you in your family? If you moved families for any reason, think about all of them. For this questionnaire, it doesn't matter at the moment about for how long or how many times any of these happened. What we are asking about here is: 'in general, did any of these things happen to you in an unfair way?'

Please tick any of these you recognise

Never got told anything, or only told when it was too late
No laughter at home, or only laughing at nasty things
Hiding feelings, putting on a brave face
Too much telling off and punishment
No togetherness, no friendliness
Pretending important things did not happen when they did
Pretending events/things did happen when they didn't
Needing to keep eyes and ears open all the time
Having to please others, even if you didn't want to
Being made to feel guilty too often
Being turned against brothers or sisters
Being told other people are dangerous when they aren't
Being blamed for things you didn't do
Being made the baddie for everything
Not being allowed to be a real person
Not being allowed to go out to see friends and clubs
Never being put first, always second or last
Never being listened to, always ignored
Too much violence in the family
Being told 'Do what I say, not what I do'
Too many broken promises, people 'changing their minds', or lies
Too much worrying about someone else
Adults always away, out, asleep
Adults putting you down because they want to be boss
Adults rowing and fighting too much

TOTAL (of 25)   NAME   DATE

The results of living in an unhealthy family

Thinking about your adulthood – after leaving home – do any of the following apply to you nowadays? If you have changed partners or families for any reason, think about all of them. For this questionnaire, it doesn't matter at the moment about how long or how many times you have thought or felt these. What we are asking about is: 'in general, have you reacted to your past in any of these ways?'

Please tick any of these you recognise

I keep asking 'Who am I?'

I keep expecting to fail

I never hope for what I really want because I know I won't get it

I still have nightmares about it

I still hide my feelings

I still feel confused about it

I keep thinking 'It was probably my fault anyway'

I manage to fool most people with my brave face

I keep putting myself second

I hope to goodness my kids do better

I am worried in case I make my kids the same

I often worry about boyfriends/girlfriends/husband/wife/partner

I sometimes wish I wasn't here

I sometimes wish I was somebody else

I can't have fun with sex

I am still so ANGRY!

I feel nobody takes me seriously

I feel all crowded in, weighed down, trapped

I sometimes think everyone's out to get me

I use too many cigarettes, drink too much, eat badly

I'm not a proper person

I still have to watch out and be careful with my old family

I find it difficult to give love

I'm not at all sure who I can trust

I keep asking 'Why me?'

TOTAL (of 25)   NAME   DATE

APPENDIX VI

Some More Poems

I have included some poems here in the Appendix to add to those I have used in the main text of the book. While I chose those in the main text to show some particular point, they all show several points. The similarities between them are as interesting as the differences.

I would like to stress that while I have called them all 'poems', some may not rhyme, some may not have the rhythm you might expect, some may have spelling mistakes, etc. I think we must be careful to avoid thinking of them as poems written by professional poets and authors. They have been written by ordinary people who have been sexually abused and who have been brave enough to show me their work and permit it to be published here.

B.6: Poem example – Is there no end?

There's a hole in my heart
How will I cope?
Fill it with alcohol, pills and dope.
But when they're not there I'm full of despair
Do I deserve the help that I need
Or am I suffering from an unknown greed?

The love that I got was just not right
But who was I to fight
Be a 'good' girl and do not tell
Cause if you do you'll go to hell.

But he was wrong you see
Cause the hell I live leaves me hard to breathe,
My breath gets shorter, the pain gets stronger
Can I take this for much longer

My dreams have gone, the nightmare's back
And somehow I lost all track
The pain and the shame seem to last forever
If there's a god I'll pray until I reach the end of my tether.

                                        Louise

B.7: Poem example – Living in my mind

Living in my mind
is a cold and empty place,
full of doubt and fear.
Giving double meaning
to everything I hear.

Darkness reaches out again closing in,
not velvet darkness, softly enfolding
but hard dark, full of sharp tearing edges.

Why has the fear returned
has all this trying, been for nothing?
Have I not learned anything?

Through the darkness time unfolds
bringing tomorrow nearer
and the awful fear
that there will be no one
who can talk and laugh with me
in safety.

R.A.S.

B.8: Poem example – Hidden

Hide away a secret,
Lock it up tight.
Clear away the evidence,
Keep it out of sight.

Hidden in an attic,
Hidden deep down,
Hidden in a smile,
Hidden in a frown.

Hidden in a hanky,
Hidden in a tear.
Hidden from my memory,
Hidden in fear.

Hidden in silence,
Hidden behind a wall.
Hidden in another world,
Hidden beyond recall.

These are some of the places
I hid it all away.
What did I hide there?
I could never say.

                                        Anna

B.9: Poem example – He picked me

Of all the people in the world
He picked me.
I should have known it then it was plain to see
A drink with a friend
turned out to be the beginning of the end.

A powerful man in a high place
On my own in a room as black as space
I am so sorry if I led you on
I didn't know you were so strong.

Money and drugs made it go away
Nothing let me face the day
I call on the man as a last resort
Bruised and beaten here I lay.

Confused my pride has gone
I feel no pain I close my eyes and hold on.
Time passes by – I ask why?
Time to change or die
Now people listen to my story of pain
Bad and insane they say he's to blame.

At this point I feel I need to get my own back
Anger is something I do not lack
I don't know how but some day soon
I will be rid of all this doom and gloom
All I know is that your mind gets weak
And it helps to speak.

James White

B.10: Poem example – The auto-thoughts of a robot

I feel just like a robot
No feelings from within
My movements they are stilted
My emotions kept within

I work on autopilot
To get through every day
With the help of cigs and whisky
I guess it's just my way

I do what is expected
Of that there is no doubt
But so much time is wasted
No wonder they want out

We are meant to be a family
Even though there is no dad
But I just cannot function
No wonder they feel so sad

When you're on auto-pilot
You learn how not to feel
Your life takes on a living lie
And nothing is quite real

You just go through the motions
It doesn't matter how
For there is no tomorrow
Just the here and now

Your mind is full of auto-thoughts
Which way should you go
Programmed from the day you're born
The seeds sown row by row

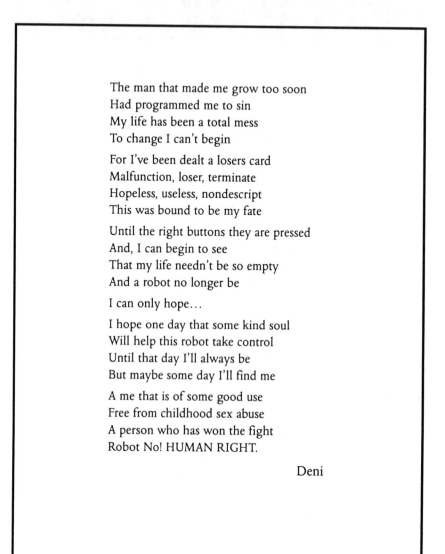

The man that made me grow too soon
Had programmed me to sin
My life has been a total mess
To change I can't begin

For I've been dealt a losers card
Malfunction, loser, terminate
Hopeless, useless, nondescript
This was bound to be my fate

Until the right buttons they are pressed
And, I can begin to see
That my life needn't be so empty
And a robot no longer be

I can only hope...

I hope one day that some kind soul
Will help this robot take control
Until that day I'll always be
But maybe some day I'll find me

A me that is of some good use
Free from childhood sex abuse
A person who has won the fight
Robot No! HUMAN RIGHT.

                              Deni

B.11: Poem example – Someone

Someone stole my life from me
Whom I did not know
I blamed it all on anyone else
But I didn't know where to go

Someone took away my life
I just cannot recall
I blamed it all on little me
But then she was only small

Someone robbed me of a life
They committed me to sin
I could of been a normal wife
If it hadn't been for him

Someone didn't value my life
To him I could be used
An ugly worthless person
A nothing he could abuse

Someone made me hate my life
I just wanted to die
To live a life of total sham
All of it was a lie

Someone made me hate all men
No-one that I could trust
I tried to put away my thoughts
That was all it was – lust

Someone totally wrecked my life
I'm glad he now is dead
For no longer can he control me
Or rear his ugly head

Someone did invade my dreams
The nightmares went on and on
But now I don't feel quite as small
Some battles I have won

Someone stole my life from me
Father was his name
A vile disgusting monster
My life will never be the same

Someone gave me back my life
ASCSA is the name
A Group of like minded people
They've given me back my name

                                        Deni

B.12: Poem example – If you bought damaged goods you'd go and complain

If you bought damaged goods
you'd go and complain

But a child can't do this
When they have been abused
Because of the fear and pain

Nobody to listen
Nobody to believe
Nobody to trust
Nobody to understand
Nobody seemed to care
Children seen but not heard
Even made to feel and believe
Fault and blame
For what's been done to them

Growing up in fear and pain
To find the real love
And stop believing that love is
The using and abusing and being thrown away
All those things from the past
I wish they would go away

And then to find
Somebody to believe in you
Somebody to understand
Somebody to trust
Somebody to listen
Somebody who cares

To find that you can complain about
the damage done to you

To find the blame is not yours
that help is at hand

                    Anonymous

B.13: Poem example – The lamp post on the hill

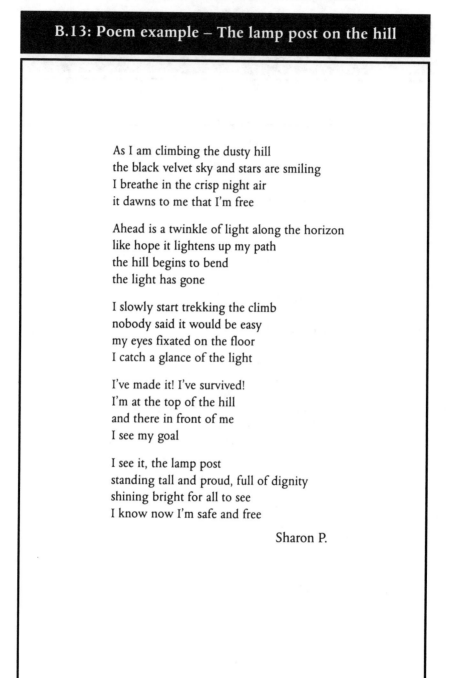

As I am climbing the dusty hill
the black velvet sky and stars are smiling
I breathe in the crisp night air
it dawns to me that I'm free

Ahead is a twinkle of light along the horizon
like hope it lightens up my path
the hill begins to bend
the light has gone

I slowly start trekking the climb
nobody said it would be easy
my eyes fixated on the floor
I catch a glance of the light

I've made it! I've survived!
I'm at the top of the hill
and there in front of me
I see my goal

I see it, the lamp post
standing tall and proud, full of dignity
shining bright for all to see
I know now I'm safe and free

Sharon P.

B.14: Poem example – The result

I did it, I got help.
After all my counselling sessions
I am able to control my feelings.
I have less depressions and worries,
All my relations say I am a changed person,
Even my friends have passed comments.
My boyfriend and I have a calmer, closer relationship.
I can cope much better with my children's behaviour.
'Don't keep it inside', this is my advice
Thanks to counselling I like to class myself as normal now.

So...
GET HELP – FEEL BETTER – I DID

Listen to the song called... Holding back the Years

If you fit the bill get counselling, – set yourself free; I did

There's someone there to help YOU
Don't be afraid to do it. I DID

Cheryl

APPENDIX VII

A Cross Index of Survivors

Survivors

These survivors have been very generous in allowing me to include their work. I must thank them again for their contributions. I have tried to avoid making any of them identifiable. I would have liked to say how old they each were, how long ago the abuse was, how long the abuse went on and what happened, etc, but that would spoil their anonymity. So, I will generalise: they are between mid-twenties and mid-fifties, they are mainly women, they were abused for several years at least, they are all recovering – some faster than others – and most of them have good relationships with partners and children.

APPENDIX VIII
An Alphabetical Index of Metaphors

APPENDIX IX
A Cross Index of Metaphors

This is intended to show the cross-linking of the various ideas presented. It is simply a set of likely connections that could be made from the heading in capitals.

The Counselling Agreement
    Trust – make your own decision about trusting me
    Basic philosophy – you deserve help
    Counselling programme – metaphors
    Separate 'you' from 'it'
    Does anything about me remind you of abuser(s)?

Hopelessness
    Guide – therapist's role
    Compass – noticing progress
    Starting point – next step
    The Fogbank – the boomerang
    Normal reactions – 'Flu, Bruised knee and Broken leg
    Variants – The Maze, The Forest, The Pit

Normal Reactions
    The 'Flu – bruised knee
    Talked about – not isolated
    Confusions
    Symptoms –
    Temporary – more like bereavement
        – get used to it, do not get over it
        – get in control of it all
    Permanent – Post Traumatic Stress responses

The Wall
    Lost and lonely – the Fogbank
    Stuck – the Trap
    Variants – The brave face, the hard face, the happy smiley face

Why Me?

Confidence – Monty Python Foot
Stealing a pencil
Victim spotting – not the school bully!
The Trap – variations on the theme
PTSR questionnaire – see appendix

Confidence

Courage and determination
Normal development
Having your confidence bashed down
Expecting to fail
Well-shaped objectives

Confusion

Going round in circles
Stealing a pencil
Ups and downs of change
I'm Stupid! – the 'forbidden word' rule
A normal reaction to sexual abuse

Guilt

Circles of Confusion
Why did it happen to me?
What if I enjoyed some aspect of it?
Survivor Guilt

Stupid

Circles Sexual abuse is always complicated
The 'forbidden word' rule
See also Crazy!, Guilt, Confusion

References

Bandler, R. and Grinder, J. (1982) *Reframing*. Moab: Real People Press.

Bateson, G., Jackson, D., Haley, J. and Weakland, J. (1956) 'Towards a theory of schizophrenia.' *Behavioural Science 1*, 251–63.

Bettleheim, B. (1976) *The Uses of Enchantment*. Harmondsworth: Penguin.

Finkelor, D. (1984) *Child Sexual Abuse: New Theory and Research*. New York: Free Press.

Laing, R.D. (1970) *Knots*. Harmondsworth: Penguin.

Seligman, M. (1973) 'Fall into helplessness.' *Psychology Today 7*, 1, 43–48.

de Shazer, S. (1985) *Keys to the Solution in Brief Therapy*. New York: Norton.

Zeig, J.K. (1980) *A Teaching Seminar with Milton H. Erickson*. New York: Brunner/Mazel.

Further Reading

It is difficult to recommend books about child sexual abuse. There are various subjects within the area: statistics and research, theories and therapies, politics and punishments (for abusers) and so on. The list is growing. From a subject that no one wrote about, it has suddenly become the subject of a lot of articles and books over the past ten years. This is another book – a useful addition, I hope.

As a way of providing something to help those interested, I have a list of the books stocked in local public libraries in my area. They are probably similar to those in other areas of the country. Very few survivors feel brave enough to go to libraries or bookshops and ask an assistant what books they have in stock about sexual abuse. This is because they worry about who will see or hear them asking. They imagine that anyone watching will guess the secret and somehow make things worse – even unintentionally. It is interesting to see the growth of information about child abuse, and child sexual abuse, on the Internet. For people who are connected – and that number is growing incredibly fast – this is an easy and anonymous way of getting information and even 'talking' to other survivors through the computer keyboard and screen.

The Courage to Heal	Bass and Davies
Rescuing the Inner Child	Penny Parkes
Cry Hard and Swim	Jacqueline Spring
Strong at the Broken Places	Linda T Sanford
Surviving Sexual Abuse	Deirdre Walsh
The Trauma Trap	Dr. David Muss & Rosemary Liddy
How to Survive In Spite of your Parents	Dr. Margaret Rinhold
Becoming Whole Again	V Gallagher
Child Sexual Abuse	C Bagley
The Death of Narcissus	M Fraser
Breaking Free	C Ainscough
Only Words	C A Mackinnon
Broken Boys / Mending Men	S Grubman-Black
Child Sexual Abuse	M Hancock
The Last Taboo	G Search
Female Sexual Abuse of Children	M Elliott

Two poems by other *ASCSA* group members have been published in Malone, C., Marce, L. and Farthing, L. (1996) *The Memory Bird*. London: Virago.